D1537965

THE NORTH EAST

Industrial Britain

THE NORTH EAST
JOHN W. HOUSE

Augustus M. Kelley Publishers
New York

Published in the United States of America by
Augustus M. Kelley Publishers
New York 1969

Standard Book Number 678 05569 6
Library of Congress Catalog Card Number 77-91239

Printed in Great Britain
by Clarke Doble & Brendon Limited Plymouth

TO MY WIFE

who has contributed in so many ways to make
possible the preparation of this book

Contents

List of Illustrations

Plates

9

Figures in Text

Preface

THIS INTERPRETATION OF the Industrial North East as a distinctive and traditional industrial region within the British economic system starts from a consideration of its national rôle, its internal and external linkages, and rests on an assessment of the basic resources of place and people and the way in which these have evolved to define the present character of the North East and the heritage of its many-sided problems. Because the region has long been a 'pilot-zone' for successive governmental location and employment policies these have been reviewed and assessed in their cumulative impact on sub-region and landscape.

The main substance is an analysis of the way in which the major strands of the industrial structure have developed in post-war years, seen against a backcloth of the essential traditional characteristics from earlier times. A study of the sinews of the economy, coal, iron and steel is the prelude to an interpretation of the dynamics of industrial change, first with regard to the rapid growth industries and their regional contribution, secondly in respect of the much more difficult issues of the traditional industries in course of transformation and, in some cases, dramatic decline.

The contrasting economic structures, landscapes, planning problems and prospects of the major industrial districts on Teesside, Tyneside and at Sunderland therefore merit review as do the five New Towns of the North East, those harbingers of that new living environment of which the regional planners have spoken so often and at such length in the past few years. Indeed a main purpose of the book is to attempt a contemporary industrial stocktaking, an appraisal of assets and liabilities in the major industries and in the sub-regions, finally indicating an outline of the way ahead to the end of this century— North East Phoenix.

The book is the product of two decades of living and working in the North East, increasingly preoccupied with social and economic problems in conurbation, mining district and rural area, an interest first stimulated and constantly encouraged by my association during many of those years with that most skilled interpreter of the North East, Emeritus Professor G. H. J. Daysh.

A particular feature of the great majority of the figures in the book is that only two scales have been used, one for the diagrams of the North East, the other for the diagrams of its industrial heart. The set of figures on the employment patterns of individual industries in 1966 (Figs 18, 20–24, 25–28) are on the same scale and the symbol scales are identical so that the figures are visually cross-comparable.

John W. House

Department of Geography
University of Newcastle upon Tyne
January 1969

1

Region and System

IN ANY ECONOMIC sub-division of the United Kingdom the North East stands out clearly as one of the major, traditional heavy-industrial regions. It is territorially distinct, perhaps more remote than most, and has an industrial structure for long based on coal, iron and steel, shipbuilding and heavy engineering. The essentials of its present economic character were strikingly fashioned during the latter half of the nineteenth century but the imprint and legacy of earlier and later phases of industrial development and decline are also writ large in both the landscape and the lives of the people. There are few regions in Britain where present economic and social problems have so clearly been derived from a complex industrial past, and indeed have arisen from the very facts of early prominence and nineteenth-century status in mining and manufacturing. The North East is a microcosm of the fortunes of industrial Britain, to some extent a museum-piece of its former glories, more recently a laboratory for regional development policies by governments.

Since the economic depression of the early 1930s the North East has had a continuous record as one of the national problem areas and has been the recipient of economic and social aid under a variety of governmental industrial-location and regional policies. In the most recent phase, following the White Paper of 1963, the North East initially shared with central Scotland 'pilot-zone' status in the formulation of regional policy to promote growth and redress the balance between the more affluent and the less prosperous regions of Britain. This policy culminated in the definition of a network of national economic planning regions in 1964 and the development since then of a rudimentary framework for regional planning of an advisory and consultative character.[1]

The North East has thus for some decades been attempting, with limited, but nevertheless significant, success, a radical transformation in its industrial structure as part of a programme of rehabilitation and preparation for more stable and substantial economic growth. Traditional branches of industry still strongly colour the structure of regional employment and, for that matter, the trends of unemployment. Yet traditional industries are themselves undergoing fundamental changes, by growth and decline in some branches, streamlining or reorganisation of production in others, through search for new markets and new products; for some industries and individual firms however the outcome has unfortunately been dramatic decline, even closure. Industrial progress in the region is thus only partially the story of new industries introduced into the North East in the past thirty-five years with government aid, valuable and significant though such a broadening of the industrial base has undoubtedly been.

At the present time the regional economy is at a critical stage. Growth in some industries is scarcely offsetting the effects of decline elsewhere. Coalmining is entering a phase of even more rapid pit closures, iron and steel stands on the brink of a rationalisation and probably a substantial reduction of its labour force. Shipbuilding is in course of radical reshaping and faces an uncertain long-term future, whilst the character of heavy engineering is constantly changing in its efforts to adjust to new types of product and non-traditional markets. On the other hand the tempo of economic growth is rising in the North East, both from the implantation of new growth industries and from the mounting contribution by those introduced as the result of earlier government policies. An assessment of the present situation is thus timely, giving perspective to the contribution of both traditional and newer ingredients in the regional industrial structure.

The industrial North East conventionally includes the Tyneside conurbation, Sunderland, Teesside and the coalfield—a compact area set within a broad rural hinterland stretching to the Cheviots in the north, the Pennines in the west and across the Cleveland hills in the south. For many administrative purposes the North East is defined as the counties of Northumberland, Durham and the North Riding of Yorkshire, an identity accepted for most purposes in this book. These three counties in turn form the economic heart of the Northern economic planning region, coterminous with the Northern standard region, both definitions enlarging the North East by the addition of Cumberland and Westmorland. Whenever possible statistics refer to the North East, but in some cases the Northern region is the minimum unit for which official data is available, and is the

Page 17: (above) *A1 (M) – A66 (M) junction, near Darlington*; (below) *Team Valley industrial estate, looking north.*

Page 18: (above) *Pallion industrial estate, Sunderland*; (below) *Board of Trade advance factory, Newburn industrial estate.*

conventionally-accepted basis for inter-regional comparisons within Britain.

Though the North East is the subject of the book clearly the region is no island in the national economy even though it is one of its most clear-cut formal and functional units. Although for long considered in isolation and as isolated, the North East fully merits an interpretation related to the links and bonds it has with other parts of Britain, the North Sea lands and other overseas countries. These are as important a part of the assessment of regional prospects as they are vital to an understanding of current problems. In defining its character it is as vital to see what differentiates the North East from elsewhere as to survey its human and natural resources in their own right.

The North East as Region

The identity and coherence of the North East and its distinctiveness among British regions result from a long and complex development, referred to more fully in Chapter 2. There is sharp, even abrupt, contrast between the broad, thinly-peopled rural zone and the compact, densely-peopled city-clusters on the lower Tyne, Wear and Tees. The rural zone is bordered by an upland rim widely breached only southwards by the Vale of York; the urban heart of the North East is set within the triangular coalfield, with its closely ordered pattern of mining settlements and small towns. There is thus throughout the region a strong central focus on the lower reaches of the three rivers, with Tyneside by its size and position serving as its metropolitan centre.

An antithesis to the highly developed urban and coalfield core the broad rural hinterland has a declining population and an extensive hill, dale and lowland economy; it is the custodian of many historical traditions and monuments of the Border status of the region throughout the centuries. Focused on a small number of scattered market towns the rural zone has its own problems of agricultural adjustment, social provision, decline in its youthful population, and the need to develop new forms of employment at suitable centres. Rural problems are of lesser scale than those of coalfield or older industrial city but they are none the less equally indicative of marginal conditions within the economy of the North East.

The theme of the economic and social problems of marginality will be recurrent in this interpretation of the region today. The term margin may refer to the high costs of production, lower profitability or it

B

may equally indicate resources which have lapsed or are going out of use on the land, in the mines, in the factories or in land use in the cities. The North East is perhaps distinctive in the wide range of marginal conditions, many of them interrelated and indeed helping to define the region as a whole.

Regional policy has particular relevance to the problems of the margins but its central purpose is investment and prosperity for the economic core, from which benefits may be expected to radiate later throughout the rural and mining hinterland. A feature of the 1963 Hailsham White Paper was the designation of a 'growth zone' from Tyne to Tees into which increased central-government investment was to be concentrated; it might be, however, that in the short run such a concentration policy would adversely affect areas outside the growth zone. In the event the policy lacked implementation and the test has not been made.

The economic core of the North East from Tyne to Tees has two major nodes, one at each end. Tyneside, together with Sunderland, is larger, more diversified and the logical metropolitan centre; Teesside has had the more vigorous general economic growth since 1945 and has the greater range of underused assets. No assessment of a present regional strategy can ignore the clamant demands for growth at both ends of the Tees–Tyne axis.

Tyneside is internally diverse with metropolitan functions focusing on Newcastle, the centre for administration, the professions, higher education, shopping, wholesaling, banking and insurance facilities. Downstream there are more specialised industrial settlements, with vigorous civic traditions contributing to the still-unresolved problem of local-government reform on Tyneside. Physically separated from this continuous built-up area Sunderland has a measure of self-contained community life and a distinct industrial blend, with greater problems in general, though the degree of dependence on shipbuilding and the need to widen the range of industries further are little different from the problems of Tyneside. Indeed increasingly the planning for these towns requires interpreting at the level of a Tyne–Wear city region with a commuting hinterland perhaps up to twenty miles to the north, south and west.

Tyneside and Teesside each contribute vitally but distinctively to the output and wealth of the North East. The industrial structure differs for each sub-region but the contrasts have not been such as to lead to intensive complementary exchange of products. Teesside has long been based on iron and steel, chemicals and the constructional-engineering industries. It has extensive estuarine land and great port potential, indeed considerable development of its potential industrial sites has taken place in the past few years. For these reasons the regional economic planning council recommended that Teesside should be investigated as a national growth area in the same way as Humberside, Severnside or the Dundee area. The Rochdale Committee, and subsequently the National Ports Council, also recommended that the Tees should be developed as a major port in the north. In contrast Tyneside seems to have the less promising economic future, certainly if emphasis is laid on the traditional manufactures of shipbuilding, marine and heavy engineering. Yet on closer comparison with the Tees the Tyne has benefited from a greater variety of growth industries introduced since the war. Furthermore the structure and range of local engineering is changing and there are in any case profitable lines in heavy electrical engineering even among the traditional branches of the engineering industry. In terms of future job provision from established industries indeed the Tyne may have the longer-term advantage. If economic growth is measured in terms of capital investment, or output per unit of labour, the Tees contrasts with the more labour-intensive economy of the Tyne and is likely to be the site of most dramatic developments during the remainder of this century.

The importance of the Tyne–Tees axis or growth zone is widely accepted but it is difficult to measure the flows of goods and people along it with any precision. Fig 1 indicates road and rail freight densities, but only a general visual comparison is justified since the basis of the statistics is necessarily different. A map of bus services might be expected to indicate a similar functional relationship but with an even greater emphasis on internal flows. Rail passenger movements bring out the strength of commuting within the Tyne–Wear city region and around Teesside whilst tonnage freight-flows by rail highlight not only the considerable short-distance internal movement, including hauling of coal to the rivers, but also the significance of the Tyne–Tees link and the strong flow southwards out of the region.

The effects of government policy, allied with market trends, are likely to result in further centralisation of investment, and of industrial location in particular, thus reinforcing the sense of separate social and economic identity within the growth zone of the North East. Such a development would add to the already well-marked sense of regional consciousness, based on tradition, an awareness of common problems, and a deep-seated wish to further the interests of the region through a strong regional planning mechanism.

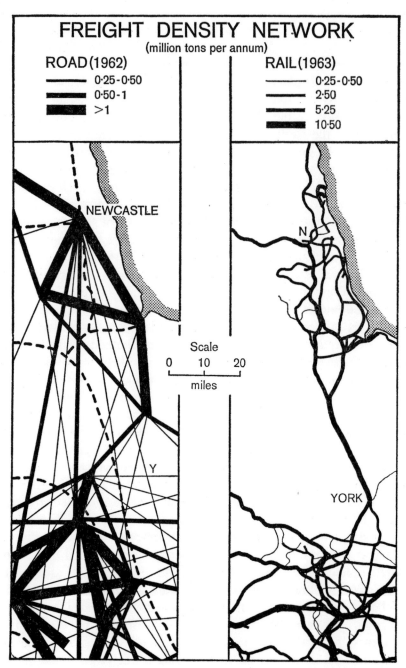

Fig 1. The broken line in the left-hand section indicates main roads. (Source: data from *Survey of Road Goods Transport* 1962 and *The Reshaping of British Railways* 1963.)

The North East and the UK

It is easier to identify the regional characteristics of the North East, whether by natural resources, historical character, industrial development or present problems, than it is to assess the relative strength of the linkages with other regions of Britain, with the North Sea lands or with the outside world in general.

National Status

The most straightforward comparison of North East and nation lies in its proportionate rôle in the national economy as interpreted by a selected range of economic and social indicators; for some criteria the Northern region is the only available basis for such comparisons. As a yardstick the indicators should constantly be referred to the size of the regional population and its purchasing power.[2]

Table 1

NORTH EAST AND NATION. SELECTED ECONOMIC AND SOCIAL INDICATORS, AS PERCENTAGE UK, 1966 UNLESS OTHERWISE SPECIFIED

	North East
Population	4·9
Population 1981 (est)	6·0
Electricity sales	5·3
Sales through manufacturing plants 1958	5·7
Sales through retail outlets 1961	5·9
Deep-mined coal (tons)	16·6
Crude steel	17·7
Shipbuilding	51·2
Unemployed, as a percentage of national total	9·5†
Unemployed, rate, national=1·6	2·6
Average weekly income, national=100	80·0†
Activity rate,*	
male, national=76·0	72·7†
female, national=40·4	34·9†

† Northern region figure.
* Proportion of employed and unemployed expressed as a percentage of all those in working age groups.

Source: Various.

Table 1 brings out salient traits of the North East, both good and bad. Population will continue to grow and, by 1981, may well outstrip

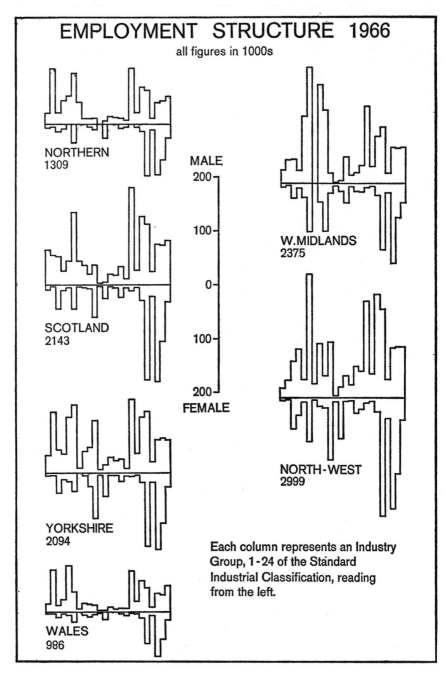

Fig 2. (Source: data from the Department of Employment & Productivity.)

new job provision. Average weekly incomes, at 80 per cent of the national average, are among the lowest for British regions. Furthermore the North East carries, and has long carried, a disproportionately heavy burden of the national unemployed and yet there is at present more of an untapped labour reservoir, as the activity rates for both males and females show. On the other hand the prominent contribution to certain staples of the British industrial economy is clear and in both retailing and manufacturing the region has a status slightly above that suggested by the size of the regional population.

Fig 2 shows graphically the comparison in volume and type of employment between the Northern region and comparable British industrial regions. In industrial structure the Northern region shows similarities with Scotland or Wales. Wales has a correspondingly strong concentration on coalmining and iron and steel and dearth of adequate variety in other manufacturing. A further similarity, less common to Scotland, is the lack of industrial employment for women in the North, though they are well-represented in service industries, a sector in which all heavy-industrial areas are deficient when compared to the national average. The comparison of the North, Scotland or Yorkshire with the West Midlands industrial structure strikingly highlights the greater variety and representation of growth industries within the latter area. Scotland further shares with the North a more independent economic identity and a strong engineering sector, but shows more variety in manufacturing and in jobs for women. Yorkshire and the North West both have more balanced regional economies though the weaknesses in Lancashire textiles are well-known.

Economic Growth Status

In Table 2 the proportions employed in growth and decline industries reinforce the similarities and contrasts with other regions. Figures for the West Midlands and the UK highlight the contrast with the older industrial regions of the North and Wales, and among these traditional regions the Northern region shares with Yorkshire an unenviable ratio between decline and growth industries. The marginally higher figures for slower growth in Yorkshire and for faster decline in the Northern region are nevertheless significant. Scotland, the North West and Wales show small but meaningfully better ratios between growth and decline, whilst Yorkshire again scores on its better balance between the two categories of growth industry in comparison with the narrower specialisation in the Northern region.

Table 2

INDUSTRIAL GROWTH AND DECLINE SECTORS, BY STANDARD
REGIONS, 1966

	Total Employment (1,000s)	Faster growth per cent	Slower growth per cent	Slower decline per cent	Faster decline per cent	Total growth per cent	Total decline per cent
Northern	1,309	50·8	18·5	9·9	20·8	69·3	30·7
Scotland	2,143	53·5	18·2	9·9	18·4	71·7	28·3
Yorkshire and Humberside	2,094	48·5	20·6	10·0	20·9	69·1	30·9
North West	2,999	56·9	16·7	11·4	15·0	73·6	26·4
Wales	472	47·9	23·7	9·3	19·1	71·6	28·4
West Midland	2,375	62·9	21·2	6·5	9·4	84·1	15·9
UK	23,781	55·9	18·9	10·4	14·8	74·8	25·2

Source: Calculated from Department of Employment & Productivity data.

Faster growth: Professional services; Distributive trades; Insurance, banking and finance; Engineering and electrical goods; Other manufactures; Paper, printing and publishing; Metal goods; Construction; Vehicles; Chemicals.

Slower growth: Miscellaneous services; Metal manufacture; Gas, electricity, water; Bricks, pottery, glass; Food, drink, tobacco.

Slower decline: Timber and furniture; Transport and communications; Clothing and footwear.

Faster decline: Public administration and defence; Textiles; Leather, fur; Shipbuilding and marine engineering; Mining and quarrying; Agriculture, forestry and fishing.

Linkages within Britain

The extent to which the North East is tied into the British economy by flows of goods, services, or people is hard to establish: indicators are fragmentary, rarely comprehensive, and often available only in ways which make comparability difficult. Interpretation of the linkages raises the question of the economic and social meaning of isolation, a term much used and misused in connection with the North. It is more important at all times to see the relative importance of intra-regional, inter-regional and foreign exchanges if the rôle and status of the North East is to be adequately assessed.

Freight flows (Fig 1) are perhaps the best general indicator of economic linkage,[3] though data on tonnage may mislead unless value can also be added, which is rarely possible. About 35 million tons of rail-borne freight crossed Northern region boundaries in 1962, 23 million tons entering and leaving southwards, including about 10 million on the section Northallerton–York. These figures take account of goods and commodities in transit to and from Scotland and are thus greater than the traffic originating in, or delivering to, the

Northern region. More detailed analysis is not possible but the distinct thinning of rail freight on the main-line section south of York as far as Doncaster suggests both limited rail-trading relationship of the North East with the East Midlands and the South East and also the strength of two-way interconnection with the West Riding, Lancashire and, to a lesser extent, the West Midlands. Rail-freight flows north and west from Newcastle are both slight and almost equal in tonnage, but the traffic with Scotland contains less coal and is probably higher in value. Under the Beeching proposals the Newcastle–Carlisle freight link was to be strengthened, that with Edinburgh curtailed, at least in terms of passenger movement.

Data on road freight (1962) is fuller but not in any sense statistically comparable with that of rail, even in tonnage; for example a national count some three years later showed 1,430 million tons of freight travelling by road, only 229 million by rail—figures for the Northern region should show something of this predominance of road freight movements. Some 11 million tons flowed out of the Northern region, compared with 10 million tons entering and 70 million tons circulating within. The strong ties with Yorkshire are once again clear, whilst rather more than two-thirds of outward flows and three-quarters of inward flows were with immediately adjacent economic regions

Table 3

DIRECTION OF ROAD FREIGHT MOVEMENT IN THE NORTHERN
REGION, BY PERCENTAGE, 1962

	Tonnage road freight (per cent)	
	Out	In
E. and W. Ridings	33	38
North West	17	22
Scotland	19	14
Midlands	15	16
South (including Wales)	16	10

Source: Calculated from *Survey of Road Goods Transport* 1962.

(Table 3). The low ratio of flows to and from London and the South East, 6 per cent out of and 5 per cent into the Northern region, may surprise some but are likely to be much higher in value terms. The greater net inflow from Yorkshire and the North West is in contrast to the surplus of goods moving out by road to Scotland.

In contrast to internal flows within the Northern region where crude materials account for 32 per cent and fuel for 24 per cent of tonnage by road, the outward movement of freight has only 25 per cent in these two categories combined; but it has 28 per cent in chemicals, iron and steel and other intermediate goods and 14 per cent in manufactures, the latter providing only 5 per cent of tonnage moving internally. Freight inflows of manufactures however are higher at 18 per cent. Internal movement of foodstuffs is 17 per cent compared with an outward flow of 18 per cent and an inflow of 25 per cent.

A 1963 survey of Tyneside longer-distance road freight movements[4] showed some differences. In one-half of both outward and inward journeys by goods vehicles from Tyneside Yorkshire is more strongly emphasised, though these figures include the south bank of the Tees excluded from the 1962 count. Scotland (8 per cent out, 7·7 per cent in) is less prominent, but the South East is more (12·7 per cent out, 12 per cent in); other areas retain their 1962 proportions.

Coastwise shipping carried 15 million tons from and 2·5 million tons into North Eastern ports in 1965.[5] Dominating coastwise exports was the coal trade, 13 million tons mainly to the Thames estuary; petroleum products formed 2 million tons of coastwise imports (Fig 3). The contrast in structure of coastal trade as between the Tees and the coal-export ports further north is clearly indicated.

To sum up, road and rail freight data brings out strongly the close participation of the North East in a North of England economy, with less developed, though still significant ties of about the same proportions with Scotland, the Midlands and the South. The special nature of the southward coastwise shipments of coal and the movement of petroleum products northwards does not invalidate this generalisation.

Is this closer linkage with other industrial areas of the North an indication of the extent of economic isolation from the Midlands and the South? Even more directly, has the isolation of the North East, real or assumed, affected its ability to attract new industry and impeded its industrial transformation? With the rapid and flexible growth of road-hauling of freight any answer to these questions might be sought in road-traffic data. There are but fragments of information which suggest that the costs generated by increased line-hauling to the North East are easily exaggerated and likely to be location-determining costs in relatively few industries, least of all in many of the light manufactures which have proliferated since the war. Use of firm's transport, high-cost low-bulk relationship of product, low freight cost related to total production costs have all reduced any disadvantage of distance to and from the North East, whilst the northward extension of the M1, the considerable extent of the A1 at motorway

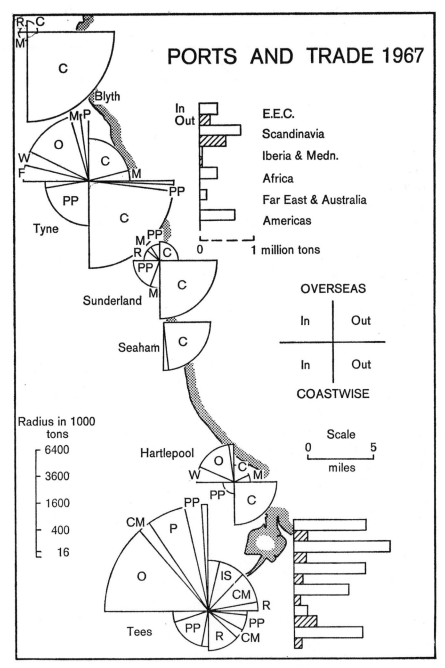

Fig 3. Key: C coal, CM chemical manufs, F food, IS iron and steel, M manufs,
O ores and scrap, P crude petroleum, PP petroleum products, R raw materials, W wood.
(Source: data from *Digest of Port Statistics* 1967.)

standard and the work on the Durham motorway are contributing to minimising the time-distance element which may have lain at the basis of unfavourable costs as seen hitherto. There nevertheless remains a strong psychological belief among some industrialists that location in the North East is likely to incur telling transfer-cost disadvantages. Proof is lacking and the argument is suspect.

The alignment of major routeways, the main Edinburgh–London rail link and the A1, has tended to favour some development of an eastern flank economy in Britain, weakened only by the lack of substantial industrial development between Greater London, Humberside and Teesside. The coastal fuels trade, soon to be reinforced by piped natural gas, the northward movement of foodstuffs and the return flow of meat from the hills, the setting up of branch plants in the North East by firms from Newark and Grantham, or the location of a motor-components firm intermediate between the car plants of the Midlands and Scotland are indications of such a rudimentary but developing east-coast linkage. The channelling of heavy freight traffic off the A1, by the M16 to the M1, affords closer contacts than hitherto with the Midlands industrial areas, further diminishing the isolation of the North East. Such isolation is difficult to put into economic terms and is not without powerful emotional undertones so long as industrialists continue to believe that they cannot prosper at sites more than even a few miles east or west of the A1 where it passes through the region.

Passenger movements may be a less reliable indication of economic linkage. Density of rail passenger traffic thins once again between York and Doncaster on the main Newcastle–London line, emphasising not only the West Riding–Lancashire linkage with the North East, but also the metropolitan focusing common to the BR network. Fig 4 is based on an interpretation of the winter rail time-table 1967–8 and the iso-chrones are related to fastest service, including changeover times when appropriate. The east-coast linkage is strikingly shown, with Brighton as accessible as Aberdeen, Birmingham as near in time to Newcastle as Glasgow; conversely, the 4 hours to the west Cumberland coast or to pockets of the Lancashire Pennines indicates islands of remoteness, at least in time. Within 12 hours only the furthest corners of the North West Highlands, Milford Haven or Lands End remain just out of reach.

Air services based on Newcastle (Fig 4) bring London, Liverpool, Belfast, Dublin and Amsterdam airports within little more than 1 hour's flight time; the London–Newcastle time was recently reduced by a further 10 minutes on the introduction of jet aircraft. Flights to

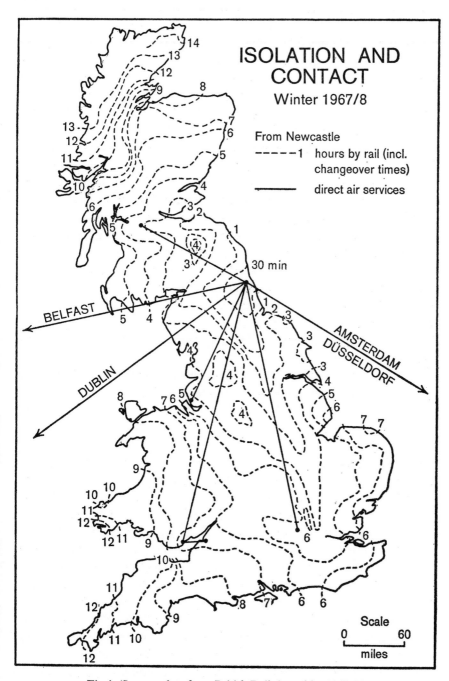

Fig 4. (Source: data from British Rail timetables 1967–8.)

the South West, Cardiff and Bristol take longer, but Glasgow airport lies within 40 minutes flying time from Newcastle. The frequent direct service to London puts the North East closely in touch with the great inter-war and post-war development of industry north and west of the metropolis. In the case of at least one firm the setting up of a production unit north of Newcastle was stimulated by this inter-regional air link. Teeside airport also is linked to London (Heathrow).

A final illustration of the inter-regional links of the North East lies in bulk interchange of people by migration.[6] The latest complete data, for the years 1960–1, enabled interpretation of gross movements between regions for the first time. Compared with the nation the Northern region showed a lower level of mobility, in common with most industrial areas north of the Wash–Severn line and in contrast to the more affluent areas to the south. Much of both in- and out-migration in respect of the Northern region was with immediately adjacent areas, particularly with the East and West Ridings which sent more to the North than they received from thence, to a lesser extent with Scotland. Longer-distance movement to London and the South East was a further prominent feature, but it was more selective and smaller in volume.

It remains to examine the overseas links of the North East, both its North Sea face and its deep-sea linkages (Fig 3).

The North East and Overseas

Bulk handling figures largely in the trade of North Eastern ports, including coal for both coastwise and export trades and iron ore inward-bound from overseas. A comparison of the ports by tonnage and value of trade (Table 4) shows the primacy of Tyne and Tees, both being substantial bulk-handling ports with a similar total value of trading. Fig 3 shows that the Tees has sizeable iron ore imports from across the oceans compared with the Tyne, which has its major bulk trading in coal shipments, particularly coastwise to the Thames. The rise in imports of petroleum and its products is seen at both ports, and on a smaller scale at Sunderland, with an important representation of petroleum products coming in from other coastal refineries in Britain. The establishment of refineries on the Tees will increase the circulation of petroleum products substantially within the next decade. Other bulk imports are foodstuffs and wood into the Tyne, wood and iron ore into Hartlepool and chemicals into the Tees. The specialised coal-exporting ports of Blyth and Seaham stand out with virtually no

Table 4
TRADE OF NORTH EASTERN PORTS 1966

| | | Tonnage (1,000 tons) | | Value (£ million) |
		Overseas	Coastwise	
Tyne	In	1,963	1,240	72·2
	Out	575	3,669	37·0
Tees	In	5,993	872	40·4
	Out	1,487	811	63·6
Sunderland	In	118	281	3·2
	Out	114	1,903	3·6
Hartlepool	In	660	61	6·0
	Out	189	809	1·6
Blyth	In	37	2	0·4
	Out	43	3,260	2·1

Source: Digest of Port Statistics 1967.

overseas coal trading; Sunderland and the Tyne share in a larger over-seas coal trade. The coastwise export of raw materials, chemicals and petroleum products from the Tees is noteworthy, albeit less in tonnage than from the coal ports further north.

Though small in tonnage, exports of manufactures rank high in value. The contribution of iron and steel and the chemical industries gives the Tees some export precedence over the Tyne, a tribute to the regularity of cargo-liner sailings, though the overseas sales of com-pleted ships gives considerable additional tonnage and value if included in the trade of the Tyne and Wear.

Port Forelands

In short sea trading Scandinavia and the Baltic take pride of place over links with the EEC countries.[7] About 16 per cent of British imports from and 8 per cent of British exports to Scandinavia passed through North Eastern ports in 1965, compared with 9 and 7 per cent respec-tively to the EEC countries. Iron ores and concentrates moved from Sweden to the Tees, whilst Tyne imports from Scandinavia included lumber and wood as well as a smaller quantity of ore. Coal formed the bulk of Tyne exports to the Baltic and Norway whereas the Tees sent petroleum products, iron and steel and chemical manufactures. Hartle-pool, a smaller port, is closely tied in trade with Scandinavia, import-ing wood and iron ore and sending coal in return. The Tyne is a principal passenger port for Scandinavia, with 169,000 travellers passing through the port in 1965. Links with EFTA partners do not yet seem to have either increased or diversified the trade between the North East and Scandinavia but the potential is there and is beginning to be reflected in the figures for interchange of manufactured goods, at least from the Tees.

Trade with the North Sea-basin countries of the EEC is most prominent to and from the Tees, with substantial imports of petroleum products from the Netherlands, to a lesser extent from Italian and French refineries; in return, trade is strongest with West Germany in chemicals, and then in metal and chemical manufactures with the Netherlands. The Tyne on the other hand has closest regional trade in EEC with the Netherlands, importing notably unmilled cereals and petroleum, but rather more petroleum comes from Italian and, to a lesser extent, Belgian refineries; coal exports to the Netherlands are a striking feature. Such North Eastern trade with the EEC is linked particularly to the raw material needs of Tyne and Tees industry and, bilaterally, with fuel exports and outflow of Teesside manufactures.

The larger-scale and more diversified trade from the Tees to the deep-sea areas contrasts with the lesser, import-orientated trade of the Tyne. Again the raw material needs of Teesside industry stand out: iron ore from West Africa and Canada, less so from Venezuela; petroleum from the Persian Gulf and South America; fertiliser materials from West Africa. In return there is a strong movement of chemical products to the Far East and of metal manufactures to North America, the Far East and South Africa. In contrast, the Tyne draws iron ore from West Africa, South America and Canada, and limited supplies of petroleum from the Persian Gulf, but has virtually no long-distance export trade in manufactured goods. For this reason it remains a medium-sized port serving mainly local needs and the National Ports Council has made no recommendation for immediate investment. On the other hand the Tees is recognised as having great potential and is already the third largest port in Britain for the export of manufactured goods.

Port Hinterlands

Study of the source origins of dry cargo exports underlines the regional nature of trade through the North Eastern ports: four-fifths of Newcastle and nine-tenths of Teesside exports come from the Northern region; 6 per cent come to the Tyne for export from the West Riding and 4 per cent from the South West go out through Teesside, probably originating in ICI plants on Severnside. Conversely, three-

Page 35: (above) *Mining village, Thornley (county Durham)*; (below) *Ashington, Northumberland.*

Page 36: (above) *Vane Tempest colliery and coastline*; (below) *British Steel Corporation, Lackenby, in the foreground and Cleveland works.*

quarters of Northern dry cargo exports go out through North Eastern ports, but 13 per cent pass through Liverpool, 4 per cent each through other North Western ports and through Hull. These figures underline strongly the self-contained nature of the overseas links from the North East and also the limited links with other north of England ports. Raw material needs, including food for the regional market, minerals and petroleum are balanced by export of traditional manufactures, the latter confined at present largely to Teesside. The favourable position relative to Scandinavia has been capitalised upon only in regional trading to and from the North East and, in national terms, is limited to passenger traffic. Otherwise port trade reflects the lack of diversity in North East manufacturing but does show that the needs of local heavy industry, beyond those met from local resources, are served importantly by international imports.

The North East has been identified as a territorially distinct, but not really remote heavy industrial economy, focused on Tyne, Wear and Tees and set within a major, if declining, coalfield. It probably has a greater self-contained flow of economic life than any major British industrial region, other than perhaps Northern Ireland or Scotland; in particular it is most closely linked externally as part of a north of England–south of Scotland economy, illustrated both in the flows of freight traffic by rail and road and in the regional interchange of workers and general migrants. Links with the North West come out in the use made of the port of Liverpool and in the incorporation of Cumbria within the Northern economic planning region. Passenger links with London and the eastern flank of England are closer in time than elsewhere at comparable distance, though perhaps surprisingly limited in volume, and there is slight evidence of an incipient east-coast economy along the axial line from London to Newcastle. The coal trade to London is a special case of linkage but otherwise the port of London plays little part in North-eastern economic links.

In overseas trade the North East operates regionally in meeting the needs and sending out the products of its industries. It scarcely inter-prets or serves a national purpose in either the hinterlands or the fore-lands of the ports of Tyne and Tees. Links with EFTA and EEC are soundly based on raw materials and fuels but as yet only the Tees is realising some of the possibilities of exchange of manufactures, and that mainly with Scandinavia.

References to this chapter are on page 239.

c

2

Resources and Development

THIS CHAPTER interprets the natural and human resources of the North East,[1] with some assessment of their revaluation through time.

The Natural Endowment

Physical Elements

About 130 miles from Berwick to York and around 40 miles in width through Northumberland and Durham, land is, in general, not a scarce factor in the North East; but much land is high, poor in quality, and remote from the main centres of population. The bordering rim of upland, from the Cheviots in the north, through the Border fells and Cross Fell to Great Whernside in the south-west, is generally above 2,300 ft falling below 1,500 ft only where it is cut through by the Tyne gap and at Stainmore (Fig 5). On the southern border access to the North East is through the broad Vale of York, flanked to the east by the tableland of the North York moors, rising to between 1,300 and 1,400 ft. To the north the narrow coastal plain gives a lowland corridor into the Merse of Tweed and so beyond the Lammermuirs to the Lothians and Edinburgh.

The physique of the North East is dominated by the three perimeter hill massifs: the Cheviots–Border fells, the Alston (North Pennine) block and the Cleveland hills. The ridge trending south-west from the andesite lava and granitic mass of the Cheviots is composed of tabular lower-carboniferous sandstones and shales. From it the upper courses of the North Tyne and Rede flow south-east in broad basins, in contrast to the radial drainage of short tributaries from the Cheviots to the north. Much of Northumberland is composed of a succession of tablelands and scarps with an easterly dip towards the coal basin, swinging towards a southerly dip along the Tyne. The fell sandstone

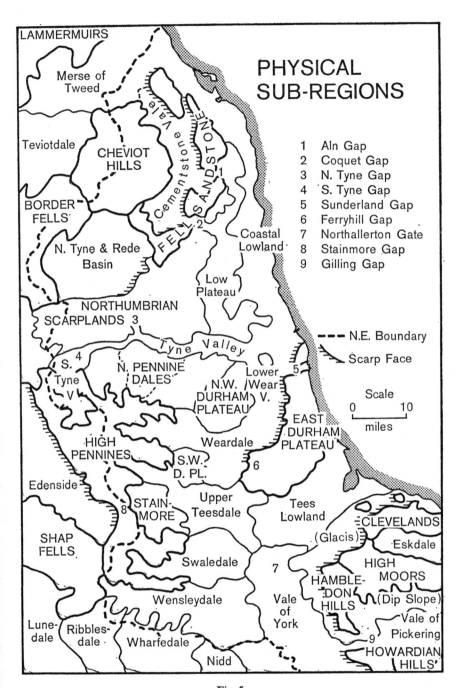

PHYSICAL
SUB-REGIONS

LAMMERMUIRS
Merse of Tweed
Teviotdale
CHEVIOT HILLS
BORDER FELLS
N. Tyne & Rede Basin
Cementstone Vale
FELL SANDSTONE
Coastal Lowland
Low Plateau
NORTHUMBRIAN SCARPLANDS 3
Tyne Valley
S. Tyne V
N. PENNINE DALES
Lower Wear V.
N.W. DURHAM PLATEAU
EAST DURHAM PLATEAU
HIGH PENNINES
Weardale
S.W. D. PL.
Edenside
STAIN-MORE
Upper Teesdale
Tees Lowland
CLEVELANDS
Eskdale
SHAP FELLS
(Glacis)
HIGH MOORS
Swaledale
HAMBLE-DON HILLS
(Dip Slope)
Wensleydale
Vale of York
Vale of Pickering
Lune-dale
Ribbles-dale
Wharfedale
Nidd
HOWARDIAN HILLS'

1 Aln Gap
2 Coquet Gap
3 N. Tyne Gap
4 S. Tyne Gap
5 Sunderland Gap
6 Ferryhill Gap
7 Northallerton Gate
8 Stainmore Gap
9 Gilling Gap

- - - N.E. Boundary
⊣ Scarp Face

Scale
0   10
miles

Fig 5.

and the great limestone are strong landform builders with intervening vales on shales and softer sediments, the lower slopes being usually cloaked in glacial drift. The coastal plain, mainly of glacial drift, broadens in south-east Northumberland and continues into north-east Durham; in its estuarine section the Tyne crosses this plain after emerging from a gorge tract at Newcastle.

County Durham is strongly influenced in its relief by the tableland of the north Pennines, on carboniferous-limestone formations (Fig 6), with short, northward-trending valleys and long west-to-east dales in the upper Wear and Tees. The lithology of the rock is varied and merges into the gritstones of the north-west and south-west Durham plateaus; in the upper dales, including Swaledale and Wensleydale to the south, there are true limestones with a characteristic scenery.

Central and eastern Durham are underlain by the triangular coal basin which has its northern apex around Amble in Northumberland. The coal measures slope eastwards, to pass as the 'concealed' coalfield below the magnesian limestone (permian) of the east-Durham plateau. The northward trend of the middle Wear lies in a drift-floored vale, occupied by the main road and rail links from Darlington to Newcastle; from this section valleys trend westwards up into the plateaus of west Durham. The coastline of east Durham is composed of limestone cliffs, topped by drift and breached by the deep, narrow valleys locally termed 'denes'. The coalfield terminates abruptly by a fault-line on the south. At the surface the magnesian limestone dip-slope passes gently into the broad, fluvio-glacial and alluvial Tees lowland underlain by triassic sediments (bunter and keuper), and which in turn blends southwards into the drift and alluvium of the Northallerton gap and the northern Vale of York.

The Cleveland hills rise steeply to the south of Teesside, a tabular massif of jurassic sediments, limestones, shales and sandstones, sloping gently southwards to the broad west-east Vale of Pickering. The deeply-trenched Esk valley flows eastward to Whitby; its tributary vales bring out strikingly the tabular, flat-topped structure of the northern Clevelands. On the west the scarps of the Hambledon hills overlook the Vale of York; beyond lies the Yorkshire dales country, Swaledale, Wensleydale and Nidderdale.

Natural Zones

The relief and layout of the North East is thus strongly differentiated, with striking contrast in land use and capability as between

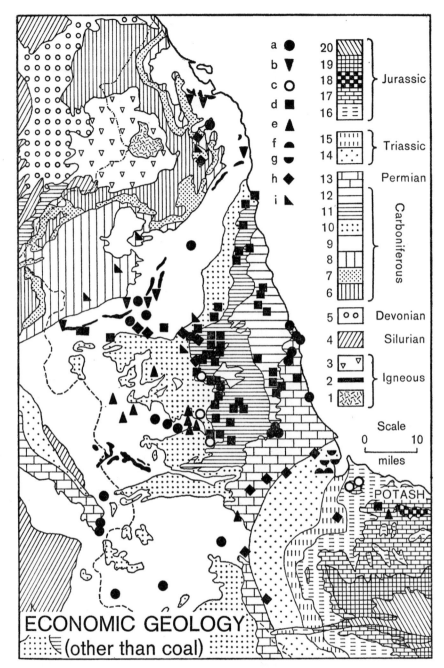

ECONOMIC GEOLOGY
(other than coal)

Fig 6. Key: a. limestone, b. whinstone, c. iron ore, d. fireclay, e. ganister, f. anhydrite, g. salt, h. sand and gravel, i. freestone.

1 granite, 2 quartz dolerite (dykes, sills), 3 andesite and basic lavas, 6 cementstone, 7 fell sandstone, 8 scremerston group, 9 carboniferous limestone series, 10 coal measures (and millstone grit), 11 coal measures (main productive), 12 coal measures (upper), 14 bunter, 15 keuper, 16 lower lias, 17 oolites, 18 cornbrash/Oxford clay, 19 corallian, 20 kimmeridge clay. (Source: *Scientific Survey of North East England*, British Association 1949.)

upland and lowland.[2] With an average of 45 in or more precipitation per annum, allied with thin, poor, leached soils and a short, cloudy growing season, with a late start and risk of early terminal frosts, the High Pennines and Cheviots lie above the limits of cultivation or even of intensive pasturing. The foot-hills, from around 1,000 to 1,500 ft, have an almost equally severe climate but lesser precipitation, 35 to 45 in per annum. This is the zone of major Forestry Commission planting in post-war years, with a commercial timberline between 1,250 and 1,500 ft. Oats will not ripen above 1,200 ft, even with favourable soil and aspect, and there is virtually no permanent habitation above 1,000 ft.

The intermediate regions, with 25 to 35 in of rain each year, are variable in quality, depending on aspect and exposure. Between 800 and 1,000 ft agriculture may be practised and settlement is possible if the aspect is favourable, if some protection from the north and east is afforded and if slopes are not too steep. The valleys of the main rivers, such as that of the Tyne, afford locally more-favoured conditions with high farming and dense rural settlement.

The coast lowlands, the middle Wear valley, the Tees lowland and the Vale of York usually have less than 25 in of precipitation per annum. In Northumberland and Durham cloud, rainfall in July and August, and humidity near the coast, reduce the dryness of the growing season; on the Tees lowland and the Vale of York the growing season is perceptibly longer, summer temperatures are higher and the lighter soils may dry out. The cool coastal climate covers the major population concentrations of Tyne, Wear and Tees, and this tends to type the area in the eyes of those from outside, particularly when popularly associated with high levels of atmospheric pollution, and a marked tendency towards grey, overcast skies.

Land Quality

Environmental conditions mean that first-grade land in the North East is rare and limited to patches in the coastal plain of south-east Northumberland, the middle Wear and the Tees lowland. The east-Durham plateau, the coastal lowland around Belford and the Merse of Tweed is good quality land (II + 1 category)[2] but much of the intermediate land is second-grade and, as might be expected, the plateaus and hills are almost uniformly and extensively third-class in quality; their entrenched vales usually rise in status to III + 2 grade. Mining subsidence introduces patches of poor quality land into the coast lowlands and the lower plateaus. Fortunately the highest quality land is not often threatened by uses alternative to farming, though the expansion of Teesside and the new towns at Peterlee, Washington and Cramlington are all necessarily taking place on good farmland. The North Tyneside green belt, one of the few approved in Britain outside Greater London, has hitherto limited urban sprawl on the grade II land around the conurbation.

The physique, structure and layout of the North East have furthered the concentration of settlement and industry into the lower reaches of Tyne, Wear and Tees. Isolated centres of manufacturing have been few and confined either to the processing of local minerals or agricultural raw materials or to a service function for a restricted market hinterland.

Minerals

The range of local minerals is considerable, many of contemporary importance (Fig 6). The coal industry itself is considered in detail in Chapter 6. Ironstone, once prolific in the northern flank of the Cleve-lands, is today worked out in economic terms both there and in more scattered deposits in west Durham, or as far away as the upper North Tyne. Building and road-making materials include limestone, whin-stone (from the igneous whin sill), and freestone, the latter in declining use today. The voracious needs of the construction industry have hitherto been met from large sand and gravel deposits south-west of Newcastle, in central Durham, the middle Tees valley and around Richmond and Catterick. Indications are that a scarcity is developing and hauls, conventionally around 20 to 25 miles, will need to be increased shortly. Limestone is also used agriculturally and for furnace linings; as regards the latter the large quarries on the face of the east Durham scarp are favourably placed for the Teesside steel industry. Fireclay and ganister are widespread through the coalfield but the North East has to import quality bricks. The salt and anhydrite deposits of Teesside were influential in the growth of the table-salt and, more substantially at a later date, the heavy inorganic chemical industry at Billingham. More recently the discovery of vast potash reserves at great depth under and off the coast of north-east Yorkshire suggests a further notable addition to regional mineral resources once the decisions on the economics of brining or deep-mining as a method of extraction are taken. Opencast coal extraction has contributed some of the most dramatic temporary landscape changes since 1945

(Fig 12). Today its contribution is diminishing but the smooth, rolling contours and fenced fields indicate its passage throughout much of the lowland North East. Unlike in the Greater London area, land-use conflict involving minerals is relatively rare in the North East. Dereliction of land is however much more common and the legacy of long-term coalmining has left sizeable tracts of unstable land. Few new developments, including the new towns of Peterlee and Washington, can ignore the effects of strata movements in designing a programme for the expansion of their built-up area.

Hitherto regarded as universally abundant, water is a mineral of increasing scarcity and rising cost. Tyneside draws its water from the series of reservoirs from the upper Rede to Whittle Dene; Teesside from the upper Tees and, to a small extent, from the Clevelands. Sunderland and Hartlepool have also drawn on the deep water-table below the magnesian limestone and more recently the Derwent reservoir has provided both additional supplies and a developing centre of recreation. Teesside faces the greatest prospective water shortage and the Cow Green reservoir proposal in upper Teesdale, an exception to the lack of land-use conflict, brought bitter opposition from those wishing to protect the area's unique flora from encroachment by a storage reservoir. Within the concept of the Solway barrage project on the west coast there may be some provision for piping water across to Tyneside, but at present the Solway scheme seems likely to rank well behind the Morecambe Bay project in precedence and both seem destined for longer-term development.

Peopling and Development

Though the North East has an industrial history stretching back through the centuries it was the impact of the late eighteenth-century industrial revolution and its flowering during the nineteenth century that gave the region its heaviest imprint of factory, town and mine,[3] that created the narrowly-based but for a long time prosperous industrial structure and laid the foundations of the problems of adjustment, decline and rehabilitation which have emerged and persisted in the twentieth century.

In 1801 the North East had barely 0·33 million people and still slightly less than 0·66 million forty years later. The great economic momentum from iron and steel, metal shipbuilding and heavy engineering developed thereafter, with 1 million people in the region by the mid-1860s, 2 million by 1901 after the most rapid crescendo of growth, and 2·5 million at the time of the economic depression of the early 1930s. This scale of economic development was prodigious requiring a major transformation in the landscape, the burgeoning of industrial cities, a spreading rash of densely-peopled mining villages (Fig 15), and an immense and swelling tide of in-migrants during its most formative stages. The early railway age was partly responsible for the sharp influx of people in the 1840s and early 1850s, supplemented by the effects of the Irish famines and the start of a movement off the land that was to rise to flood-tide by the early 1870s. By the 1880s the large and youthful population of the region was providing its own entrants to the vast labour force and there then began that slight net exodus of people which has characterised the North East ever since. A net loss trickle of 19,000 in the 1880s became a net outflow of 33,000 in the decade before the First World War, rose to a great net ebb-tide of 141,000 in 1911–21, and culminated in a massive net out-migration of more than 190,000 between 1921 and 1931.

The turbulent flow of nineteenth century in-migrants peopled the coalfield and the towns. In 1821 two-thirds of the North Easterners lived in settlements of less than 2,000 persons; by 1931 more than half lived in towns of more than 50,000. Accompanying the change there were profound internal redistributions and changes in the employment structure. In the early nineteenth century the concentration of mining around the lower banks of the Tyne and Wear was already well-established, linked by wagon-ways to the coaling staithes— the link from south-west Durham to the Tees awaited the Stockton & Darlington railway. Factory employment was limited to Tyne and Wear though several market towns showed a variety of small industrial establishments; the lower Tees was in large measure still under marshes and green fields downstream from the small port of Stockton.[4] The concentration of the North East's economy on extractive activity, mining, and farming, associated with commerce and limited but varied manufacturing, persisted until the early 1850s.

From the mid-nineteenth century the framework of the present economy rapidly took shape, in structure, location and also in incipient problems. A major industrial boom lasted for some forty years, with a rising tempo of expansion in iron production, then steel, and a steady increase in the varied trades and manufactures using these as raw materials. By 1861 the boom was already in full swing, with shipbuilding employment emerging strongly on Tyne and Wear, though accompanied there by the pottery, glass, and alkali chemical industries.

The expansion of Teesside was meteoric—among the most dramatic in Britain during the Industrial Revolution—based on the advantage of combining Cleveland iron ore with south-west Durham coking coal for the manufacture of iron at an estuarine site with ample land for industrial and urban expansion. Population in the coalfield thickened steadily as the railways put more distant pits in touch with tide-water coaling staithes and the demand for coal in Britain and abroad rose steadily and sharply. The middle Wear, the margins of the east-Durham plateau, and the steam-coal district of south Northumberland, all became heavily populated in the early 1850s; the Tow Law and Derwent (later Consett) ironworks had been started on the bleak west-Durham plateau some ten years earlier. The population of the North East has never since been so cosmopolitan and included Irishmen, miners from south Wales and Staffordshire, Cornishmen, and unemployed tin-miners from Derbyshire.

Table 5

ECONOMIC GROWTH INDICATORS FOR THE NORTH EAST
1841–1931

	1841	1861	1881	1901	1931
Population (NE) (1,000s)	617	942	1458	1995	2515
Coal (million tons)	9	19	35	45	42
Coal miners (1,000s)	23	50	96	165	188
Iron ore (million tons)	–	1·5	6·3	5·6	1·5
Pig iron (million tons)	–	0·7	2·0	2·8	1·1
Steel (million tons)	–	–	0·3	1·3	1·1
Iron and steel workers (1,000s)	–	13	31	34	23
Shipbuilding workers (1,000s)	–	7	15	42	51
Lead (1,000 tons)	14	19	15	5	4

Source: Various.

The crescendo of industrial expansion continued through the later nineteenth century, attracting a rising flow of rural workers into the towns and mines. Depopulation of the countryside caused abandonment of some isolated farms, decay of outlying hamlets and the downward creep of the moorland boundary. The output of pig-iron rose steadily until the turn of the century with the supply of rails, ships and machinery in a generally prosperous market. During the 1880s the problems of converting the phosphoric Cleveland ores to steel were overcome with the aid of the Thomas-Gilchrist process, and markets for iron and steel products at home and abroad rose meteorically and diversified as the engineering industry proliferated its products.

The thirty years to the First World War saw the zenith of the coal, shipbuilding and traditional heavy-engineering industries of the North East and in this period the regional contribution to the national export economy was also close to its peak. Much of the industrial and urban landscape was fashioned at this time and the last phase of major coalfield development was ushered in. Fig 15 (page 105) shows the pattern of employment in 1914 at Northumberland and Durham pits, a striking contrast in its density and numbers to the situation today. Districts ranked as marginal now, in north-west and south-west Durham or in south-east Northumberland, were then in maximum production whilst large new sinkings had taken place through the east-Durham plateau in the late nineteenth and early twentieth centuries. The effects of mining are still manifest even on those landscapes where production has long ceased, in the colliery yards, the drab pitmen's terraces, the wagon-ways and the subsidence 'flashes', a sombre legacy for the modern planner. Similarly the monotonous red-brick terraced fabric of the large cities, the geometrical patterned suburbs of Tyneside, Sunderland and the Teesside towns date from the period 1880 to 1914. The rapid urban sprawl conveniently, though with bye-law salubrity, housed the industrial workers and the middle class, linked to workplace by the urban tramway system and the beginnings of rail commuting.

Around the turn of the century the shipyards were producing some two-fifths of the national tonnage, with a degree of internal specialisation on each of the three rivers. Passenger liners and warships were the pride of the Tyne, cargo liners and tramp steamers were more characteristic of Wear and Tees. The engineering industry of the later nineteenth century also showed variety in the individual industrial areas of the North East. Tyneside was characterised by the marine, early heavy-electrical, and general branches of engineering; Darlington by locomotive manufacture, only recently demised, and railway repair work; whilst the Tees predominated in constructional engineering, bridge-building, iron and steel founding and many small branches of the metal trades.

From the First World War to the economic depression of the early 1930s the North Eastern economy underwent its first stages of agonising reappraisal. The mining industry progressively lost its large overseas export markets, its labour force began to fall, pits in the outer margins closed or were flooded and decay set in among the pitmen's villages. The iron and steel industry suffered fluctuations whilst shipbuilding, forever a cyclical manufacture, experienced unemployment, smaller yards failed and depression spread to other heavy industries. New growth industries, such as heavy electrical engineering or the heavy inorganic chemical industry at Billingham from 1928 onwards failed to offset instability, unemployment, recurrent crises and progressive out-migration of workers from the traditional mining and manufacturing towns. The stage was set for the traumatic experience of mass unemployment in the early 1930s, a vivid recollection for some to this day and an evil part of northern lore and legend. This precipitated government interest and action, the substance of Chapter 4, and thus began the slow, progressive transformation from a leader rôle in nineteenth-century Britain to a changed, but not substantially diminished status in the mid-twentieth century.

References to this chapter are on pages 239 and 246–8.

3

People and Work

Population

Distribution

Approximately 3,000,000 (2,973,760 in 1968) the population of the North East shows striking contrasts in distribution and density (Fig 7). Only central Scotland and south Wales show a comparably sharp break between urban concentration and wide dispersal through a thinly-settled rural hinterland.

The Tyneside conurbation (842,630) with Sunderland (219,710) totals more than 1 million, tightly grouped along the banks of Tyne and Wear. By comparison Teesside, as defined in *Challenge of the Changing North*, is a more open city grouping with rather more than 0·5 million people. Between Tyne and Tees the coalfield has a close mesh of settlement, nucleated in mining villages or mining service centres for the most part; the characteristic North Eastern small or medium-sized town in the population bracket of 10,000 to 40,000 is well represented. Similarly specialised coalfield towns are found in south-east Northumberland, with a close interurban interval.

Within the towns of the North East densities of population vary by the ward and reflect both the age of the urban fabric and the socio-economic composition of the residents. Some of the highest residential densities per acre in the nation are recorded on Tyneside and in central Middlesbrough, a clear indicator of statutory overcrowding, which is being progressively improved by the process of urban renewal. The high concentration of people in the towns and cities, a product of the boom development of the area during the past hundred years, has produced its own growth momentum and with almost two-thirds of the regional population in the larger cities it is difficult to envisage a radical redistribution during this century. The sparse population around,

49

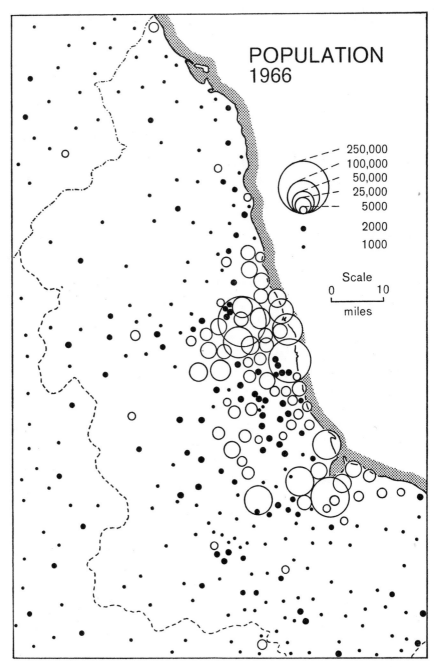

POPULATION
1966

250,000
100,000
50,000
25,000
5000

2000

1000

Scale
0   10
miles

Fig 7. (Source: data from *Census* volumes for the North Eastern counties 1961 and 1966.)

and the limited size and scattered nature of the market centres, offer little as potential growth centres; in this sense the gap in the hierarchy of urban settlements and the outworn character of some central areas is something of a regional handicap.

By contrast with the urbanised core the outer rural zone has extensive tracts with population densities of one person per twenty-five acres, or less. Even taking into account the higher actual densities along the valley floors and lower slopes these densities are among the lowest in Britain. Dense rural populations correlate well with the higher quality of farmland in the coastal areas and westward along the main valleys. Within the more closely-settled rural area lie the main market settlements, irregularly-spaced and with three size categories: 5,000; 7,000; 11,000–13,000. Nucleation in rural settlements is well represented through villages down to hamlet level; dispersal of population is seen in the former lead-mining dales of the northern Pennines but is not generally characteristic.

Structure

In socio-economic structure, as shown by the census classification, the Northern region in 1966 had a deficiency of executive and white collar grades (census socio-economic groups 1–4 and 5–7 respectively), but an above average representation of blue collar workers (groups 8–11); semi-skilled manual workers, group 10, are high in proportion to skilled workers when compared with the national average.[1] A similar contrast with the United Kingdom is seen in personal income levels (before tax), for 1964–5: below £1,000, Northern region 66 per cent, UK 62 per cent; £1,000–2,500, 32 per cent and 36 per cent respectively; over £2,500, 1 per cent and 2 per cent.

The age composition of the Northern region has slightly higher proportions below 15 years, illustrating the continuing rather larger natural increase rate and fractionally fewer people above retirement age. A socially telling statistic is the low proportion of Northern children staying on at school beyond the age of 15, (1967 North 36 per cent; UK 46 per cent).

Change

Table 6 shows that in spite of a post-war rise in the surplus of births over deaths a net loss of migrants to other parts of the country or abroad has kept the North East's population increase to modest

Table 6

THE NORTH EAST. POPULATION CHANGE 1938–67

	Estimated population (1,000s)	Total change (1,000s)	Natural increase (1,000s)	Migration	
				change (1,000s)	net rate per annum
1967 (6 year)	2,965	+ 72	+115	− 43	−7·2
1961 (5 year)	2,893	+ 71	+ 98	− 27	−5·4
1956 (5 year)	2,822	+ 44	+ 84	− 40	−8·0
1951 (13 year)	2,778	+101	+204	−103	−7·9
1938	2,677	—	—	—	—

Source: Census Reports and Registrar General's Annual Estimates.

proportions, only 288,000 in almost thirty years, or slightly less than 4 per 1,000 per annum. Nevertheless there have been more sizeable short-term fluctuations, in keeping with the state of the national and regional economy: in 1951–2 there was a net loss of 15,100 migrants, in 1960–1, 16,700; by contrast the net loss was down to only 2,100 in 1955–6 and 1,900 in 1958–9. During the same period levels of unemployment were characteristically double the national average, a clear indication that the rate of job provision was inadequate both in its range and volume. Between 1962 and 1966 the net loss of migrants varied from 9,000 to 14,000 per annum, the latter figure being reached in 1963–4. The latest figure, 1966–7, recorded a net migration loss of only 4,000.

The higher post-war birth rates are now bringing increasing numbers into the labour force, notwithstanding the continuing loss of migrants from the North East. Population projections imply a rapid rise in the regional population by 1981 and an accelerating trend towards the end of the century. Indeed it is a feature of regional policy to reduce the level of net outmigration by the mid-1970s and stop net loss altogether at a later date. This will necessarily require a very considerable increase in the rate of new job provision and the rise in population by the end of the century involves major decisions on its location in the very near future, if these are to differ at all noticeably from the present pattern, a possibility which seems increasingly unlikely.

The process of migration is central to the study of regional populations and provides a general barometer of economic and social change.[2] Though the figures of net loss of migrants are never dramatic these days, unlike the mass of outward movement in the depression years of the early 1930s, they conceal a much larger total movement and the process is a selective one, with consequently more serious effects

Page 53: *British Steel Corporation: (above) Hartlepool South works of South Durham Steel & Iron Company; (below) Consett iron and steel works.*

Page 54: (above) *Teesport and Shell oil refinery*; (below) *ICI Wilton works, looking north to the Tees estuary.*

both on employment and social structure and on the health and well-being of particular communities and sub-regions.

The numbers of employed persons in movement into and out of the Northern region have been increasing steadily, about 60,000 annually in the late 1950s, 70,000–80,000 in the early 1960s, a volume which is between six to eight times the net loss of employed persons. It is not possible to break down the Northern region data into separate figures for the North East. The scale on which people are moving is not in itself disturbing, indeed high turnover often indicates an affluent society but the steady net loss, particularly since 2 of every 5 lost are under 30 years of age, is potentially more serious for the economic health and welfare of the region. Slightly more girls and women are leaving than men (112 to 100), particularly from the countryside and the mining areas, where jobs for females are scarcer. The socio-economic composition of migrants to and from the Northern region shows general similarity with the structure of the regional population, ie the greatest movement is among skilled manual workers, followed by junior non-manual employees, both male and female. Curiously there is also an above average to-and-fro movement in precisely those categories which are deficient in the region. The executive and white collar groups are both groups which it is vital to conserve, even attract, if regional development policies are to be effective.

The currents of migration are complex, with compensating flows and counter-currents, but certain net trends are apparent: the drift from the countryside continues, though it is rarely spectacular in scale; the most affected areas are in the more remote dales of the upland rim and in the lowland hinterland of Berwick on Tweed. Regrouping of the coal-mining population is beginning, in response to the rising volume and widespread incidence of pit closures supplemented by the rehousing policies of the respective councils: the areas most affected are south-east Northumberland and west Durham but south-east Durham, with its modern, larger collieries, several of which have recently closed, is also important in this respect.

The 'flight to the suburbs' and the loss of population from almost all the city central areas is a national phenomenon and one characteristic alike of the lower Tyne, Wear and Tees. Loss from the centre is the counterpart of the rehousing in peripheral estates, with limited but controlled urban sprawl (Fig 8 page 56 and Fig 12 on page 95). These outlying estates tend to perpetuate the single-class communities of the inner suburbs, wealth being equated with distinctive housing standards and a congregation of the like-minded.

D

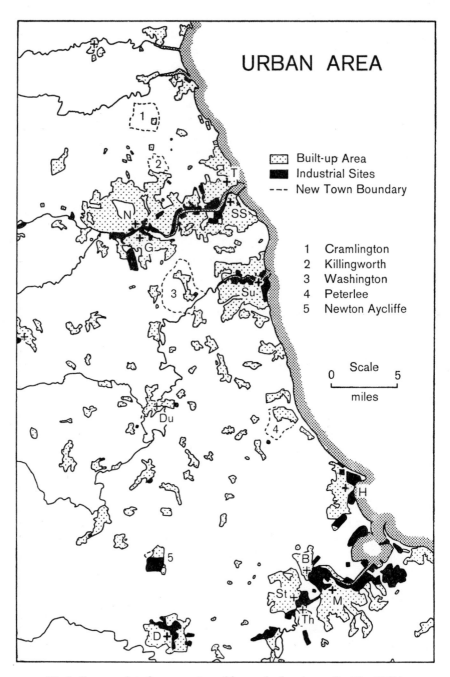

URBAN AREA

Built-up Area
Industrial Sites
New Town Boundary

1 Cramlington
2 Killingworth
3 Washington
4 Peterlee
5 Newton Aycliffe

Scale
0   5
miles

Fig 8. (Source: data from county and borough planning authorities 1968.)

Illustrating sub-regional contrasts Teesside has grown in population, Tyneside has developed more slowly and there has been a relative decline in the more marginal areas, both rural and mining districts alike. These trends reflect intra-regional movements, which in total exceed those across the boundaries of the North East. The greatest volume of migration indeed is that between streets and suburbs in the large towns.

Interchanges of North Easterners with other parts of Britain bring out once again the importance of immediately adjacent economic regions, the East and West Ridings, the North West and Scotland, but also show the attraction of Greater London, though this is less prominent than might have been expected in view of its size and affluence. Similarly the scale of interchange with the prosperous Midlands is in a minor key.

Reasons for the complex movements of people cannot readily be simplified. Within journey to work distance, interpreted as up to eighteen miles from place of work in the North, personal reasons such as housing, marriage, desire for a better living environment predominate; over eighteen miles either still within the same economic region or outward to another region, the search for work, for a new job, or for promotion becomes paramount. In reality single motives are rare but nevertheless most movement tends to be triggered-off by a particular cause among many that might have been significant. An interesting outcome of migration analysis is the detection of a compensating counter-current for almost every flow, differing little in its composition by age, sex, occupation or social status from the movement in the opposite direction. In rural areas or marginal industrial districts however there is usually a perceptibly older, less privileged group in the inflow compared with those who are leaving.

The implications of migration for the development, economy and social composition of sub-regions of the North East are dealt with later where relevant—ability to influence the process is the most vital consideration for the regional planner at the present time.

Work

Some reference has been made to the general employment structure of the Northern region, in comparison with other British heavy industrial regions. The North East accounts for the bulk of the Northern insured population; 1,133,000 of 1,309,000 (87 per cent) in 1966.

Table 7

THE NORTH EAST. INSURED EMPLOYMENT 1948–66
(In thousands)

	Male	Female	Total	Female as a percentage of total	Change Male	Change female	Total	Percentage annual change NE	GB
1966	757	376	1,133	33·0	−21	+51	+30	+0·4	+0·9
1959	778	325	1,103	29·5	+15	+25	+40	+0·6	+0·8
1953*	763	300	1,063	28·3	−25	+14	−11	−0·2	+0·6
1948*	788	286	1,074	26·7	—	—	—	—	—

* adjusted figures.

Source: Department of Employment & Productivity data.

The overall rate of employment growth in the North East since the war has been slower than the national average, fluctuating with national and regional conditions of prosperity and depression, and with an unemployment rate typically double that of the UK. The apparent decline in employment between 1948 and 1953 in the North East (Table 7) indicates the effects of transition from a wartime to a peacetime economy. The increases during the 1950s and 1960s are a compound of the internal trends of growth and decline in locally-based activities and the result of the introduction of new industries under stimulus of government industrial-location policies. They further conceal some quite marked changes in the service industries of the North East.[3]

A striking feature is the extent of the 'petticoat revolution' in post-war years, with notable growth of female jobs, especially during the 1960s. The overall decline in male jobs during the past seven years is a most disturbing feature of the general employment situation, a decline it is imperative to stop and reverse since many further male jobs are going to be lost in the near future with the continuing rundown in certain basic industries. The two-job family for some North Eastern households would be a poor recompense for the loss of the only bread-winner employed in others.

During the post-war years there has been a broad structural change in the economy of the North East (Table 8). Employment in mining and quarrying, dominated by coal mining, has declined from one-fifth of all employment in 1939 to less than 10 per cent in 1966. Agriculture has always been less represented regionally than nationally and its labour force has also declined both proportionately and absolutely. Manufacturing employment has fluctuated in its proportionate status whilst the numbers employed in the service industry, commensurate with some increase in affluence and the influence of the State in economic life, have scarcely ceased to rise, though with marked changes in internal composition. The impact of these broad changes on the sub-regions and on the landscapes of the North East are discussed later.

Within the critically important manufacturing sector, on which the prosperity and prospects for the North East firmly depend, changes have been striking. Though employment figures are with great difficulty comparable over the entire post-war period it is clear that shipbuilding and marine engineering, together with certain heavy-engineering

Table 8

SECTORS OF THE NORTH EAST ECONOMY 1939–66, PERCENTAGE OF INSURED EMPLOYMENT

	Mining and quarrying	Manufacturing	Services	Agriculture	Other	Total
1966	9·0	36·8	52·1	1·7	0·4	100·0
1959	14·5	35·9	47·3	2·3	0·0	100·0
1953	16·0	37·4	44·1	2·4	0·1	100·0
1948	16·0	33·9	46·6	3·4	0·1	100·0
1939	21·4	32·2	43·4	3·0	0·0	100·0

Source: Department of Employment & Productivity data.

branches, notably vehicle manufacture, have declined whilst other industries, including electrical engineering and electrical goods, metal manufacture, cotton textiles and clothing, timber, paper and miscellaneous manufactures have increased their representation in employment terms.

Bound up with these changes in industry groups discussed in the next chapter is the entire course of regional policy and the progress of the North East's readjustment, from being one of Britain's most vulnerable economic regions, to being one of greater diversity and balance, with new growth elements to compensate at least in some measure for the effects of continuing decline in traditional manufactures. Broadly summarising this change a specialisation index has been compiled,* for the North East and for its component sub-regions. The figures for the North East: 1936 = 36·7, 1953 = 33·9, 1959 = 32·2, 1966 = 31·5 indicate a general but slow rate of diminishing specialisation; but it must be remembered that these changes are com-

* *Specialisation Index* $= \sqrt{P_3^2 + P_4^2 \ldots P_{16}^2}$ where P indicates % representation of each industry group (III-XVI) of the Standard Industrial Classification. Minimum index (i.e. maximum diversification) = 25·0.

plex and include the running down of some long-established and specialised branches of manufacturing as well as the introduction and expansion of others.

As an expression of the relationship between the rate of growth of population, provision of new jobs, and the frictions and impediments in the process of regional economic and social change the level of unemployment is a useful general indicator. The level must be consistently measured against national as well as regional circumstances.

Economic Sub-regions (Fig 9)

Just as the North East is a functioning part of the national and international economy so its constituent sub-regions are integral parts of the working regional economy, itself, as has been seen, an open-ended system. Sub-regional definition must for this reason involve a degree of arbitrariness and abstraction but is justifiable to the extent that there is valid internal diversity in economic structure, trends and problems. The broad principles in definition relate to distinctive blend of employment, settlement pattern and hierarchy, position and status in regional policies and strategies. Since the employment analysis is the foundation of sub-regional assessment it is necessary to adopt groupings of employment-exchange areas. Those adopted are essentially the sub-regions recognised by the economic planning council, with minor modifications.

The sub-regions (Table 9) may be classified as follows:

Rural hinterland	North
	West
	North Riding
Coalfield	Northumberland
	north-west Durham
	north-east Durham
	south-west Durham
	south-east Durham
Conurbations and major towns	Tyneside north
	Tyneside south
	Wearside
	Darlington (with Teesdale)
	Teesside
	Teesside (Cleveland)

The mainly rural economy employs one-tenth, the coalfield one-fifth and the urban concentrations rather more than two-thirds of the regional labour force. Female jobs are one in three throughout the

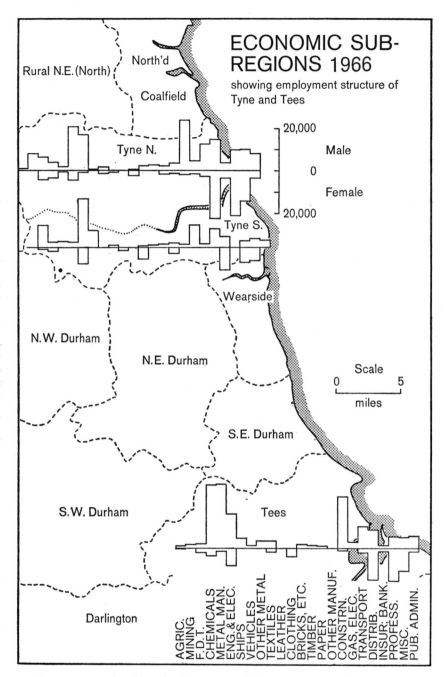

ECONOMIC SUB-
REGIONS 1966
showing employment structure of
Tyne and Tees

Rural N.E.(North)

North'd
Coalfield

Tyne N.

20,000

Male

0

Female

20,000

Tyne S.

Wearside

N.W. Durham

N.E. Durham

Scale
0   5
miles

S.E. Durham

S.W. Durham

Tees

Darlington

AGRIC.
MINING
F.D.T.
CHEMICALS
METAL MAN.
ENG. & ELEC.
SHIPS
VEHICLES
OTHER METAL
TEXTILES
LEATHER
CLOTHING
BRICKS, ETC.
TIMBER
PAPER
OTHER MANUF.
CONSTRN.
GAS, ELEC.
TRANSPORT
DISTRIB.
INSUR: BANK.
PROFESS.
MISC.
PUB. ADMIN.

Fig 9. (Source : data from the Department of Employment & Productivity 1966.)

Table 9

ECONOMIC STRUCTURE OF SUB-REGIONS OF THE NORTH EAST 1966

1966	Employment (1,000's)	Percentage of females	Percentage in agriculture	Percentage in mining and quarrying	Percentage in manufacturing	Percentage in services	Percentage in other activities	Specialisation index	manufacturing		3 major industrial groups (SIC)		
									Percentage in major industrial group	Percentage in 3 major industrial groups			
RURAL													
Rural North	27	34·4	15·3	9·4	10·8	64·3	0·2	36·5	19·7	52·4	3	6A	10
Rural West	15	36·5	11·8	5·2	17·8	65·2	0·0	36·4	25·9	51·8	4	14	16
Rural N. Riding	63	38·0	9·7	0·9	12·8	76·3	0·3	38·3	43·6	63·8	3	8	6B
COALFIELD													
Northumberland	45	26·4	0·8	40·4	18·6	39·8	0·4	40·5	28·7	61·9	6B	12	7
NW Durham	33	28·0	1·6	19·1	35·8	43·2	0·3	54·9	47·6	83·6	5	6A	16
NE Durham	72	30·6	1·1	21·8	25·1	51·8	0·2	36·4	24·8	51·4	6A	12	4
SW Durham	42	32·2	1·6	15·5	40·2	40·0	0·3	40·2	29·9	61·5	6B	8	12
SE Durham	26	26·0	1·3	52·4	11·5	34·3	0·5	50·8	38·8	78·8	12	3	10
URBAN													
Tyneside North	255	36·3	0·5	3·2	33·8	62·0	0·5	34·9	20·8	51·6	7	6A	3
Tyneside South	150	33·8	0·2	7·8	48·0	43·7	0·3	36·4	22·2	55·2	6B	6A	7
Wearside	107	35·0	0·2	13·3	39·1	47·1	0·3	37·5	24·4	58·6	7	6B	6A
Darlington	44	33·6	2·6	0·5	40·7	56·0	0·2	38·8	23·8	60·7	6A	10	5
Teesside	237	30·3	0·5	0·9	51·4	47·1	0·1	41·6	27·4	66·5	4	5	6A
Tees (Cleveland)	10	40·0	2·7	0·2	45·7	51·1	0·3	62·4	59·9	80·6	5	12	6A
NORTH EAST	1,133*	33·2	1·7	9·0	36·8	52·1	0·3	31·5	16·5	41·4	6A	6B	5

(* includes unrounded 100s.)

Source: Department of Employment & Productivity data.

SIC identifications: 3 food, drink, tobacco; 4 chemicals; 5 metal manufacture; 6A general engineering; 6B electrical machinery and goods; 7 shipbuilding and marine engineering; 8 vehicles; 10 textiles; 12 clothing and footwear; 14 timber, furniture etc; 16 other manufacturing.

North East, lower in the coalfield and more fully represented in the rural areas, with a high ratio of employment in service population. Provision of new jobs has for some time been more buoyant for women than for men.

The three rural sub-regions differ in degree, but significantly in the proportions engaged in agriculture, in the service industries and by type and spread of industrial establishments. The Rural North lies between Morpeth and the Scottish border and includes the market towns of Morpeth, Alnwick and Berwick; part lies within the coalfield and the southern margins have commuter populations from the Tyne-side city region. Both these features conceal the characteristics of truly rural populations. Rural problem areas emerge further north particularly around Berwick on Tweed where the development commission is currently implementing a pilot scheme for rural stability and growth. Employment in manufacturing is low and biased to food and drink and the engineering industry. The service population has a high ratio and the truly rural character of large tracts is indicated by the highest sub-regional percentage engaged in agriculture. The Rural West is principally the Tyne valley west of Prudhoe. It has a higher commuter population, a lower ratio in agriculture and almost no mining today, though pits have closed within the past decade. Apart from the problems of rural isolation in the Pennines and Border fells there are pockets of former coalmining communities and there has been an undue dependence on the ICI chemical plant at Prudhoe (closed 1967) in a limited range of industry, to which a recent addition has been the chipboard factory at Hexham, located there to use wood from the north-Tyne forests.

The Rural North Riding contains the resort towns of Scarborough, Whitby, and Saltburn, together with commuter settlements from Tees-side and immediately north of York. Three-quarters of all jobs are thus in the service industries, a much higher proportion than a normal rural area with its market towns could justify. The military establishments at Richmond and Catterick add a distinctive, though declining, ingredient to the service population. Though low in proportion manufactures are diverse, with food and drink, electrical goods and vehicles clearly represented—a useful balance of growth industries, yet mostly in fairly small and scattered establishments; apart from Cleveland the Rural North Riding has the highest sub-regional percentage of female employment. The problems of the sub-region concern rural transport and social provision, the needs of the resort areas, and the pressure for development on rural land to which commercial potash mining is being added in the near future.

The coalfield sub-regions have seen some of the most dramatic employment changes during the past decade, with the progressive contraction of the mining labour force since 1957. Dominance of mining varies locally, but sub-regionally is highest in the area of many large twentieth-century collieries in south-east Durham and in the Northumberland coalfield. The employment trends are much more diverse among coalfield localities and are less masked by manufacturing than in other non-coal sub-regions of Durham. The coalfields are characterised by high specialisation indices which means a lack of variety in manufacturing, often also a deficiency in the number of jobs available. Female employment is always, and at times conspicuously, below the regional (33 per cent) and the national (37 per cent) averages.

Government industrial-location policy has made some notable achievements in the coalfield, illustrated by the dominant types of manufacturing, for example: clothing, food and drink, textiles in south-east Durham; electrical goods and clothing in south Northumberland. The most vulnerable coalfield sub-regions are south-east Durham, with its over-dependence on mining and lack of sufficient alternative jobs for men, and the north-west Durham plateau where the Consett steel plant dominates manufacturing and is itself faced with an uncertain future, at a time when local mining decline is again accelerating. The presence of commuters travelling daily to Tyneside or Sunderland is responsible for the above-average service population in north-east Durham.

The division between north and south Tyneside, among urban sub-regions, is justified by a contrasting economic structure (Fig 9 and Table 9). On the north bank the metropolitan status of Newcastle is reflected in the 62 per cent service population, well above any other urban sub-region, and a fuller representation of female jobs. Conversely the south bank of the Tyne has a higher manufacturing percentage than all urban regions other than Teesside. Specialisation indices vary little though Teesside, with 41·6, has the least diversified manufacturing and north Tyneside has the most varied, with a useful range of new growth elements.

The strength of traditional manufacturing is seen in the ingredients of sub-regional specialisation: on the Tyne, shipbuilding and marine engineering, heavy engineering and the heavy electrical industry, with food and drink next in status; on Wearside a similar structure but with electrical goods, a major post-war development, second in status after shipbuilding. Darlington has a slightly less diversified industrial structure with heavy and constructional engineering, followed by woollen textiles and steel manufactures. Teesside strikingly shows the twin pillars of iron and steel and the heavy chemical industry, both inorganic and organic, these industries together employing more than half those in manufacturing; heavy engineering, 13 per cent of the labour force, is less significant than on the Tyne.

Contrasts between the Tyne and Tees sub-economies represent a common theme in the later study of employment changes, and an assessment of the differing prospects of each is vital to development of an effective regional strategy for the North East. The Tees has the merits of two major industrial sectors, both containing leader firms with great growth potential in terms of output but much less so in jobs; its demerit is the potential weakness caused by a lack of diversity in supporting manufactures. The Tyne suffers from its high ratio of declining industries but, since the war, has seen the introduction and development of a range of new manufactures which may give a more coherent and balanced development over the next few decades.

The Cleveland sub-economy is again marginal in character. Iron mining has ceased and the immediate proximity of Teesside has probably weakened rather than strengthened the prospects of introducing a more varied range of manufactures. Dependence on the Skinningrove iron and steel works for almost two-thirds of industrial jobs is a sign of vulnerability when the rationalisation of the steel industry is under active consideration and smaller or marginally located plants are the most likely to be eliminated. Textiles is the industry second in status, with only 12 per cent of jobs, and these mainly for women.

References to this chapter are on pages 240 and 248.

4

Development and Government Policy

SINCE THE economic depression of the early 1930s governments throughout the developed world have become steadily more involved in alleviating, though rarely finally curing, economic and social distress. More recently they have turned their attention to maintaining full employment or positively stimulating economic growth and seeking to improve regional living environments. In the process of economic and social 'first-aid' governments have never been entirely free agents, being affected often inexorably by international circumstances. Varying internal priorities and the changing political complexion of the decision-takers have added further variety to the often tangled skein of development. Consistently within the programmes of government involvement there has been a regional strand—perhaps more effectively termed a locality-based element of policy-making—often applied to unusual, even bizarrely defined, administrative entities. Since 1963 the ingredients of true regional planning have been introduced in Britain though it is still too early to speak of a coherent or even effective process of regional development.

Together with Clydeside, Merseyside and South Wales the North East has been a perennial experimental ground for full employment policies, industrial location programmes, aid to diversification, projects for improving living environment and, indeed, so often a test-bed for the variants of multi-strand government regional pilot-schemes. The development process is complex and many-sided, the product of countless, and often scarcely related decisions at government, local authority and private entrepreneurial level.

This chapter examines the course of government involvement with the North East and attempts a general assessment of the effects on the regional economy and the broad distribution of resources. It interprets the criteria for measurement of growth and change and suggests how far particular successive policies or non-policies have been beneficial to North Eastern industry. As yet no clear or final verdict is possible since it is difficult if not impossible to estimate what might have happened but for certain government involvements at critical times.

From Area to Regional Policy

Throughout successive policies the objective has remained similar; namely to reduce regional unemployment by introducing new and varied employment, thus helping to diversify the economy and to reduce the excessive dependence on a narrow range of long-established manufactures. Since the early 1960s a more positive policy of stimulation has been emphasised, rather than the traditional defensive elements of strategy, and phrases such as 'self-sustaining economic growth', 'increased development momentum', 'break-through to growth' have become fashionable, even practicable.

Pre 1939

The earliest government involvement in the regional conditions of the North East was born of acute distress and massive unemployment, resulting in the Special Areas Act of 1934, under which the central area of the North East was scheduled together with south Wales, west Cumberland and central Scotland. The measures were modest indeed, the objective most ambitious: 'to facilitate economic revival' of an area with 37 per cent of its insured employees out of work in June 1932.[1] Though industrial land could be purchased and communications improved by the special-area commissioners it was not until the government decided to experiment with trading estates, to build factories for letting to private firms, that industrialists were persuaded to move to the special areas and then only to a very limited degree in the early years. In May 1939 about 3,100 workers were employed on trading estates at Team Valley (2,500), St Helen's Auckland, Sunderland (Pallion) and Tynemouth. Several of the new firms were established by refugee industrialists from Europe, often with novel products; some of these firms have since developed into staple industries of the new North East and proved most fortunate introductions at a most timely juncture.

By September 1939 some 5,000 workers were employed on trading estates in the North East, more than half of them women. Jobs for

men proved harder to attract, unfortunately so, since the structural
unemployment was invariably among men. In some compensation,
employment in iron and steel, shipbuilding and heavy engineering
improved steadily after the rearmament programme began in 1937.
Nevertheless pockets of deep unemployment persisted: Tyneside,
Haltwhistle and the greater part of County Durham had been scheduled
for special aid in 1934; in parts of south-west Durham more than one-
third were still unemployed by 1937, whilst in Sunderland in the same
year the figure had not fallen below one-fifth.

The pre-war regional aid policy was embryonic but it contained
the principles which were to persist: the successful rôle of the trading
(later termed industrial) estate in attracting new firms or plants; the
priority given to location of new industry close to the localities with
highest unemployment rates; the success in providing hitherto scarce
jobs for women—the harbinger of the two-job family in the North East.

Also during the pre-war period, from 1936–8, there was uniquely
a short-lived and scarcely successful policy of encouraging, even
aiding, migration away from the North East as a means of alleviating
unemployment. Such aided migration proved expensive and meagre
in its effects, replaced after the 1944 White Paper on Employment
Policy by a general programme of 'taking work to the worker' which
has prevailed more or less ever since. Indeed in current thinking on
regional planning it is a declared objective to 'hold the natural increase
within the Northern Region' and to eliminate net outmigration within
the next fifteen years, a rather hopeful hostage to fortune.

1939–1945

During the 1939–45 war demand for the products of heavy industry
boomed and combined employment in coal, iron and steel, shipbuilding
and general heavy engineering rose from 35 per cent of all jobs in 1938
to 40 per cent in 1943, falling back to 34 per cent by 1946. Some
modernisation had taken place in the shipyards and steel plants and
the government policy of strategic dispersal of ordnance factories had
led to the setting up of important sites at Aycliffe and Spennymoor,
centres at which many females took jobs in manufacturing for the
first time. These acquired skills and factory experience were later to
be converted to employment in the new post-war industries. By mid-
1945 employment on industrial estates in the North East had risen to
about 12,000.

Changes Since 1945[2]

Stemming from the Royal Commission on the Distribution of the Industrial Population (Barlow Report) 1940, the White Paper on Employment Policy 1944, and the Distribution of Industry Act 1945 there developed in early post-war years a remarkably comprehensive planning process. The Board of Trade became, and has since remained, responsible for industrial location policy, with the power to schedule or remove from the schedule areas for priority government aid, termed development areas. The North East Development Area was on the original list in 1945 (Fig 11 on page 87) and remained a beneficiary until the lapse of the legislation in 1958–9. It covered the greater part of the industrial North East as defined in this book and extended westwards along the Tyne valley to Haltwhistle.

In interpreting the general effects of the development-area policy upon the North East it is important to appreciate the limitations of the criteria by which an assessment may be made and, secondly, that the policy was applied with very varying effectiveness, both in time and by locality.

The Measurement of Growth and Change

Several criteria are needed to give a fair picture; none is satisfactory by itself and each has certain limitations. Most typically in Britain volume of insured employment and activity rate (proportion of civilian employees employed plus registered unemployed in a given population age-group) is given pride of place as an indicator. If more jobs have been made available this is reckoned to be confirmation of economic growth. In reality, of course, this must be qualified by the productivity and profitability of such jobs, the extent to which they are male or female and the degree to which increasing employment may be an indication of over-manning as well as a move away from unemployment towards full employment. Additionally the new jobs should be in the right place, either where unemployment is high or where economic growth can be most effectively stimulated.

Chapter 3 showed that total insured employment has risen modestly in the North East since 1948 but that jobs for men have actually decreased slightly whilst those for women have increased substantially. It remains here to underline that the rate of employment increase in the North East, after an early post-war spurt, has lagged behind that of the country as a whole. The annual rate of increase of regional employment 1953–61 was only about one-half that of the nation and if the national momentum is to be achieved, within the next 5 years, employment will need to increase in the North East by an improbable rate of 1 per cent per annum. Activity rates in the Northern region have remained consistently about 4 per cent below the national average (1961 GB 57·4, North 53·7; 1966 GB 57·6, North 53·3). The female activity rate is still slightly less favourable than that for males in comparison with the respective national rates.

Reference has also already been made to the extent of diversification, broadening the base of the manufacturing economy, from a specialisation index figure of 36·7 in 1936 to 33·9 in 1953 and 31·5 in 1966. The marked change occured in the early post-war years but thereafter the process was only very gradual and due as much to the changing internal balance in employment structure as to the inflow of new industries, plants and firms.

Extent of diversification, introduction of balance or new growth elements into manufacturing industry, and contribution of new industry according to area occupied (floor-space index), are hallmarks of the achievements of industrial-location policies since the war. To these might be added relief of unemployment—a credit at least on the welfare side of the equation of regional development. Change in value of sales (turnover) in manufacturing industry is equally a directly positive indicator of achievement.

Table 10

THE NORTH EAST. PERCENTAGE EMPLOYMENT IN GROWTH AND
DECLINE SECTORS 1939–66

(For definitions see Table 2 on page 26)

	1939	1947	1953	1959	1962	1966
Faster growth	41·3	38·1	38·5	44·6	45·4	50·8
Slower growth	15·4	18·2	19·3	17·8	18·3	18·5
Slower decline	9·1	9·8	11·3	9·5	10·4	9·9
Faster decline	34·1	33·9	30·9	28·0	25·8	20·8

Source: Department of Employment & Productivity data.

The general improvement in balance of the employment structure is not entirely, or even dominantly, the result of government industrial-location policies, but rather the product of the interaction of new jobs in growth industries with the often substantial decline in tradi-

Page 71: (above) *A. Reyrolle switchgear works, Hebburn*; (below) *General Electric Company telephone works at Hartlepool*.

Page 72: (above) *Morganite Resistors Ltd, Bede industrial estate, Jarrow*; (below) *Cummings Ltd diesel engine works, Darlington.*

tional forms of employment. Table 10 shows that in both periods of more rapid change, 1953–9 and 1962–6, there was decline in basic industries, latterly very striking in coal mining; this contributed in a purely statistical way to the notable percentage increase in the 'growth' sector. Nevertheless the growth sector includes the valuable diversification afforded by new job provision under successive industrial-location policies. Since service industries are also included in the figures and government policy has only indirectly influenced many of these the contribution of new jobs in manufacturing is less apparent.

A useful though by no means comprehensive indicator of new manufacturing growth is the floor-space index of new factories or additions to existing factories. This may be measured from Board of Trade figures of industrial building completions for all schemes in manufacturing industry exceeding 5,000 sq ft. The data does not always show which completed buildings have been occupied, nor how intensively the new buildings are being used; buildings for storage rank equally with machine shops or canteens. There is, however, usually some correlation between extensions to floor space and commensurate increase in employment.

Table 11

INDUSTRIAL BUILDING COMPLETIONS 1945–68

(In million sq ft; schemes exceeding 5,000 sq ft in manufacturing industry)

	NE Development Area (Fig 11)	Percentage of Great Britain	Percentage Treasury financed	Percentage privately financed
1945–9	10·0	16·7	41·5	58·5
1950–4	12·6	7·9	11·1	88·9
1955–9	14·2	6·2	8·7	91·3
	Northern Region			
1960–4	13·7	6·5	—	—
1965–mid 68	14·0	11·2	—	—

Source: Board of Trade data.

The sharp stimulus of the development-areas policy in the early post-war years gave the North East its highest-ever proportion of government regional aid (Table 11). The industrial estates expanded rapidly and new growth elements came into North Eastern industry on a considerable scale, including light electrical products, plastic goods, clothing and textiles and manufacture of motor vehicle components. The government's direct contribution in financing new jobs appeared

E

to diminish through the 1950s. As industrial momentum was gained and post-war readjustments were made the ratio of Treasury-financed economic development fell during the last few years of the development-areas policy; the policy itself was relaxed and the rate of building completions fell seriously behind the national tempo. The later 1950s was a period of slowing down in the national economy, a time of accelerating coal mine closures and of the onset of problems of over-capacity in the steel industry; thus there was little relocation of industry nationally, and relatively few movements of new firms into the North East.

Late in 1958 the government began to reinflate the sagging national economy, leading to a higher rate of industrial completions in the early 1960s. Since then the Local Employment Act (1960) has replaced the more regionally-based policies of the Distribution of Industry Act (1945) and new industrial growth has in principle been channelled towards designated but more localised and changeable development districts (Fig 11 on page 87), localities with deeper pools of unemployment and often marginal in location, amenities and utilities. Older industries benefited under the 1960 legislation, however, and in its early stages almost all expenditure went into extensions to existing establishments. In contrasting the regional impact of the Local Employment Act and the earlier legislation one must take into account the fact that throughout the 1950s the development-area policy had been progressively less rigorously applied and that it had virtually lapsed as a regional instrument by the time it was replaced.

After the North East White Paper of 1963[3] the principle of streamlining the regional economy was envisaged, with strong emphasis on a 'growth zone' between Tyneside and Teesside. This was a reversal of previous priorities which had been devoted to locality-based unemployment problems; the policy however was never really implemented and relief in economic aid to development districts of particular hardship continued. In 1964 the foundation of the Department of Economic Affairs led to more comprehensive proposals for regional planning for the North East at the level of the wider Northern economic planning region, whilst the Industrial Development Act of 1966 replaced development districts by larger development areas which this time included the designation of the Northern region. The effects of recent legislation, including the novel concepts of selective employment tax and the regional employment premium, must work powerfully in favour of the development areas but their effects are not as yet detectable in the short-run.

Table 12 emphasises both the outstanding importance of moves to the North in the years 1945–51 and the very significant rôle in all periods of moves from the South East to the North, tributes to the effectiveness of government policies of restricting industrial growth in the more affluent areas and promoting transfers to the development areas. Even in the most recent period the South East provided more than double the number of moves compared with the next most important source of origin, Yorkshire and Humberside. Still dealing with movement inside England the affluent areas of the Midlands came next in originating moves to the North, increasing somewhat in proportion in the latest period. A further encouraging feature is that since 1952, though the numbers have been less, a higher proportion of new jobs has been for men. The 89,000 jobs in transferred establishments has represented a valuable and significant infusion into the employment structure of the North and further benefits will accrue as many of the transplants continue to develop in their new location. The fact that the average number of new jobs per transplant is lower in the latest period should not mislead; in the early years the labour force tends to be low, building up more rapidly after about three years in the new location. The number of transfers from abroad in the period 1960–5 may be an interesting harbinger for the future. The North East in particular has hitherto attracted fewer foreign-based firms than has seemed its due.

The industrial estates have had a key rôle under successive industrial-location policies. Though there has been some movement from the congested sites of existing North Eastern cities, and some firms have set up storage facilities only, the provision of new jobs on industrial estates has been the most outstanding success of post-war industrial planning and a distinctive British contribution to development policies which have since been followed in many parts of the world.

Though the proportion of jobs on estates to total regional employment may seem small it is employment that might often never have come to the North East without the attractions of the industrial estates as a spearhead of government industrial-location policy. The ratio of male jobs on estates is improving but still less than one-half overall, (Table 13). Though male jobs are peculiarly precious in view of the decline of jobs for men in mining, shipbuilding and certain branches of heavy engineering the industrial estates have nevertheless been very important in providing a rising employment activity rate among women and yet have also introduced substantial new job possibilities for men.

In the post-war years full-employment policies have been promoted

Table 12

MOVEMENT OF MANUFACTURING ESTABLISHMENTS INTO THE NORTHERN REGION BY STANDARD REGION OF ORIGIN 1945–1965

(In thousands)

Standard region	1945–65			1945–51			1952–9			1960–5		
	moves	Employment male (1,000s)	total (1,000s)	moves	Employment male (1,000s)	total (1,000s)	moves	Employment male (1,000s)	total (1,000s)	moves	Employment male (1,000s)	total (1,000s)
South East	94	16·5	35·8	49	11·7	28·4	12	1·9	3·0	33	2·9	4·5
Yorks and Humberside	51	13·9	26·7	31	10·2	20·9	7	1·8	3·1	13	1·9	2·8
East Midland	17	4·3	9·6	8	2·2	6·3	3	1·7	2·5	6	0·4	0·7
Abroad	19	3·8	5·2	3	0·6	1·2	6	1·6	2·0	10	1·5	1·9
West Midland	10	3·1	5·0	2	1·1	1·5	2	1·1	1·2	6	0·9	2·3
North West	14	1·0	2·5	7	0·6	1·5	1	—	—	6	0·4	0·9
Other	15	2·8	4·8	7	1·6	2·9	3	0·9	1·4	5	0·4	0·6
TOTAL	220	45·4	89·6	107	28·0	62·7	34	9·0	13·2	79	8·4	13·7

Source: Board of Trade.

Table 13

EMPLOYMENT AT INDUSTRIAL ESTATES IN THE NORTH EAST
1939–68

	Total (1,000s)	Percentage of males	Percentage of total NE insured employment
1939	3·5	44·0	0·4
1948	22·0	38·9	2·0
1953	44·6	41·5	4·2
1958	52·6	43·9	4·8
1963	65·8	45·8	5·9
Jan 68	86·1	49·6	7·6

Source: Data supplied by courtesy of the Industrial Estates Management Corporation for England.

by all political parties and thus the unemployment level has often been regarded as the sensitive barometer of the success or failure of regional policies. Levels of unemployment are usually beyond regional control, fluctuating nationally in both the short and the longer term.

Table 14 shows that, after the high levels of unemployment in the immediate post-war years there was rapid improvement, but bad patches in the early 1950s and again in the early 1960s. It is thus not possible to say that the unemployment problem in the North East has either been solved or improved relative to the national level, except for short periods. It is almost equally certain, however, that without successive location policies for new industry the situation would have been far worse, underlining the deep-seated and difficult problem of transforming the local economy and the necessarily long-term nature of the solution.

Summing up on the development-area policy from its inception in

Table 14

PERCENTAGE UNEMPLOYMENT IN THE NORTH EAST AND
GREAT BRITAIN 1946–66

	1946	1948	1950	1952	1954	1956	1958	1960	1962	1964	1966	1968
North East	7·7	3·0	3·1	4·2	3·4	2·0	2·3	2·9	3·7	3·3	2·6	5·1
Gt. Britain	2·4	1·8	1·5	2·0	1·3	1·2	2·1	1·7	2·1	1·7	1·6	2·9
NE ± GB	+5·3	+1·2	+1·6	+2·2	+2·1	+0·8	+0·2	+1·2	+1·6	+1·6	+1·0	+2·2

Source: Department of Employment & Productivity data.

1945 to its demise in 1959 its general effects on the North East were substantial and varied. The early post-war years saw a considerable implantation of new industries and these have since grown, to provide in many localities the basis of new industrial specialisations. The scale of new job provision, particularly that for women and girls, offset part of the decline in the basic industries and the industrial estates played a leading rôle in economic development. The employment structure of the North East has been diversified since the war, not dramatically, but none the less quite usefully. It remains a heavy-industrial region but there are significant and substantial new elements of growth industries, whose contribution in further new jobs is likely to be great over the next fifteen years. Out-migration has not been stopped, scarcely even slowed down, but the rate of net loss, today running at about 4,000 per annum, is not presently critical for regional prospects. Nor is the level of unemployment dramatic and it is clear that without the policies from 1945–9 both out-migration and unemployment would have been more serious, even catastrophic, and the future prospects that much bleaker. It remains to be seen if the basis has been laid for a rising momentum of self-sustaining economic growth—the happy incantation of planners—and if the degree of industrial diversification achieved will prove adequate to cushion the further downturn in basic industries and, at the same time, provide the means of attracting new firms to transform even more effectively the industrial structure in the North East in the present generation.

The major elements of employment change 1959–66 are now reviewed as a prelude to considering, in the next chapter, the sub-regional impact and the changing landscape resulting from government policies (Fig 10).

The figures in Table 15 confirm that during the 1960s the North East has been undergoing a scale and rate of employment change that compels modification of some of the established generalisations about its economic character. The structural change is deeply-founded and still has further to run; in some activities it is even likely to escalate in tempo. Though stability in numbers working in shipbuilding may shortly be in sight, and the vehicle industry is re-emerging in a radically changed form, the contraction in mining is likely to accelerate in the next decade and perhaps a further 10 per cent will leave agriculture in the North East in the same period.

On the credit side the rapid growth in 'other manufactures' and in electrical engineering is most apparent, the latter perhaps the greatest post-war employment growth industry in the region, with 43 per cent

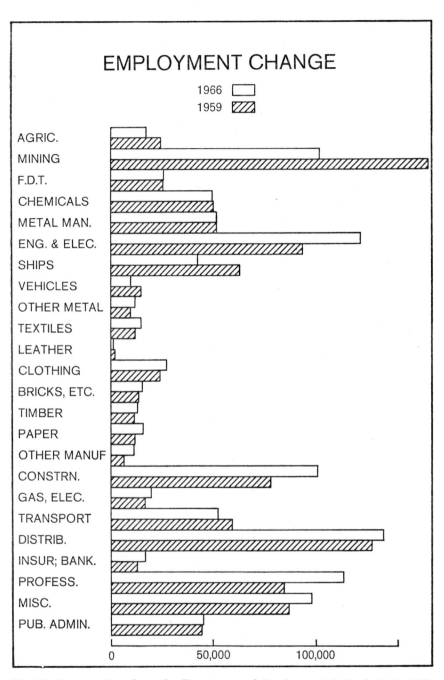

Fig 10. (Source: data from the Department of Employment & Productivity 1959 and 1966.)

Table 15

THE NORTH EAST EMPLOYMENT CHANGES 1959–66, BY SIC GROUPS
(1959=100)

GROWTH		DECLINE	
Other manufactures	150	Mining and quarrying	63
Electrical engineering	144	Shipbuilding	67
Professional and scientific	135	Vehicles	67
Paper, printing and		Leather	77
publishing	131	Agriculture, fishing, forestry	78
Construction	130		
Other metal manufactures	125		
Textiles	124		

Source: Department of Employment & Productivity data.

of its jobs for women. The status of the construction industry is in itself a general barometer of relative prosperity.

A warning must be issued against regarding rising employment in any industry as indicative of commensurate improvement in the economic health of a region. This may be true in some labour-intensive industries but in not a few industries, such as steel-making or some branches of engineering, there is presently over-manning by as much as 30 per cent on some estimates. Any further job provision in such industries, without increased productivity per man, would tend to make an already bad situation worse. On the other hand there are industries, as diverse as chemicals and agriculture, where very great improvements in productivity have been accomplished with a stable or declining

Table 16

NORTHERN REGION CHANGES IN SALES AND EMPLOYMENT, 1954–8, BY SIC ORDERS IN MANUFACTURING (1954=100)

Growth in sales, slower growth in employment		
	Sales	*Employment*
Chemicals	148	127
Metal manufactures	129	102
Engineering	138	113
Growth in sales same or less than growth in employment		
Food and drink	106	105
Timber, furniture	79	82

Source: Census of Production 1958.

labour force. This can be confirmed at the level of particular plants and firms but is more difficult to establish for entire industries. The only available data comes from the periodic censuses of production but even this is partial in its value or reliability (Table 16).

References to this chapter are on pages 240 and 248–9.

5

Growth and Change in Sub-region and Landscape

Sub-Regions

THE NORTH EAST has always had variety within its regional economy and for this reason the course of economic and social change since 1945 has been uneven, the effects of government location policies variable in their localised incidence. Teesside has been one of the most noticeable post-war boom areas in the British economy, whilst Tyne and Wear have had only slight overall economic growth in the past twenty-five years (Table 17). Rundown in employment in the rural zone has been negligible in a general sense, though the rural West has declined rather more than other rural areas. Among other slow decline areas the Cleveland margin, the Northumberland coalfield and the vulnerable sub-economy of south-east Durham all contain the problems of coalmining decline. The marginal mining and industrial districts of west Durham have seen the most marked decline in labour force since the war in spite of vigorous government promotion of new industry in these areas. The table emphasises starkly the problems of the wasting away of jobs for men, often compensated for by the 'petticoat revolution' taking over a marked proportion of jobs in new industries and service occupations. The picture on Tyneside is dramatic and in strong contrast to Teesside where male employment has risen even more markedly than for women. Since 1959 particularly the clear growth in jobs for women highlights an actual slight decline in jobs for men on Tyne and Wear.

The changing balance between men and women conceals complex changes in the employment structure, some of a very fundamental kind. On the Tees four industry groups have traditionally employed four-fifths of those in manufacturing: chemicals, iron and steel,

Table 17

SUB-REGIONS OF THE NORTH EAST. EMPLOYMENT GROWTH AND
CHANGE 1948–66

(In thousands)

	'66 Index 1948=100	Total change		1948–53		1953–9		1959–66	
		M	F	M	F	M	F	M	F
FAST GROWTH									
Teesside	135	+32·5	+25·6	+4·1	+4·7	+14·2	+6·3	+14·2	+14·6
SLOW GROWTH									
Wear	112	± 0	+11·6	− 0·9	+3·5	+ 2·7	+2·6	− 1·8	+ 5·5
Tyneside	105	− 4·0	+25·2	−10·3	+0·2	+ 8·1	+7·3	− 1·8	+17·7
STABILISATION									
Rural North	100	− 1·6	+ 1·5	+ 0·8	+0·1	− 1·7	+0·1	− 0·7	+ 1·3
NE Durham	100	− 6·4	+ 6·6	+ 0·4	+1·2	− 3·0	+2·2	− 4·0	+ 3·2
Rural N. Riding	98	− 4·2	+ 3·3	− 5·0	−1·3	− 0·7	+1·7	+ 1·5	+ 2·9
SLOW DECLINE									
Tees (Cleveland)	94	− 2·0	+ 1·3	+ 0·3	+0·6	− 1·4	+0·1	− 0·9	+ 0·6
Rural West	93	− 2·4	+ 1·1	− 0·9	+0·1	− 0·3	+0·2	− 1·2	+ 0·8
Northumberland coalfield	92	− 7·5	+ 3·3	− 1·6	+0·2	+ 0·2	+0·9	− 6·1	+ 2·2
SE Durham	92	− 4·9	+ 2·6	− 0·7	−0·08	− 1·2	+1·0	− 3·0	+ 1·7
FASTER DECLINE									
Darlington*	86	− 7·8	+ 0·5	− 4·0*	+1·4	+ 1·2	+1·1	− 5·0	− 2·0
NW Durham	82	− 9·6	+ 2·3	− 1·5	+0·7	− 1·4	+0·9	− 6·7	+ 0·7
SW Durham	81	−14·2	+ 1·4	− 2·4	+0·3	− 2·6	+0·6	− 9·2	+ 0·5

Note: Figures adjusted for changes in insurance and employment classifications.
* 1948 figure not adjustable, data thus doubtful.

Source: Department of Employment & Productivity data.

engineering and shipbuilding. The figures in Table 18 show that the labour force in the highly capital-intensive chemical industry rose during the 1950s but since 1959 has remained much the same even though major expansion in plant and product range has taken place. The manpower in iron and steel decreased slightly between 1953 (31·6 per cent) and 1966 (26 per cent), yet that industry nationally is still over-manned by one-third according to the *Benson Report* and there has been a good deal of talk of forthcoming redundancies recently, both nationally and locally. The shipyards declined in proportion of manufacturing jobs but electrical engineering, particularly the tele-communications side, increased powerfully between 1959 and 1966.

Nevertheless compared with the Tyne the Tees remains a markedly less diversified economy.

Tyneside has a more important regional service function than Teesside, buttressing its more diversified manufacturing structure with a greater range of growth elements in employment. In contrast to Teesside the Tyne has almost double the proportions working in engineering

Table 18

EMPLOYMENT IN MANUFACTURING ON TYNE, WEAR AND TEES 1959–66 EXPRESSED AS A PERCENTAGE OF ALL MANUFACTURING EMPLOYMENT

		Food and drink	Chemicals	Metals	Engineering	Electrical	Shipbuilding	Textiles	Clothing	Others
TYNESIDE										
North	1966	12·1	7·9	2·3	18·7	10·5	20·8	1·1	3·8	22·8
	1959	11·1	6·6	1·9	16·8	9·9	27·4	1·3	3·5	21·5
South	1966	5·5	4·6	4·2	21·2	22·2	11·8	2·7	8·6	19·2
	1959	5·4	5·6	4·2	22·5	18·8	17·0	1·1	8·4	17·0
North and South	1953	10·0	5·2	3·1	52·0			1·5	5·9	22·3
WEARSIDE										
	1966	6·3	1·5	3·4	15·1	19·1	24·4	1·7	7·7	20·8
	1959	8·2	1·3	4·2	6·9	11·0	35·4	2·1	9·5	21·4
	1953	11·3	0·7	2·4	48·2			1·9	10·3	25·2
TEESSIDE										
	1966	3·3	27·4	26·0	13·1	7·2	4·1	4·4	3·7	10·8
	1959	3·9	28·0	28·1	12·2	2·6	10·7	2·7	3·2	8·6
	1953	4·4	21·7	31·6	26·3			1·5	4·3	10·2

Source: Department of Employment & Productivity data.

and shipbuilding, though in both areas the balance within this group has changed distinctively with the decline in shipbuilding labour and the growth of the electrical industry. Electrical engineering on Tyneside contains an important heavy sector, manufacture of generators and switchgear, as well as rising employment in light electrical goods. The food and drink industry, partly a reflection of the service status of

Tyneside in the North East, has maintained its relative importance and varied chemical manufacture has increased its representation; on the other hand textiles and clothing are less prominent employers in comparison with the early 1950s.

South Tyneside (Fig 9) has a higher proportion in basic industries, though the area is less dependent on shipbuilding than the North bank and the clothing and electrical engineering groups are more fully developed. Differences in work structure north and south of the river are increasing. Between 1959 and 1966, for example, there was a sharp fall in employment in vehicles manufacture and in the leather industry on the North bank, with a rise in employment in bricks, pottery and glass. South of the river the principal features were the considerable growth in textiles and the paper and printing industry and, to a lesser extent, in electrical engineering. North Tyneside has a much larger service sector, with a most pronounced growth over the past decade in professional and scientific services.

Wearside has an economy somewhat intermediate in structure between north and south Tyneside, with the heaviest dependence on shipbuilding of all three areas, a rapidly rising electrical goods sector, telecommunications and television or radio parts, and a developing variety within branches of engineering. Even so the spectrum of engineering remains less diverse than in either Tyneside area. The clothing industry is on the scale of south Tyneside but is falling in proportion of employment, as is also the food and drink industry. The degree of Sunderland's dependence on shipbuilding has been a persistent weakness in the economy of the town.

Areas of stabilisation in employment numbers since the war include the rural North and rural areas of the North Riding, together with north-east Durham (Table 17). In all these cases the loss of male employment has been almost exactly taken up by the increase of women at work. Both rural sub-regions include part of the commuter fringe of adjacent conurbations and the rural North includes part of the Northumberland coalfield. In the past decade sharp changes have taken place in manufacturing jobs in the rural North, decline in chemicals and metal-working, rise in engineering and textiles. The rural North Riding has experienced rapid growth in electrical goods and vehicle manufacture, whilst in north-east Durham rising employment in paper and printing, bricks and pottery and electrical goods has taken place without noticeable decline in other existing manufactures.

The slow decline areas since the war include the rural with mining margins of the rural West and Cleveland and the specialised mining areas of the south-east Northumberland coalfield and south-east Durham. In these areas decline in male employment has not been offset by commensurate growth in jobs for women, though in the past decade, when pit closures have sharpened the problem, more female jobs in manufacturing have become available. Food and drink, metal-working and timber (chipboard) processing have grown in the rural West during the past ten years and miscellaneous metal-working in Cleveland. The Northumberland coalfield and south-east Durham have already been described as vulnerable sub-regions, with excessive dependence on coal mining at a time of accelerating rundown of the mining labour force. The past decade has seen a more positive policy, with growth in engineering and metal-working and in the clothing industries in south-east Northumberland. The south-east Durham problem is much more difficult for manufacturing is not only inadequate as regards number of jobs but also unstable in structure with a fall in chemical employment and a rise in the food, clothing and timber industries over the last ten years.

Darlington is not correctly identified with the areas of faster decline, though on the statistical tests presented it appears as such. The truth is that statistical problems invalidate direct comparison with trends in other sub-regions. It is however clear that from being perhaps the most prosperous sub-region of the North East throughout the 1950s the problems of unemployment have emerged rather dramatically in the 1960s, with the decline of locomotive manufacture, carriage and wagon repairs, and the recent closure of Darlington Forge coupled with a diminution in jobs in chemicals and in some of the metal-working trades.

It will not be surprising that both north-west and south-west Durham emerge as the combined area of greatest post-war employment decline, with heavy falls in male employment uncompensated for by jobs for women. Until 1959 government policy had contributed substantially to reducing the unemployment and redeployment problem but during the 1960s the scale of contraction in mining has further aggravated a difficult situation. In both north-west and south-west Durham engineering has provided usefully more jobs in recent years, aided by a small growth in vehicles and timber processing in the north-west and textiles and brick manufacture in the south-west. The uncertain future of the Consett iron and steel plant in north-west Durham is the more serious in view of its status in providing almost half the present jobs in manufacturing there.

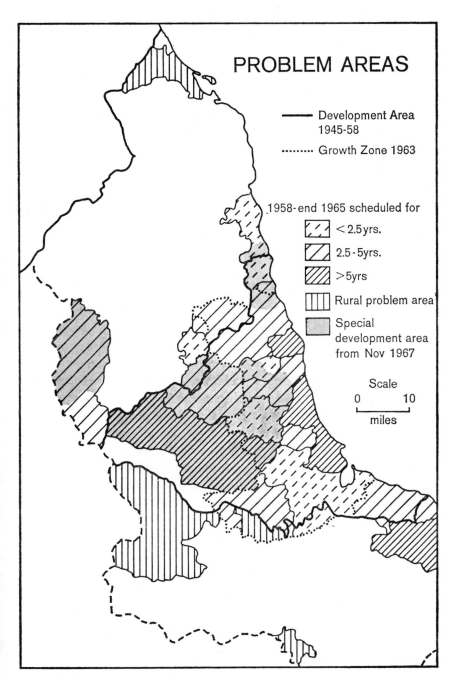

Fig 11. Special Development Areas date from November 1967. (Source: data from lists in Board of Trade *Journal* 1945 to date.)

Problem Areas

Regional policy since the war has rested upon the belief that certain areas, mainly the hearths of the Industrial Revolution with their traditionally narrow dependence on coal mining and limited branches of heavy industry, required priority aid for industrial diversification and the relief, at the point of hardship, of higher than average levels of unemployment.[1] In such a sense the North East is a marginal regional economy within the national economy, whether with its development-area designation (1945–58), its collection of scheduled development districts (1958–66), or its current status since 1966 within the development area represented by the Northern region.

Given the contrasts in resources, varied impact of the Industrial Revolution and differential location in relation to the main arteries of communication, certain localities and sub-regions are, and have long been, marginal within the economy of the North East. Some of these have been identified in the account of employment structure and its changing trends. The pattern of problem localities has been a changing one, broadly but not in detail corresponding with the areas shown on Fig 11, comprising the former development area, development districts and the areas outside the 1963 growth zone. To these are to be added the special development areas created in November 1967.

Fig 11 shows that, with few exceptions, the problem areas of the North East in recent years have lain within the boundaries of the development area as it was designated under the Distribution of Industry Act between 1945 and 1958. The length of time that localities or sub-regions were scheduled as development districts under the Distribution of Industry (Industrial Finance) legislation 1958–60 and the Local Employment Act 1960–6 was very variable. The areas with the highest and most persistent unemployment were Weardale and south-west Durham, south-east Tyneside, the coastal fringe of east Durham south of Seaham and the Whitby area; all these areas had been scheduled for more than five years before the legislation changed in 1966. The common criterion of high unemployment covered strong contrasts in the nature and severity of the underlying economic and social problems. Basically these were concerned with either rural farming in isolated areas, decaying coalmining settlements, or marginal industrial districts excessively dependent on a narrow range of traditional manufactures, often in localities fairly remote from the

Page 89: (left) *Furness shipyard, Haverton Hill (Tees); (right) ship repair yards, North Shields.*

Page 90: (above) *Austin & Pickersgill shipyard at Southwick, Sunderland*; (below) *Whessoe Ltd engineering works, Darlington.*

main towns. Frequently these unfavourable ingredients were all present in some measure, as in the upper reaches of the valleys of west Durham.[2] The special development areas defined coalfield districts where difficult social and economic problems were resulting from the decline in mining.

Rural problem areas are those with a marked trend of continuing out-migration, particularly of young folk, and a deteriorating social provision. These are the localities where public transport facilities have been seriously curtailed in recent years. They are not necessarily the areas of the poorest quality farmland but rather those where the farm labour force threatens to fall to dangerously low levels on reasonably good land and where some increased public investment provision is required to stabilise the situation.[3] With the exception of the Berwick on Tweed hinterland where the Development Commission in 1966 introduced a pilot-scheme to develop industry in a declining rural area, the predominantly rural margins have not been scheduled under government industrial-location policy, and indeed the prospects for their attracting industrial plants must be very limited.

'Rural with mining' districts such as the Haltwhistle-Alston area,[4] Weardale, or the 'rural-coastal holiday resort' problem area of Whitby,[5] have nevertheless provided some of the more intractable problems for industrial reconversion or the introduction of new firms into the local economy. The basic difficulty is relative inaccessibility, combined with a smallish locally available labour force willing and capable of reconversion into new jobs at a particular point in time, and a generally limited attractiveness of living environment as seen by the entrepreneur. Furthermore the pressures which can be brought on small firms to move into the outer marginal localities are likely to be limited, and general dispersal policies into small branch plants are rarely favoured except at times of acute national labour shortage.

The west-Durham problem is a more serious variant of the general problem of mining decline and pit closure taking place in a locality whose position is a few miles off the major routeways and whose social capital is sub-standard and unlikely to be replaced. It poses the issues of rehabilitation, perhaps involving longer-term priority economic first-aid from government sources, or a carefully programmed decline. Since 1945 west Durham has probably had greater aid relative to its population size than any area in the North East. The policy of developing the grouped factory sites on industrial estates has been successfully followed. In addition, individual locations such as that of Ransome & Marles Ltd at Annfield Plain, or more recently Ever

F

Ready Ltd at Stanley, show that it is possible to follow a forward-looking industrialisation policy. Nevertheless the economy of west Durham has been only partially transformed and mining decline continues to increase the number of new jobs required; of those made available a fair proportion have been for women. Furthermore any radical employment change at the Consett steelworks would seriously aggravate the local problem of jobs for men. The county planning policy is to regroup the population and permit some of the older, less viable settlements to work out their remaining life without other than minimàl increase in public investment. From the more accessible settlements journeys-to-work in Tyneside or Darlington have increased, whilst Newton Aycliffe and its large associated industrial estate have helped both directly and indirectly, through rehousing, to stabilise the employment situation in south-west Durham. The longer-term future of such a marginal mining and industrial area touches on the antagonism between a policy of continuing to preserve social capital and bring the work to the worker on the one hand; on the other hand the consequences of concentrating industrial growth in the major centres, at the most accessible sites in the former growth zone between Tyne and Tees, imply that growth elsewhere must imply a measure of decline in areas like west Durham. A compromise policy of attempting to spread growth thinly everywhere could only possibly succeed at a time of rapid national economic growth and even then must be expected to have limited appeal to those industrialists who would at such a time exercise a stronger bargaining position on choice between alternative locations.

The problems of the east-Durham coastal tract have already been related to excessive dependence on coal mining and a rather narrow range of manufacturing, much of it introduced by government aid but not all proving to be stable. The New Town of Peterlee (Fig 8) has the twin rôles of providing an attractive environment for new industries on its estates and of regrouping the mining population from surrounding sub-standard settlements. In the early stages there was some reluctance to abandon the mining villages and exchange the traditional close-knit community for the New Town environment.

Changes in the coalfield are more fully analysed in the next chapter but the problems of industrial reconversion in mining areas, which in the past led to high unemployment and scheduling of localities as development districts, will spread more widely in the next decade. Since the development area is today no less than the entire Northern region it may well be that the solution of local problems will be less in the locality itself or even within daily travelling distance, longer though that is expected by officialdom to become, but rather in a greater degree of movement within the region from areas which are declining to those which are growing, perhaps involving a revival of the dormant growth-zone concept.

South-east Tyneside, particularly around Jarrow and Hebburn, has been traditionally associated in many minds with the more dramatic aspects of the 1930s economic depression. The area had significant proportions in coal mining, shipbuilding and repairing and, to a lesser extent, in marine engineering. These were the industries that produced the characteristically high unemployment levels but, fortunately, heavy electrical engineering has been an indigenous growth industry since the early years of the century, whilst even in the past decade the electrical goods industry has grown very rapidly on the Bede industrial estate. The direction of change within the local economy is shown by the figures in Table 19.

Table 19

SOUTH-EAST TYNESIDE. EMPLOYMENT CHANGE IN SELECTED
INDUSTRIES 1959–66

Per cent insured population	1959	1966
Coal mining	9·8	8·6
Shipbuilding and repairing	14·2	11·4
Electrical engineering	11·5	12·5
Electrical goods	4·0	5·1

Source: Department of Employment & Productivity data.

Other localities in the industrial North East have had shorter periods of scheduling as development districts. Tyneside localities have been on the list for rather longer than anywhere on Teesside and unemployment patches throughout the coalfield appeared as the process of pit closure began to develop in the later 1950s. Often the period of scheduling was too short and the availability of firms capable of being 'steered' was too low for there to be any appreciable effect on the local employment situation. This was a weakness of the system of the 'stop-list', invoked once the level of unemployment fell below a certain critical threshold, thus thereafter depriving the locality of the benefits of governmental location policies.

The scheduled districts thus roughly corresponded with the problem areas, ie the mining and industrial margins. The piecemeal application of government aid, however, probably produced a less effective overall result than would have arisen from a freer-working location policy, permitting industrialists to choose more readily sites upon the larger and more centrally located industrial estates. In any event the scheduling of a district was no guarantee of the solution of its local unemployment problem, or that new firms would necessarily be attracted or 'steered', as the case of Whitby well illustrates during the past fifteen years.

The Landscape of Change

(Figs 8 and 12)

The industrial and urban landscapes of the North East were fashioned during a long and complex history, with the events of the past hundred years particularly formative on the spread of the built-up area, the thickening of the pattern of industrial sites on the lower Tyne, Wear and Tees and the increasing density of the network of collieries with their associated settlements and rail-links.

The zenith in the rate of development in the North East was during the period from 1880 to 1914. The geometrical patterns of brick-built, high-density terraced houses in flats date from this time, an impress of minimum bye-law standards of social provision. The larger firms of today were often substantially established in the same period: steel plant, shipyard, heavy engineering or chemical works. Others active in the late nineteenth century, for example the traditional Tyneside pottery or glass manufactures, have since declined and been replaced; other earlier industrial sites remain derelict. In the city centres, until the phase of post-1947 town planning, the architecture and mass of shops, offices and banks frequently portrayed the civic pride and magnificence of late Victorian England. Similarly many of the bridges, viaducts and railway stations display the elegance and grandeur of the golden age before 1914.

Nevertheless the problems which were later dramatically to plague the North East were already in embryo in the late nineteenth century. Working out or flooding of pits led to closures and the decay of mining villages, subsidence scarred the landscape, older industrial sites were overwhelmed by technological change and abandoned, derelict land spread. The dead hand of the past continues to pose the planner with the need to transform the traditional cultural landscape, develop-

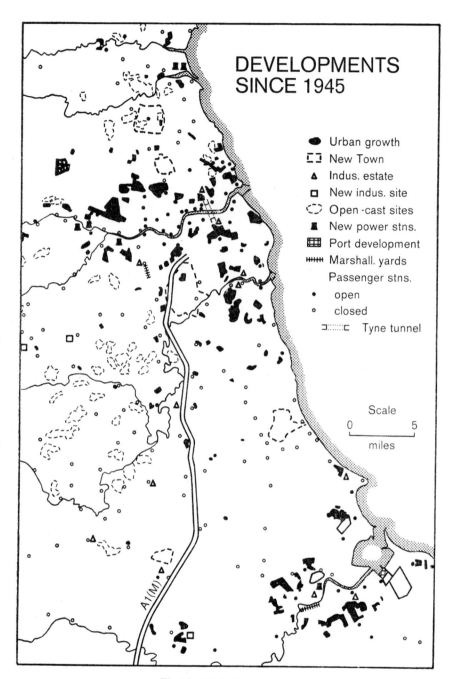

DEVELOPMENTS
SINCE 1945

Urban growth
New Town
Indus. estate
New indus. site
Open-cast sites
New power stns.
Port development
Marshall. yards
Passenger stns.
  • open
  ○ closed
  Tyne tunnel

Scale

0   5

miles

A1(M)

Fig 12. (Multiple sources.)

ing here, controlling there, running down and planting over elsewhere.

Fig 12 shows fresh elements of the cultural landscape emerging
since 1945. The spread of peripheral housing estates around Tyneside
and Sunderland is more striking than for Teesside. These new estates
have developed partly to replace the high-density slums of inner areas
under programmes of urban renewal, partly to make good the slow
growth of new housing in the period between the two world wars.
Higher-class neighbourhoods have been defined north and west of
Newcastle, at Blaydon-Ryton south of the Tyne and in the East Boldon
area between Tyneside and Sunderland; similar neighbourhoods are
found in north-west and south Teesside and in the western suburbs of
Darlington.

The New Towns now show appreciably in the landscape. Newton
Aycliffe (18,000 in 1967), Peterlee (19,800) and Washington (23,500)
have been created under the New Towns Act; Cramlington and
Killingworth are distinctively county council-inspired developments.
All are related in some measure to the regrouping of mining populations or the settling of overspill from the inner areas of the cities. With
their architecture, layout, neighbourhood structure, careful design of
traffic movement and, not least, the industrial capacity of their zoned
estates, the New Towns offer a foretaste of the transformed living
environment through which the regional planners hope to stabilise or
attract the workers and managers of the future. The take-off period
in the New Towns of the North East has been slower than in the
London metropolitan area and many will criticise the repetitive
similarities with details of the towns of the outer London ring. Others
will applaud the novel concepts of the grid-iron dispersed structure
of workplace and residence zoning at Washington or the novel
architecture and style of the existing precincts at Peterlee or Cramlington.

The government industrial estates (Fig 13) are unevenly distributed,
in part a reflection of the varying course of industrial-location policies;
partly the result of the historical distribution of unemployment already
there in pre-war years. The most substantial estates are at Team Valley,
Sunderland, and Hartlepool; the developments at Spennymoor and
Aycliffe are the result of conversion of wartime royal ordnance
factories, the site at Aycliffe giving justification for the development
of the New Town. The smaller estates in west Durham or elsewhere
in the coalfield indicate the active policies of dispersing manufacturing
jobs to the site of unemployment. In the coalfield towns there has been

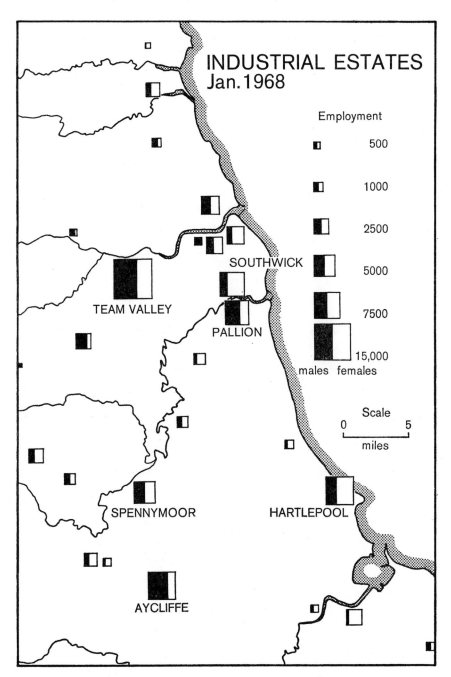

Fig 13. (Source: data from the English Industrial Estate Corporation.)

the additional need to provide jobs for women, as well as for displaced miners. The pattern and size of estates generally correspond to the employment needs of localities at particular stages of location policy for solving unemployment within or near the locality. The pattern clearly does not correspond to the more economically logical concentration at fewer, larger estates. The present trend, as in the Yarm Road development on Teesside or the further developments in progress at Team Valley does, however, indicate some perhaps belated move in that direction.

Some of the principal post-war industrial developments have been on Teesside: the ICI Wilton works, a vast chemical 'trading estate' based on organic chemicals derived from naphtha feedstock and linked by pipeline under the Tees with Billingham; the Greatham steel works of the former South Durham Iron & Steel Co; Patons & Baldwin's knitting wool factory east of Darlington. Major developments at other North East steelworks, the steel plant and universal beam mill of Dorman Long at Lackenby, Consett Iron at Consett and the reorganisation of the Tyne and Wear shipyards are other striking new features of the industrial landscape. Ransome & Marles ball-bearing plant at Annfield Plain in north-west Durham is an interesting example of a 'greenfield' development by a substantial firm in the heart of one of the marginal problem areas.

The pattern of opencast coal sites, many now returned to cultivation, illustrates a major, if temporary, feature in the cultural landscape. The concentration and close pattern in west Durham is paralleled by a strong development at some of the largest sites ever worked in the North East, at Acorn Bank or Radar Site in central south-east Northumberland. The new thermal power stations at Stella, Blyth and North Tees are linked to the post-war 275 kv supergrid, a spinal power line from Clydeside into central and southern England.

Teesport is the principal post-war development in communications, with steadily improving capacity for larger vessels. Today vessels of 50,000 deadweight tons can be accommodated and the river is to be deepened for 65,000 ton oil tankers. In rail freight movements the reorganised marshalling yards and the freightliner depots are the counterpart of the centralisation and concentration of facilities in the road haulage industry. On the debit side of transport provision the post-war period has witnessed the very large-scale decay and withdrawal of rural and mining transport links, both road and rail. These have had particularly serious social effects in the wide rural hinterland of the North East.

The Tyne road tunnel was opened in 1967 and the Durham Motor-way (A1 M) is presently being completed, enabling more rapid transit to Tyneside across the Durham coalfield and more ready links with the heart of the British economy to the south.

References to this chapter are on page 240.

6

Coal and Steel

THE CLASSICAL nineteenth-century Industrial Revolution developed from the twin pillars of coal and iron with steel. The North East was a pioneer in developing these products, with a maximum output of coal just before the First World War of 56 million tons in 1911. In 1967 the figure was 27 million tons representing 16·4 per cent of the national deep-mined total; to this should be added 2·1 million tons produced by opencast methods. Regional steel production, on the other hand, has continued to rise until very recent years, with a peak output of 4·8 million tons of crude steel in 1960. Both coal and steel, however, have now entered a phase of retrenchment, much more dramatically so in coal than in steel. Coal is a wasting asset and the effect of centuries of creaming off the best and most accessible reserves has been to increase costs, even though improved technology of extraction has worked in the opposite direction. Since the late 1950s the mounting competition from other fuels has made a more rapid contraction of the coal industry inevitable, with profound economic and social consequences for many communities in areas such as the North East. The steel industry, like coal, has been reorganised and modernised since 1945 but it also in the past ten years has been faced with falling effective market demand. With renationalisation of the steel industry in 1967 the likelihood of streamlining, concentration, and perhaps even reduction of capacity, has once more become a live issue. The over-manning of the industry is its most immediate problem.

Neither the coal nor the steel industry is standing still in meeting the challenge to its products and both remain vital sectors in North Eastern industry, providing it also with a range of exports both to other parts of Britain and internationally. This chapter concentrates on the changing face and rôle of coal and steel and their significance in proposals for regional development.

The Northumberland and Durham Coalfield

Economically worthwhile reserves of coal, some 5,000 million tons including 300 million tons of high-grade coking quality, are concentrated in the middle coal measures within a broad, shallow triangular basin (Fig 14), dipping gently eastward below a sandstone succession in the Wear valley and thence passing under the magnesian limestone capping (permian scarp) in east Durham and continuing below the sea for some miles offshore. The main coal seams occur within a vertical band of some 800 ft, which is little disturbed other than by the principal broadly east-to-west fault-lines of the Ninety Fathom dyke cutting across Tyneside, the Butterknowle fault from near Bishop Auckland to Ferryhill, and the Hauxley fault and Stakeford dyke.[1] These have vertical displacements of between 500 and 800 ft. There are shallow basins in the Wallsend–Seaham–Sunderland area and around Blyth, with a structural doming of the coal measures in the South Shields area. Most seams are thicker and of better quality in the western part of the coalfield, deteriorating and often disappearing eastwards. Since the better quality coals were at shallower depths in the west they were worked early and are now mainly exhausted.

There is a quality variation from soft bright caking coals of less than 30 per cent volatile content to harder house and steam coals with slightly more than 40 per cent volatile matter. Since the chemical composition varies laterally within the same seam rather more than between seams within the same locality, a broad sub-zoning is possible (Fig 14).

In most parts of Durham the coals have strongly-caking qualities suitable for foundries and blast furnaces, particularly west of the Wear where the coals are low in ash, sulphur and phosphorus. From northwest Durham the volatile content increases radially outwards through a zone of gas-caking quality to steam and household coals; the latter two groups are prominent in Northumberland and little to be distinguished from the coals of most British coalfields. The caking coals of Durham, on the other hand, are of particular national importance, rivalled only by those of south Wales for foundry coke, or parts of Yorkshire for coking-gas quality. For this reason these scarce quality resources have been steadily worked during conditions of rising costs and increasing technical difficulty.

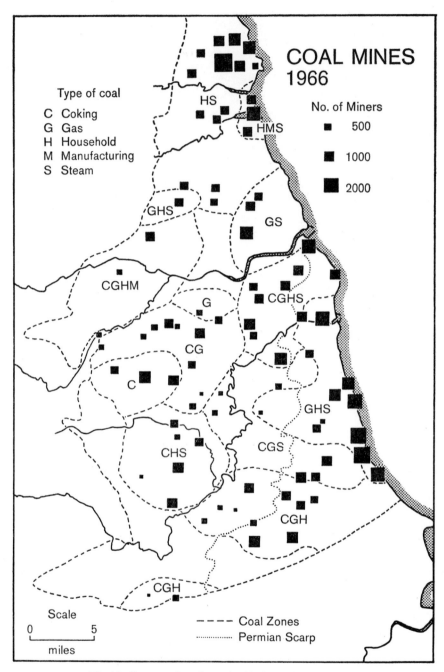

Fig 14. (Source: data from the National Coal Board.)

Development

Mining began in the thirteenth century but was sporadic until the mid-sixteenth century when markets were developed in London and other towns around the North Sea basin. The early pits were for domestic coal and were sunk close to the banks of the lower Tyne and Wear within short wagonway distance of the coaling staithes.[2] After about 1720 wagonways were driven further into the hinterland, particularly into the middle-Wear valley and the north-west Durham plateau, whilst technical improvements in steam-pumping enabled deeper seams to be mined, notably in south-east Northumberland. By 1825 the whole exposed coalfield north of Durham City was being worked to relatively shallow depths. During the same period wagon-ways were replaced by the early railways and sinking of deep mines took place in the concealed coalfield in east Durham, though progress was slow there because of the technical difficulties of deep shafts and the problem of water seepage from porous sands at the base of the magnesian limestone. This area was still coming into production up to 1914 and to this day exploration continues actively into the sea-ward extent of workable seams. Whilst mines were being opened up throughout south Durham, shafts were sunk to tap previously un-touched resources in the central part of the coalfield.

The coal trade did not progress continuously, however, for there were several periods of overproduction, followed by a lowering of price occasioning the collapse of some colliery companies. The sinking of shafts, even with improved technology, was an expensive operation and led to further financial instability. Limitation on the output (vend) of coal was several times resorted to in an effort to avoid the worst effects of depression.

During the 1840s the rail network spread and many new collieries were opened, particularly in the steam-coal area north of the Ninety Fathom dyke in south Northumberland. Production also expanded rapidly on the north-west Durham plateau and in the concealed coal-field. Nevertheless the total coal output in the North East remained fairly static due to recurrent labour disputes, including the great strike of 1844 in County Durham.

From the early 1860s there began a rapid crescendo of development. The local iron and steel industry made heavy demands on the reserves of coking coal in west Durham whilst the needs of industry for steam coal, and of shipping for bunker coals, were virtually insatiable. New pits were opened in all producing districts whilst the size of collieries was repeatedly increased in response to the requirements of an improved technology of extraction.

Towards the end of the nineteenth century the thicker and richer seams of hard coals in west Durham had been depleted; in south-west Durham flooding had greatly added to the cost of mining. In the hinterland of Blyth in Northumberland, on the other hand, the working of steam and household coals was proceeding apace and many new pits had been established. During the early twentieth century some of the largest collieries in the North East were opened in the south-eastern part of the east Durham plateau.

Fig 15 shows the distribution of miners in 1914 very soon after the peak of employment in the local coalfield—a sharp contrast to the 1966 pattern seen in Fig 14. The 1914 distribution is the composite result of the spread and intensification of mining already referred to but it also contained localities, in south-west Durham for example, which were already beset by problems of pit closure, a growing loss of migrants and the dereliction of some of the smaller settlements near worked-out pits. In many areas by 1914 succeeding phases of development or decline were already to be seen in the landscape of housing, mine workings, roads and railways. The stone-built miners' cottages in the low narrow rows of the early nineteenth century gave way to the monotonous brick-terraces of later years; abandoned workings, local subsidence hollows and overgrown spoil heaps testified to the wayward history of coal exploitation as a wasting asset.

After the First World War the total output of coal declined, most strikingly so in west Durham. The pattern of collieries began to contract by closures and there was some concentration on production at fewer larger pits, a process facilitated by the fact that, following upon a period of regrouping, relatively few companies owned the productive mines. The depression years of the early 1930s hastened

Table 20

NORTHUMBERLAND AND DURHAM COALFIELD 1931–66

	1931	1941	1951	1961	1966
Production (million tons)	42	35	39	33	27
Wage-earners (thousands)	188	172	156	118	81
Productivity (tons per man per annum)	—	—	259	269	341
Profit or loss per ton before interest	—	—	−1s 11d	−2s 4d	−2s. 5d
Percentage cleaned by machinery	—	—	53	68	66
Percentage power-loaded	—	—	3	30	66

Sources: Various, including *Colliery Trades Year Book* and Ministry of Fuel & Power *Statistical Digests.*

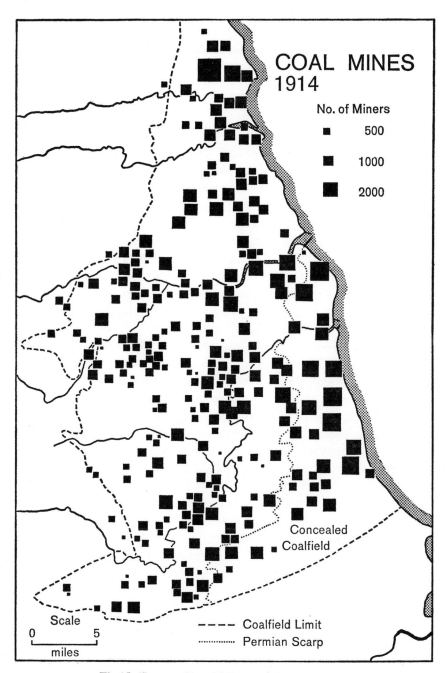

Fig 15. (Source: *List of Mines and Quarries* 1914.)

the decline of many marginal collieries and there was a sharp rise in out-migration of unemployed miners. These events were, however, the accentuation of trends which had been started many years before.

Post 1945

The fortunes of the coal industry since vesting date under the NCB have been partly the result of the changing balance of supply and demand and, partly, perhaps increasingly, of government policies on fuel and power. From 1946 to 1955 the prime purpose was to increase output, including an important quota for exports, with coal as the basis of a policy related to maximum use of national raw materials. This was the period of the *Plan for Coal*[3] with its estimates of 41 million tons output for the North East in the early 1960s. In the event the output was 33 million tons in 1961 and as low as 27 million in 1966. The *Plan* figure for west Durham, 11 million tons, was higher than could be justified on grounds of profitability, a further indicator of the special-status quality of the caking coals.

The *Plan* proposed massive investment in reorganising production with elimination of some of the higher-cost locationally marginal pits. The results have been progressively seen in the rise in productivity per manshift and per annum, and in the increased mechanisation of both cutting and power-loading. This has not yet succeeded in transforming the coalfield from a loss-making to a profit-making enterprise before charging for interest, but technical progress and the streamlining of production certainly put the coal industry on a sounder footing to face the trials of the later 1950s and the 1960s.

There was nevertheless a continuing rundown of the mining labour force, even during the most prosperous post-war years. Some 22,000 miners left the industry in the North East between 1950 and 1960, although much of this period was a time of full employment in the mines. This wastage continued to feature in later phases when pit closures came prominently into the picture; in more prosperous times wastage created a shortage of labour in the pits.

During the mid-1950s coal passed from a state of underproduction to one in which supply exceeded effective market demand. This was in part, a reflection of the more competitive price of alternative fuels; it was related also to government fuel and power policy and to the result of improved technology of fuel consumption in many industries. The most striking post-war change in consumption of coal in the North East is the growth of thermal power generation, with its most rapid

Page 107: (left) *Billingham town centre;* (right) *Patons & Baldwins Ltd knitting wool factory at Darlington.*

Page 108: (above) *Central Teesside; Middlesbrough dock in foreground*; (below) *Thornaby, shopping centre and new residential development.*

increase in the early 1960s after completion of the electricity supergrid and the commissioning of new generating stations on the Tyne
and at Blyth. Conversely gas is no longer so dependent upon coal for
its raw material; once again the change has been rapid during the

Table 21

NORTHUMBERLAND AND DURHAM COALFIELD
COAL DISTRIBUTION 1948 AND 1966

	1948		1966	
	m tons	per cent	m tons	per cent
Electricity	6·3	17·7	10·3	36·6
Gas	7·5	21·0	3·9	13·9
Coke ovens	8·6	24·2	6·0	21·3
Railways	0·9	2·2	0·1	0·4
Industry	5·8	16·2	3·7	13·1
Merchants	3·3	9·3	2·2	7·9
Miners	1·4	4·0	0·8	2·9
Colliery use	0·5	1·4	0·2	0·7
Miscellaneous	1·4	4·0	0·9	3·2
Total	35·7	100·0	28·1	100·0

Source: Ministry of Fuel & Power *Statistical Digests.*

1960s. For this reason, and also because of economies in the use of
coking coal in the steel industry the pattern of coke ovens has con-
tracted considerably in the past fifteen years. The progressive
conversion by British Rail to diesel operation, and the rise of electricity
as prime mover in growth industries, further reduced the market for
coal. All these trends are likely to develop further economies in the
use of coal and there is no compensating growth in alternative markets.
The utilisation of coal from the Northumberland and Durham coalfield
for the years 1948 and 1966 is shown in Table 21.

The years since 1957 have seen profounder changes in the
Northumberland and Durham coalfield than for any comparable
period since the depression of the early 1930s. Fig 16 shows the
pattern of pit closures and also the change in man-power at each
individual colliery for the years 1957–65. During this time almost
25,000 miners were released on closure or reorganisation of pits; four-
fifths of these were placed at other mines in the local coalfield, very
often within daily travelling distance from the miner's home town or
village. Nevertheless over 5,000 miners were declared redundant, with
particularly heavy incidence between 1963 and 1965, the earlier part

G

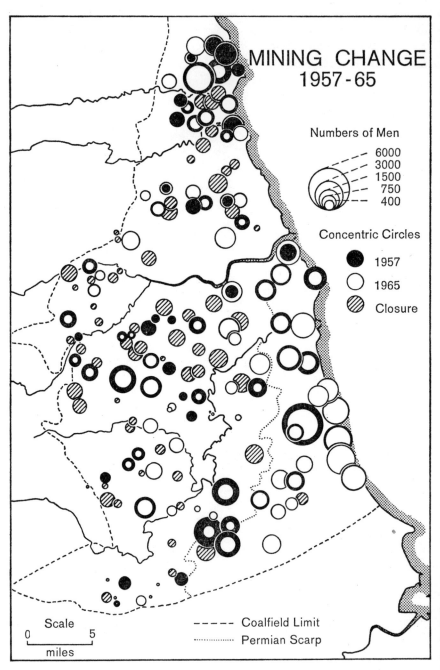

Fig 16. (Source: data from the National Coal Board.)

of this period coinciding with an industrial recession. This represents a striking change in the economic and social life of many mining settlements and the process is now entering what seems to be an even more rapid phase of pit closures.

The effect of pit closures has been widespread through all districts, but most severe in south-east Northumberland and central and west Durham. The Ashington area and the coastal strip of Durham, on the other hand, have as yet seen few pit closures, though reductions in man-power have been general at most collieries. Only at South Shields and at two of the Ashington pits was there a slight increase in man-power between 1957 and 1965.

The scale of mining contraction in south-east Northumberland has stimulated a planning programme of reconversion to other industries and an ambitious attempt to regroup mining populations in the county council New Towns of Cramlington and Killingworth. The legacy of derelict land, decaying settlements, and closed pit-head buildings, offers further physical planning problems. In the middle Wear and on the west-Durham plateau the rash of pit closures has been most intense. Noticeably during this period south-west Durham had fewer pits still working and thus fewer available for closure; nevertheless the heavy reductions of man-power in the Ferryhill area were the prelude to a more recent spate of pits to be shut down. Most of the men displaced by closures in west Durham were offered jobs in longer-life pits in east Durham, though this often meant a considerable journey to work in transport organised and subsidised by the NCB. That the economic and social problems consequent on pit closure were not very much more severe is due to the successful redeployment of all able-bodied and willing miners to other pits. This redeployment was very largely within the local coalfield and only small groups of Durham miners went to the Yorkshire–Nottinghamshire or the South Wales coalfield under the NCB inter-divisional transfer scheme.

Pit closure and Communities around Houghton le Spring[4]

The effects of pit closure can be assessed both directly on the miner's household and, more generally, on his community. Between 1963 and 1966 some 2,000 miners were released from four local pits around Houghton le Spring. In the early part of the period two-fifths became redundant but, of those leaving later, three-quarters were transferred to other pits and by 1966 only 6 per cent of those then leaving were declared redundant. Mining was the occupation of two-thirds of the local men and, characteristically in the coalfield, there was little representation of manufacturing close at hand and even service jobs occupied little more than one-third of those employed. There was a small post-war trading estate locally, and in 1963 a Board of Trade advance factory was built ahead of any prospective tenant with a view to relieving any unemployment consequent on mine closures, yet only 10 per cent of those released from mining found other jobs in the locality.

Virtually all the men transferred to other pits could remain at home and travel daily distances up to eleven miles. Even so one-fifth of these men subsequently left the mining industry, usually the younger men who could more readily command alternative employment and who had less tradition as miners. The majority settled at their new pit but showed great reluctance to go and live nearby even though there were many complaints of loss of leisure time and the break-up of old working acquaintanceships. There was also the opinion that at the new pit the transferred miner was less likely to be placed at the most profitable coal-faces and that he had lost some status on change of pit.

The 18 per cent who were declared redundant when the local pits closed created serious social problems; most of them were men over forty-five and many were approaching retirement age. Few had had any work other than mining; mostly they were men with very long service underground. Only 1 in 5 of the redundant men got other jobs but these were fairly varied, eg in engineering, electrical goods, or local authority labouring; usually however the work was unskilled or at best semi-skilled. For the majority of redundant men there was real hardship in the household, with the need for stringent economies affecting not only luxury items but often also entertainment and the general practices of social life. The change of circumstance was often met with cheerful resignation, but in other cases with bitter resentment.

Men who left mining either before the closures or soon after were typical of another of the industry's problems, even in the prosperous coalfields, namely that of the loss of the younger and abler men attracted by better conditions in other occupations. Semi-skilled machine work in engineering or the electrical industries proved the most attractive but the high wages in labouring and contracting drew others. Men leaving mining dispersed more widely and so escaped the close-knit community feeling of being locked-in on the local problems after pit closure.

The wider effect of pit closure on the local community is more difficult to assess. The mining households were affected by the need for the man to travel perhaps twelve or fifteen miles a day to a new pit, by the disturbance of social and family life, but the family continued to have a wage of similar size to rely upon. The redundant miners posed a welfare problem and had a sharply reduced power to buy in the local shops. Other men and their families had taken different jobs and left the mining village and overall the effects were deep-seated, if not always dramatic at the surface. In any case they have to be seen in the wider context of the wish of many younger folk to desert the coalfield for the towns, for better or more varied jobs, for better housing and social conditions.

The brief picture of the villages around Houghton le Spring during the 1960s indicates a current problem that is widespread and spreading, local but also regional and national. The pattern of employment at North East pits in 1966 (Fig 14) already shows a remarkable transformation when compared with that on the eve of the First World War (Fig 15), but the story is far from ended. Fig 17 looks speculatively ahead from 1965 and indeed some of the pits then declared by the NCB as 'imminently closing' have already been shut down. Discussion on national fuel and power policy, even within the past year, has made likely a much more rapid phasing out of labour in the mining industry and an acceleration of pit closures.

Considerable reserves of coal exist in Northumberland and Durham; indeed an extensive undersea exploration by boring tower has added significantly to known substantial reserves in recent years. Nevertheless the coal industry, even on its own estimates, is entering a period of further contraction and streamlining. Within fifteen or twenty years the coalfield may already have the pattern of the black circles on Fig 17. It will still be a substantial national producer and it will have seen production concentrated at fewer, but not necessarily always larger, pits. The bulk of output will then come from the Durham coastal collieries, especially those south of Seaham. Northumberland will have important production from groups of pits around Blyth, Ashington and Amble; indeed the Alcan aluminium smelter project now to be built at Blyth insures coal production and employment in the surrounding hinterland for the forseeable future. North-west Durham will continue to supply high-grade coking coal from collieries of modest size in comparison with the coastal pits, once again a tribute to the persisting importance of a unique natural resource.

Alongside the reassurance of a prosperous long-term future for some mining districts in the North East must be set the clear reality of decline and decay for others and that substantially and in the short-

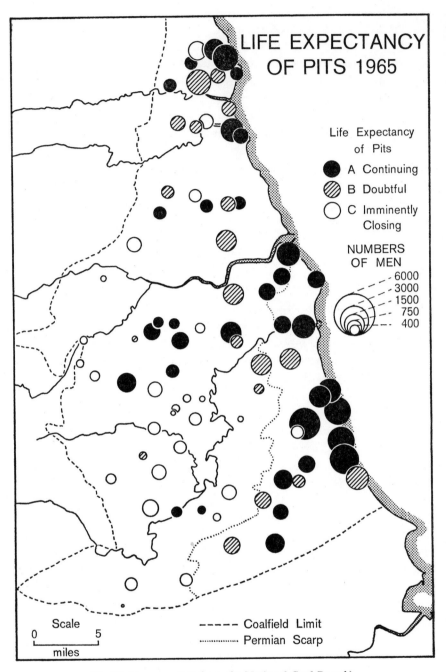

Fig 17. (Source: data from the National Coal Board.)

term. The consequential economic and social changes have been accepted by the government as justifying particular aid in the form of designated special development areas where industrial reconversion of displaced coal miners will be sought on a scale never hitherto attempted, advance factories being set up tactically as part of the programme. The successful placing of miners released on closure has been both a regional and a national success story for the NCB up to the present but with a smaller number of pits as closures continue and intensify this will shortly become more difficult.

There is considerable debate in the North East on what should be the best policy for the declining areas of the coalfield. On the one side there is the undoubtedly persuasive social argument that community spirit in the mining areas is strong and should be preserved by bringing alternative work, suitable to the ex-miner, within daily travelling distance of his present home. Less often mentioned but extremely important is the need to provide training for such new jobs, a facility somewhat scarce hitherto and far too little used by the ex-miner. Such a policy would envisage a scattering of factories through the coalfield and perhaps their grouping on small estates in more central locations. A more detached viewpoint would see the old mining community-structure as breaking up in any case, with the dispersal of mining families into council estates, would stress the hardships which held people together in the pit villages and the poor quality of housing in which so many lived for so long. With such a perspective policy might rather be to abandon many pit villages and regroup the population in the towns or around growth points at which new jobs might be more realistically provided. Indeed the difficulty of persuading industrialists to set up plants in isolated locations or on single sites in advance factories at the present time reinforces the likelihood that planning for the coalfield communities, though it may preserve where and for as long as it can, will eventually need to move towards a dramatic reshaping of towns and villages which will be as radically different as the patterns of the producing collieries themselves over the past fifty years.

Iron and Steel

Together with coal the production of iron and steel typified the Industrial Revolution in nineteenth-century Britain. During the period since 1850 the course of national and regional economic change has indeed been mirrored in the fortunes of the iron and steel industry, the supplier of raw materials to all forms of capital goods manufacture, and thus one of the fundaments of the entire national economy. Since the North East was early and dramatically associated with the Industrial Revolution its regional iron and steel industry has been one of the most consistent barometers of prosperity and depression, though the relationships between local natural resources, range of products, and location of markets have changed and become less clear-cut in the years since 1945. Nevertheless in an era of regional economic planning the iron and steel industry in the North East remains potentially a powerful instrument for influencing associated developments, the more so in that it has for long been subject to national control in its investment programmes and increasingly involved in decisions by government, culminating in the renationalisation of the steel industry in 1967. In spite of substantial increases in output, in efficiency and technological change since 1945 it is arguable that the steel industry in the North East has not yet played as prominent a leader rôle in the reconstruction of the regional economy as might have been expected. The nature of its traditional products, with emphasis on the heavier plates, beams and sections has not broadened, or perhaps been permitted to diversify from a limited range of slower growth items into a significantly wider range of lighter products, such as steel strip, for which demand has risen sharply since the war. At the present time far-reaching decisions on rationalisation and future location of the steel industry in Britain are pending, following publication of the *Benson Report*[5] in 1966. The decisions reached will be crucial not only for the economic health and prospects of a key industry in the North East but also for the continuing existence of outlying steel plants in north-west Durham and Cleveland, together with their closely-associated communities.

Location and Present Technology

Fig 18 shows the location of employment in all forms of metal manufacture. The bulk of employment, in iron and steel production, is concentrated on Teesside where the integrated steelworks of Dorman Long and South Durham together form the greatest node of steelmaking in Great Britain. Other companies within the British Steel Corporation's Northern and Tubes group are Consett Iron, on a detached site on the north-west Durham plateau, and a smaller producer, Skinningrove Iron, in Cleveland. An integral part of the group, though not within the North East, is Stewart & Lloyds who

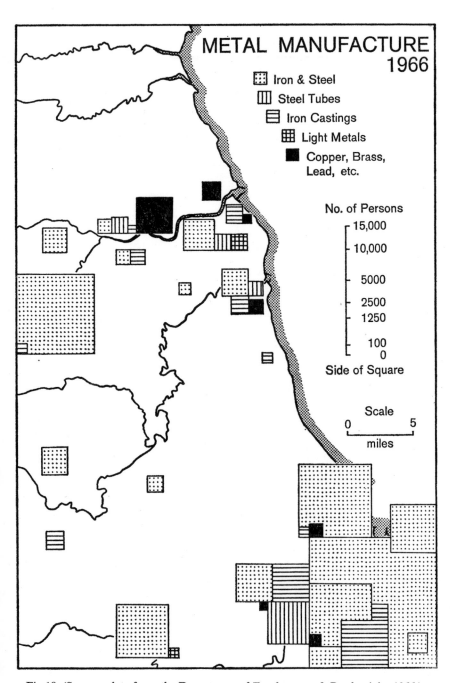

Fig 18. (Source: data from the Department of Employment & Productivity 1966.)

produce pipe and tubes at Corby in the east Midlands and with whom
Dorman Long and South Durham formed a merger early in 1967
shortly before renationalisation. Steel production figures for individual
companies are shown in Table 22.

Table 22

THE NORTH EAST. PIG IRON AND STEEL OUTPUT, 1960 (PEAK YEAR)
AND 1965 (in thousand tons) BY COMPANIES

	1960		1965	
	Pig	Steel	Pig	Steel
Consett	729	992	703	1,045
Dorman Long	1,532	2,274	1,533	1,915
Skinningrove	222	277	158	256
South Durham	810	1,080	1,004	1,430
Other	119	189	36	144
North East	3,412	4,812	3,434	4,790

Source: Company reports.

After a long and complex industrial history, involving numerous
local mergers, Dorman Long is well advanced (Stage V) in its own
post-1945 programme of rationalisation of production in a few major
plants on an integrated site at Cleveland–Lackenby, on the south bank
of the Tees estuary and close to the petro-chemicals complex of ICI
Wilton (Fig 19). Older plants in the former Ironmasters district of
Middlesbrough and at Redcar have either been closed or are being
run-down. Pig-iron production is from three large blast furnaces at
Cleveland (Clay Lane), each capable of producing 1,500 tons per day,
and from three medium-sized furnaces at the Bessemer works. At
present steel production is from a series of tilting basic open hearth
furnaces, six of them each capable of pouring 360 tons of steel at a
tap, at the Cleveland, Lackenby and Redcar works. The open hearth
furnaces are shortly to be replaced by two basic oxygen furnaces at
Lackenby, to produce 220 tons of steel per tapping and 2 million tons
of steel per annum, whilst two 100 ton electric-arc melting furnaces
are already working at the Cleveland North plant. In addition to
conventional rolling mills producing semi-finished steels Dorman Long
initiated a universal beam mill at Lackenby in 1958, followed by a
universal plate mill also making strip for tubes, and, in 1966, a new
rod mill, all trends towards more sophisticated and diversified products.

South Durham operating initially at West Hartlepool (North works)
and Cargo Fleet, added, in 1962, a major new integrated steelmaking
plant some 1¼ miles from the North works, at the former Greatham

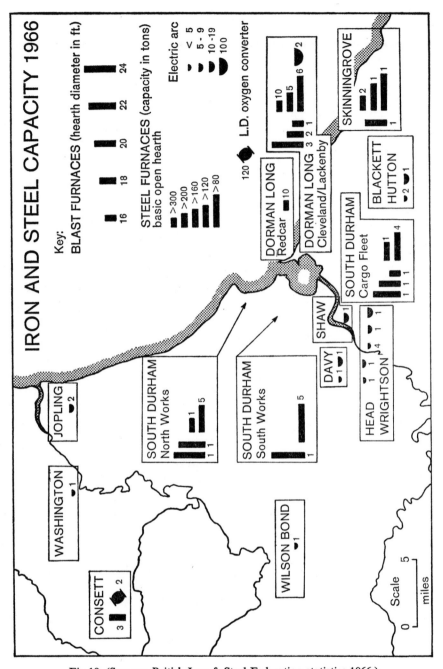

Fig 19. (Source: British Iron & Steel Federation statistics 1966.)

airfield site (South works). All three sites are equipped for pig-iron production with the largest blast furnace on Teesside (28¼ ft diameter) at the South works. Steel production is from basic open hearth furnaces, including five each of 350 tons capacity at the South works; steel production ceased at the North works in 1965. In 1955 a steel-pipe plant was developed at Stockton with a steadily developing capacity for pipes and tubes, mainly to serve the export market; at Cargo Fleet a universal beam mill was installed to roll columns and beams. By 1965 South Durham rolling-mill production was divided between 640,000 tons of steel plates, including some for pipes, and 310,000 tons of sections and rails.

The steelmaking plant at Consett, on a plateau site some 22 miles by rail from tidewater ore facilities on the lower Tyne but close to coking-coal supplies, produced more than 1 million tons of ingot steel in 1965. Its three blast furnaces use foreign ores of low phosphorus content. Oxygen steelmaking was installed in 1958 and since 1964 all steel has been made in two converters each of 120 ton capacity using the LD processes. In addition to conventional rolling facilities, a new sheared plate mill was inaugurated at Hownsgill in 1961, and in 1964 an arrangement was made with Dorman Long to share capacity at Consett and Lackenby by mutually agreeing to put 2,000 tons of rolling capacity at the disposal of the other firm each week. In 1940 Consett acquired the Jarrow mill for production of semi-continuous bar and strip, re-rolling some 5,000 tons of semi-finished steel from Consett each week.

Skinningrove works is the smallest of the North East's iron and steel plants, some 16 miles east of Middlesbrough in the Cleveland hills. There is a single blast furnace and four basic open hearth steel furnaces. The rolling mills tend to concentrate on short-run orders and special products.

Other steel-making capacity in the North East is very small in scale, associated with foundries as at Darlington, Billingham, Thornaby and Guisborough on Teesside, or Bishop Auckland, Gateshead and Pallion, Sunderland. The furnaces are usually of the electric-arc type, between 5 and 19 tons capacity.

National Status and Trends

Table 23 shows that the North East has for long been in the fore-front of national iron and steel production but that there has been some waning in relative status particularly marked between 1913 and

1920 and since the depression in steel in the late 1950s. The decline in proportionate rôle of pig-iron production has been more marked than that for crude steel, which showed a degree of stability in regional status between 1920 and 1960. The effect of the two world wars was to increase the importance of the North East during pre-war armament and to diminish its status during immediate post-war reconstruction.

Table 23

NORTH EAST AND UK. REGIONAL PIG-IRON AND STEEL PRODUCTION AS PERCENTAGE OF NATIONAL 1913–67

	1913	1920	1938	1947	1953	1960	1967
Pig iron	37·7	32·8	27·1	24·9	23·7	21·6	17·4
Steel	26·4	21·5	22·0	20·3	19·6	19·8	16·0

Source: British Iron & Steel Federation statistics and others.

The explanation of these trends is complex. The changing significance of locally available raw materials for iron and steel production, the nature of traditional products and the extent and success of attempted diversification, the policies and achievements of particular companies, the rôle of the state, the changes in markets and competitiveness of North Eastern producers nationally and internationally, all these have to be set among other less perceptible factors.

In general terms the iron and steel industry in the North East has suffered in a measure from its early start and meteoric rise during the nineteenth century. Concentration on a limited range of staple products, linked in part to the characteristics of the regional consumers in shipbuilding and heavy engineering, together with the reliable overseas rail trade encouraged continuance rather than either diversity or novelty of product—a long-standing situation which found echoes until very recent times.

It is appropriate to look first at the essential historical background and then more closely at the years post-1945. Both are ingredients of a present-day assessment and are the prelude to some consideration of the future of the industry.

The Historical Essentials

The economic history of the British iron and steel industry has been fully chronicled[6] and there is useful material on the history of particular iron and steel companies in the North East.[7] The early history of iron-making, until around 1850, concerns dispersed sites usually on or near the coalfield in association with local iron ores, or close to the Cleveland jurassic orefield which was to dominate developments during the next period. At Newcastle, the Walker ironworks was well established in the early 1830s, whilst in the following decade Tow Law blast furnaces began to work Weardale ores and at Consett the Derwent Iron Company began iron-making on a site which has been continuously occupied through to the major integrated steelworks of today. During this early phase Bolckow & Vaughan developed manufacture of iron at Middlesbrough (1840) but, ignoring Cleveland ores at first, set up blast furnaces at Witton Park in south-west Durham.

Between 1850, the date of discovery of the Cleveland main ore seam outcrop at Eston, and about 1880, when steel-making started effectively in the North East, the region developed as the major British wrought and puddled-iron producing district. Though the Derwent Iron Company took up leases in Cleveland to supply ore to north-west Durham the main weight of development took place on the south bank of the Tees with the proliferation of new companies and the gradual emergence of several leader firms: Bolckow & Vaughan at Eston, Bell Brothers at Port Clarence on the north bank of the Tees, and Dorman at Middlesbrough. The Ironmasters district in the north-western part of the town, on a bend in the Tees, developed as a concentrated grouping of iron-making plants, specialising in complementary but also some competitive products.

During twenty years to 1875 the Teesside ironmasters dominated the British industry, in production, technology, and organisation, and Cleveland ore rose to provide about 40 per cent of national output. There was a concentration on wrought iron and forge pig-iron production and indeed some opposition to the introduction of steel-making, for which the local ores with their phosphoric content were in any case thought to be unsuitable. Many smaller iron producers in Northumberland and Durham for a time bought Cleveland ores to replace worked-out local supplies but gradually these smaller firms went out of business, emphasising the prime attraction of a coastal site on the Tees estuary close to local or imported iron ore. In the 1860s Consett started using haematite ore from Cumbria, later from north-west Spain. Rather exceptionally at the same time Bessemer steel was being made at the Tudhoe works of the Weardale Company.

In the mid-1870s about 0·33 million tons of Cleveland ore was being exported and almost as much sent in the coastwise trade. The economic depression of the 1870s forced attention to steel-making in the North East and, after teething troubles, the Thomas Gilchrist process of making steel from phosphoric ores was successfully developed during the 1880s. Already in 1880 the North East coast was a pig-iron producer exporting half its output; in finished iron, however, no less than three-quarters went to the local shipbuilders.

The steel industry grew rapidly in the 1880s and 1890s using both the acid and basic Bessemer processes and the acid open-hearth method, though at this time south Wales was slightly ahead in national steel production. North Eastern shipbuilders turned late from iron to Bessemer steel materials and reluctantly were persuaded to use basic Bessemer steel produced from Cleveland ores. Large imports of Spanish haematite made acid Bessemer steel as cheap as basic steel from local ore.

The early twentieth century, 1902–4, saw depression in shipbuilding and the iron and steel industry. Closures of pig-iron making firms and furnaces had been numerous in the period from the 1870s to the turn of the century; it was now the turn of steelworks and rolling mills. Yet the status of the North East remained high within the national industry. With 3·5 million tons of pig iron in 1906 the region continued to be the largest national producer, but by the turn of the century half the pig iron made was from imported ores. The North East led the field in the technology of blast-furnace design, in size, output, and economy in the use of coke per ton of pig iron.

Further recessions in steel followed in 1907 and on the eve of the First World War, hastening a process of amalgamation and rationalisation of production which had risen in momentum since the late 1880s, and which culminated in the years after 1919. The two giants of the Teesside industry, Dorman Long and South Durham, emerged from the regroupings and increase in scale of organisation.

From a small wrought-iron and engineering business started at Middlesbrough in 1876, only one of fifteen in the town, Dorman and Long took over the Britannia works (1880), Bell Brothers at Port Clarence (finally by 1902), the Cleveland wireworks (1899), and the North East Steel Co (1890). These greatly increased iron and steel capacity and added new product specialisations. Bolckow & Vaughan grew more by expansion of their own works than by takeovers of others, though in the 1890s and 1900s they acquired Clay Lane Iron Co, a sheet and galvanising mill at Eston, the Darlington rolling mills and a constructional engineering firm, Redpath Brown. South Durham Steel & Iron Co developed in a more complex way, ie from integration backwards into coal, iron and steel on the part of the shipbuilding firm of Furness Withy of Hartlepool. In 1898 the South Durham Co was formed to acquire works at Stockton (Moor iron and steelworks and Stockton malleable ironworks) and at West Hartlepool; the Furness Withy group added the Weardale Steel, Coal & Coke Co in the next year. When the Tudhoe steelworks of the Weardale Co was closed in 1901 Cargo Fleet Iron Co was acquired. In 1905 Cargo Fleet, by reverse takeover, came to control South Durham, co-ordinating plate manufacture north of the Tees with output of rails at Cargo Fleet. Between 1907 and 1910 the outlying Skinningrove works developed steel production. Because of its site well off the coalfield, fuel economy was an important feature of its technology.

During the First World War Dorman Long took over the Redcar steelworks and built melting shops and rolling mills to develop manufacture of plate, also acquiring the Ironmasters' district site of Samuelson & Co at Newport. The economic crisis of 1920 led to further closures and amalgamations, the outstanding being the takeover of Bolckow & Vaughan by Dorman Long in 1929; South Durham acquired Cochrane & Co of Middlesbrough (1918), adding cast iron pipes to their range, and the Seaton Carew Iron Co (1919). Consett Iron Co contented itself with a major reconstruction of steel-making capacity but kept its independence.

The economic depression of the early 1930s seriously affected steel production, reflecting the slump in the capital goods industries, its major consumers. Just as the depression led to the earliest interventions by government in regional problems so it led to more centralised influence upon investment programmes in the British iron and steel industry. The saga of the abortive development of an iron and steel industry at Jarrow from 1934 onwards is well-known. Its lack of success was both a tribute to the more logical location of new capacity on the Tees rather than the Tyne and confirmation that the scale of production envisaged was too small for modern technology. Ultimately the former site of Palmer's shipyard and ironworks was developed for rolling mills, associated with Consett, a tube works (Stewarts & Lloyds), and a steel foundry (Armstrong Whitworth).

The Second World War led to further major advances in production, an increase in centralised planning in the industry, and ushered in the problems of post-war programming for meeting national needs.

Post 1945

It is not yet possible to interpret the rôles of either the individual companies, the Iron and Steel Board, or the governments of the day

Page 125: (above) *Tyne gorge at Newcastle, looking north-east*; (below) *coaling 'staithes' at Dunston.*

Page 126: (above) *Blaydon-Lemington industrial zone*; (below) *Tyne Commission quay*.

in the nature or scale of post-war developments in the iron and steel industry. Production has risen under the successive development programmes of the industry and the North East had, until after 1960, approximately kept its proportion of national output, more clearly so in steel than in pig iron.

The advantage of local Cleveland ores, important for the boom in the iron industry in the latter half of the nineteenth century, has completely disappeared, Cleveland production ceasing in the early 1960s. Degree of dependence on British ores in general has declined and the sources of foreign ore have become much diversified. The iron content of foreign ores is appreciably higher, which indicates emphatically the extent of foreign contribution to pig-iron production. No haematite ores from Cumbria have been used in the North East since the war. The percentage of home to foreign sources of supply and the major foreign suppliers are given in Table 24.

Table 24

THE NORTH EAST. SOURCES OF IRON ORE SUPPLY 1948–67
(In million tons)

	1948		1953		1960		1967
Home	1·2		1·8		1·3		1·1
Foreign	2·9		3·3		4·5		3·0
Home ore percentage	30·0		36·0		23·0		27·0
Four major suppliers:							
Sweden	1·1	Sweden	1·5	Canada	1·1	Sweden	0·8
Fr. N. Africa	0·9	Fr. N. Africa	0·8	Sweden	1·1	Liberia	0·5
Canada	0·3	Canada	0·3	Venezuela	0·7	Canada	0·5
S. Leone	0·2	S. Leone	0·1	Fr. N. Africa	0·6	Mauritania	0·2

Source: British Iron & Steel Federation *Annual Reports.*

The locational advantage of proximity to suppliers of coking coal has also on balance diminished since the war, part of a declining advantage throughout the entire history of fuel economy in iron and steelmaking. At Dorman Long for example the three blast furnaces at Clay Lane required only 10·5 cwts of coke per ton of iron produced in 1965, compared with 15·4 cwts as recently as 1960. Steel furnaces also showed economies in coal, and some substitution of alternative fuels eg oil and thermal electric power. To this extent the locational pull of the Durham coalfield has been weakened but, on the other hand, the pricing policy of the NCB has helped maintain local advantage.[8] To the advantages of regionally available limestone and

H

dolomite for fluxes in the steel furnaces has been added the manufacturing at Hartlepool since the early war years of magnesite blocks,
previously available only from Austria.

As is shown in Table 25 there has been a striking change since 1945
in the virtual elimination of haematite pig iron and the growth of the
basic quality in the North East. Foundry and forge-iron production
has largely ceased.

Table 25

NORTH   EAST   PIG-IRON   PRODUCTION   BY   TYPE   1920–67
(In thousand tons)

	1920	1938	1947	1953	1960	1967
Haematite	997	522	310	245	117	0
Basic	983	1,238	1,520	2,324	3,234	2,580
Other	659	73	104	77	61	65
Total	2,639	1,833	1,934	2,646	3,412	2,645

Source: British Iron & Steel Federation *Annual Reports.*

In crude steel production the North East has maintained post-war
its traditional high pig-iron/scrap ratio and has become more clearly a
hot metal district by the further integration between blast furnace,
molten cradle, soaking pit and steel furnace (Table 26).

Table 26

THE NORTH EAST. MATERIALS CONSUMED IN CRUDE STEEL
PRODUCTION, 1938–67, BY PERCENTAGE
(All columns total 100)

	1938	1947	1953	1960	1967
Pig—molten	37·6	37·7	43·3	48·0	50·6
—cold	8·0	6·7	3·4	2·7	1·5
Scrap metal	31·8	35·4	31·6	29·4	30·3
Oxides	11·7	8·5	9·4	8·7	7·4
Other	10·9	11·7	12·3	11·2	10·2

Source: Calculated from BISF data.

Since the war the North East has been less active in diversifying the
range of steel products than either south Wales or Scotland, with less
dramatic developments when compared with the undoubted technological achievements in the manufacture of iron and steel. Its
product range has widened somewhat (Table 27) but most strikingly
by greater variety within the traditional lines of heavy plate, heavy
sections and angles, beams and other heavy products. Demand for this

range has been slower growing than that for steel strip, the raw material for light engineering; the fortunes of North East steel producers have thus been tied more closely to the national and regional capital goods industries as well as participating, both directly and through assembly industries, in the international market. In more recent years the continuous light plate mill at Lackenby has been producing a product akin to strip, but without the cold-rolling facilities. Other limited diversification has been achieved in the traditional production of wire and by the commissioning of two rod mills at Lackenby, whilst plastic-coated steel is a pointer to the developing products of the future.

Table 27

THE NORTH EAST. PRODUCTION OF SELECTED STEEL PRODUCTS
AS PERCENTAGES OF NATIONAL OUTPUT 1947–67

	1947	1953	1960	1967
Heavy and medium plates	36·5	33·3 ⎱	41·5	38·0
Other heavy products	39·1	37·4 ⎰		
Light rolled products	13·0	12·8	11·3	8·6
Sheets	5·6	3·9	2·6	1·1
Steel tubes/pipes	4·4	5·3	1·7	1·1
Steel castings	19·7	19·3	18·1	19·1
Steel forgings	7·4	7·4	7·4	3·8

Source: British Iron & Steel Federation statistics.

Failure to diversify steel products more fully has not been the result of an excessive dependence on the regional market of the North East in shipbuilding, constructional or heavy engineering. Indeed the evidence points rather to a rising market for North Eastern steel outside the region and to some inroads in turn of outside steel producers to serve the shipyards and engineering works on Tyne and Tees. For example five-sixths of all structural steel produced in the North East in 1967 was sold to customers outside the region. In 1957 40 per cent of Consett heavy plate was sold in the North East and 30 per cent of all output went to local shipyards: by 1965 one-third of the Tyne–Wear–Tees requirements for ships plates were being met from Lincolnshire. Alternatively the development of semi-finished steels from Consett since 1953 has led to about half the billet production leaving the region for distant re-rolling.

In the more recently developed lines the emphasis on outside sales is equally striking: in 1967 three-quarters of home sales from the Lackenby universal beam mill left the North East, and slightly more than one-quarter of all output went abroad. The rapidity of expansion in outside markets is illustrated by the switch in sales of plates and section at a major Teesside firm. In the early 1960s the firm used most of its own plates and sections in fabrication but by 1967 only about one-tenth of plate and half the sections were being worked up within the firm.

Markets may also change in the short-term. In the late 1950s rather more pipes from Teesside were being exported than moving to home markets; with the development of the gas and natural gas grids during the mid-1960s however the home demand became paramount at a time when overseas markets were often unremunerative.

It may be argued that the steelworks of the North East have been extremely successful in modernising their technology and plant for pig-iron and steel production but that they have been excessively conservative in new product range and may consequently have failed to act as the spearhead of new forms of industrial development that might otherwise have been developed in the region. That iron and steel production had been organised on a most efficient basis by 1958 is undeniable and, since then, the movement towards new basic oxygen-furnace plant using the LD process has been set in train. The Cleveland Lackenby complex of Dorman Long, the South works of South Durham, and the new steel furnaces and plate mill at Consett are major features in post-war national iron and steel production.

The trend towards multi-product steel plants is gathering momentum with associated versatile rolling-mill complexes capable of producing items from heavy plates to narrow or wide strip and all intermediate products. That the North East has not already diversified more fully into light rolled products, strip, or wire for example is at least partly due to decisions at central planning level in the steel industry. Government-inspired decisions in the late 1950s, on the location of new integrated steel plants and strip mills on the Clyde and in south Wales, are at least one further reason why the North East did not emulate the fast growth of the steel industry in south Wales. The conservatism of the steel-makers cannot be ruled out, nor can the merits of a policy of supplying mainly capital goods industries be ignored, though it is certainly true that for success such a market dependence requires a steadily rising momentum of overall growth rate in the national economy that has so far eluded us since the war.

A Look Ahead

The *Benson Report* envisaged further rationalisation in the British iron and steel industry together with a concentration on a limited number of multi-purpose integrated steelworks on coastal sites, each capable of a production of not less than 3·5 million ingot tons. The recommendations about wide-strip mills of at least 5 million ingot tons capacity are unlikely to be relevant to the North East and the proposals for non-integrated works of about 1 to 1·5 million ingot tons output are clearly intended for the London–Lancashire–Midlands scrap belt. With a 1966 output of 3·8 million tons of crude steel, following a peak of 4·8 millions in 1960, and at a time when re-equipment by LD basic oxygen-furnace plant supplemented by scrap-melting facilities is in progress, the North East should have no difficulty by the mid-1970s in justifying two mammoth multi-purpose integrated steelworks, together capable of upwards of 6 million tons per annum. According to the *Benson Report* one or two such plants might be justified, probably on Teesside, with deep water ore-port facilities capable by the late 1970s of taking up to 65,000 ton tankers.

The creation of two interrelated Teesside steel complexes emerges logically from the present situation. Indeed already in 1967 prior to renationalisation, Dorman Long, South Durham and Stewarts & Lloyds had agreed to merge. The merits were then seen to be co-ordination of iron and steel making with steel-tube and pipe manufacture; rationalisation of a wider range of rolled-steel products; co-ordination of interests in the chemical, engineering, design and fabrication fields; and co-operation in overseas markets. The Northern and Tubes group of the British Steel Corporation thus carries forward an amalgamation already determined to be in the interests of the three original companies. Of the future of steel on Teesside there can be little doubt, but even there the sharp cutback in the labour force will most likely produce problems of redeployment of substantial numbers of men within the next decade.

The future prospects of the Consett and Skinningrove steel plants are much more controversial. Presently Consett is fully equipped for LD basic oxygen steel production based on the recommended low phosphorus foreign ores. It lies 22 miles from the Tyne, presently able to accommodate 40,000 ton ore carriers and capable of being developed by 1970 for 65,000 ton vessels. Prior to renationalisation it was argued that steel output could be built up to 3·5 million ingot tons capacity at Consett for a level of investment likely to be less than for some comparable *Benson Report* proposals. With Consett now a functioning part of the Northern and Tubes group the probability of its reduction and ultimate elimination as a steel producer has to be envisaged, in spite of the continuity and efficiency of its operation, its massive post-war investment and modernisation, and the serious implications for the sub-regional economy of north-west Durham already seriously threatened by the momentum of coal-mine closures.

The counter argument refers to the limitation of the North East to two 3 million ingot ton plants and the national need to run down surplus capacity. It emphasises the balance of advantage for Teesside in terms of scale of operation, tidewater unloading, linkages within the estuarine steel industry, and location closer to the economic heartland of Britain, with regular overseas cargo liner sailings from Teesport. Furthermore Consett has traditionally been limited to steel of ordinary grades and, in spite of diversification, no longer either enjoys or attempts to use the advantage of close proximity to Tyne shipyards and engineering works. Indeed the plant has sought links with other areas of Britain and has had difficulty in fully loading the new plate mill; already in 1964 an exchange of weekly capacity agreement with Dorman Long was established.

The Millom steelworks in Cumberland has recently been closed. Skinningrove in Cleveland is likewise a smaller producer but is an efficient steel plant for jobbing orders, short runs and special products. Its closure would not carry the same scale of implications as that of Consett but it would seriously add to the existing unemployment problems of the Cleveland marginal economy. Closure or run-down of production at Consett would require careful phasing, involving both redeployment of some workers to other steelmaking plants and conversion of other workers to new or growing industries within daily travelling distance. The scale of the difficulties for what has been virtually a company town since the mid-nineteenth century would provide one of the most concentrated problems that regional planners anywhere in Britain have yet had to face.

Most recently the British Steel Corporation's corporate plan 1967–75 indicated that the closure of complete works was unlikely on any large scale during that period. At the same time it hinted broadly that, even though many of the smaller or less well-situated plants are able to achieve competitive operating costs, in most cases a time-limit is set by the working life of the existing plant and equipment, which are unlikely to be replaced on the same site.

References to this chapter are on pages 241 and 249.

7

Rapid Growth Industries

THE CRITERIA for measurement of economic growth were discussed in Chapter 4. Most indicators are imperfect but, because regional economic policy has traditionally been focused on the relief of un-employment and new job provision in development areas or districts, the rise of insured employment in an industry has proved the most popular and general purpose barometer of growth. The principal alternative, net industrial product at fixed prices, is rarely obtainable from firms; in the four-yearly censuses of production it is given, for industry groups by standard regions, only in terms of value of sales. A more sensitive indicator of growth would be the ratio of turnover to capital employed but again this kind of data is jealously guarded by firms.

The weakness of an overdependence on growth in employment data is increasingly apparent as costs of labour rise, technology progresses and the trend in many industries is towards labour economy and automation. Some figures of productivity per worker would help in the interpretation of employment change as an indicator of growth but such data is once more fragmentary or lacking. This is not to say that scale of new job provision is not a useful yardstick of growth, particularly in its impact on unemployment and the problem of afford-ing alternative work for those displaced from declining industries. It is rather that the indicator must be used with some caution. Put simply it would be highly undesirable if an area like the North East were to become the home for industries seeking to avoid the costs of auto-mation by the use of cheaper than average labour, or if only labour-intensive forms of manufacturing sought to profit from government incentives to move north. In general, labour-intensive industries these days are less likely to be growth industries in other respects, and it is also possible to interpret the higher ratio of female jobs in some firms moving north since the war as one attempt to benefit from the cheap labour factor.

The rising volume of new jobs, for both men and women, is certainly required. But if steady, balanced, self-sustained, all round economic growth at maximum potential rates is to be achieved, the real need is for firms and industries whose contribution to regional wealth is also based upon scale and efficiency of output in lines and products for which there is a rising momentum of demand. These leader firms or industries may be just those in which the greatest labour economies are presently being practised. They are however also likely to be those where the multiplier effects on the regional economy are greatest, bringing further employment and accruing wealth in associated firms and thus contributing to the build-up of an industrial complex.

This kind of process has been seen earlier in the development and aggregation of traditional industries in the North East. It is important that, in the fashioning of a new industrial base, it should take place again, and on a rising scale involving industries unambiguously seen as growth industries on both the national and international scales. The nature of growth industries, identified in employment terms, has already been described in Chapter 4. The purpose of the current chapter is to illustrate, by contrast, the types of economic growth in manufacturing taking place in the North East since the 1939–45 war.

The chemical industry has been referred to as the base of the new industrial revolution, just as coal and iron and steel were the base for that of the nineteenth century. Its products proliferate, new chemical routes are found to old products, and new products constantly emerge, particularly those from the petro-chemicals plants. The industry group is extremely complex, sophisticated, often large in scale on all counts and capital-intensive by nature. It scarcely qualifies as a growth industry in employment terms but, in its doubling of wealth in output with much the same labour force numerically, it clearly has leader characteristics and can act as the base for a considerable industrial pyramid.

The electrical machinery and electrical goods industry is also in the forefront of any national growth designation, and just as in the chemical industry, certain branches have traditional roots in the North East. The heavy electrical machinery industry on the Tyne may be seen as the counterpart in chemicals of the production of acids and alkalis in earlier times. Also like the entirely new and vast growth from petro-chemicals, the electrical goods industry in all its varied forms has grown from little since 1945, and has proved one of the most important growth industries in the development areas. In particular it is an increasing employer of women and girls.

A more complex story, involving sharp decline in some branches, rapid growth in others, is that of the vehicle and vehicle component industry in the North East. This industry is an example of readjustment in traditional industry as well as of the value of the contribution to regional development of new lines of production, both direct and indirect. Paper and board manufacture and the food industries, briefly considered, complete a spectrum of the post-war growth industries of the region.[1]

Chemicals

The chemical industry has a long history in the North East, participating in successive industrial revolutions in the area. It was for long based on the local resources of coal and salt but has always been characterised by its great variety of products: among others the paint and varnish industry and the manufacture of soap were early established on Tyneside. During the twentieth century rapid and continuing technological changes have transformed the world chemical industry, some with dramatic impact on the rise of the Teesside industry.

In Table 28 the diversity of products in 1921 is well seen in the heavier branches, whilst paint, soap and fine chemicals were all then proportionately more important than since. By 1931 the inception of the ICI chemical giant had begun at Billingham on the lower Tees,[2] whilst rationalisation had eliminated some of the Tyneside producers of acids and alkalis. The 1932 Board of Trade survey[3] confirmed the remarkable variety of the contemporary chemical scene on the Tyne, with twelve major branches listed, ranging from lead products to sulphuric acid (Blaydon), zinc oxide pigment (Felling), magnesia (Washington), benzole and creosote at local gasworks, soap manufacture and chemical manures. It was reported that 'little chemical processing of coal took place' and much that did was for the export trade, eg the trade in naphthalene to the United States via Hamburg. The Tyneside paint industry still consisted of many small to medium-sized firms.

The chemical industry, precursor in its new forms of a developing industrial revolution, never experienced the mass unemployment of the early 1930s and indeed jobs in chemicals rose from 6,500 in 1921 to 14,500, excluding unemployed, only ten years later. By 1945

Table 28

CHEMICAL INDUSTRY OF THE NORTH EAST
PERCENTAGE EMPLOYMENT BY SECTORS 1921–66
(All columns total 100)

	1921	1931	1951	1954	1960	1966
Alkalis and heavy acids	30·3	56·9 ⎫				
Fertilisers	5·6	3·7 ⎬ 71·5	56·8	57·3	67·2	
Tar and wood distillation	7·2	2·9 ⎪				
Other chemicals	16·0	8·7 ⎭				
Coke ovens and by-products	—	—	12·0	11·9	8·4	6·6
Drugs, pharmaceuticals	8·3	5·4	2·9	3·3	3·6	5·1
Paint and printing ink	15·1	10·8	6·9	6·5	7·0	6·1
Soap, detergents, etc	7·7	5·3 ⎱ 4·7		4·9 ⎱ 6·0		⎰ 4·7
Polishes, gelatine, etc	1·7	0·9 ⎰		0·2 ⎰		⎱ 0·6
Synthetic resins/plastics	—	—	—	16·4	16·9	9·2
Other products	8·1	5·4	2·0	—	0·8	0·5

(− No information)

Sources: 1921, 1931, 1951 Industry tables of the *Census;* 1931 excludes unemployed. 1954 *Census of Production* (Northern region figures). 1960 and 1966
Department of Employment & Productivity returns.

employment had risen to over 44,000. By-products from the coke
ovens were still of minor significance but the ties between the ICI plant
at Billingham and the south-west Durham coalfield became steadily
closer as the manufacture of ammonium-based fertilisers increased. In
1929 the anhydrite process for sulphuric acid was introduced, using the
locally mined raw material, whilst between 1935 and 1939 the manufacture of petrol from coal took place. Since 1945 the major developments in chemicals have moved away from coal, either as raw material
or fuel, and increasingly towards light distillate oil or naphtha as
sources of alternative chemical routes to an increasingly wide range of
synthesised products.

In 1945 the chemical industry was already employing as many as
it was ten years later. Concentration on materials for the war effort,
including production from royal ordnance factories, meant a considerable narrowing in the base of the pre-war industry. After 1945 a
major change in structure took place and considerable redeployment
of labour was necessary, numbers employed in the industry falling by
4,400 between 1945 and 1950, mainly due to the closure of ROFs and
cessation of large-scale manufacture of explosives.[4]

Since the war the chemical industry in the North East has had a
boom development on a generally accelerating momentum, interrupted
only by brief recessions in 1958 and 1966. The most striking growth

has been at the mammoth ICI plants at Billingham and Wilton, respectively on the north and south banks of the lower Tees, creating the largest petro-chemicals and general chemicals complex outside the USA. Within the ICI complex the changeover to petroleum feedstock raw materials has been pronounced, ties with the Durham coalfield being progressively and substantially weakened. Associated with the growth of petro-chemicals, for many years dependent on coastwise movements of feedstock from refineries elsewhere, there has been establishment of refineries on Teesside, coming into production in the very recent past: Shell on a 170 acre site at Teesport with a throughput of 6 million tons per annum and capable of docking 65,000 ton tankers within a few hundred yards; Philips-Imperial Petroleum on the north bank of the Tees with a crude oil distillation throughput of 4 million tons per annum, an important part of which is to serve ICI with naphtha feedstock. The approach channel to the Tees is being prepared for 85,000 ton tankers.

From the petro-chemicals plants new products have proliferated; artificial fibre polymers, polythene and polypropylene, the aromatics, ethylene, pharmaceuticals, paints and anti-freeze, to name only some important items. Traditional lines in fertilisers have been reached by substitution of organic chemical routes with petroleum replacing of coal as a raw material. Indeed one of the striking features of the post-war period has been the decay of the coke-oven industry, very dramatically since the 1958 recession; in the early 1960s ICI at Billingham alone decided to economise 600,000 tons of coking coal a year in processing. Decline of the coke ovens is also related to the change in demand for town gas produced from new raw materials and to decreased demand from the steel industry. The freeing of the chemical industry from its direct coalfield linkages however is perhaps the most notable feature.

Employment in the chemical industry has risen but in no wise commensurate with the volume, value and variety of manufactured products. Technological change has produced dramatic economies of labour: at ICI Billingham, for example, between 1946 and 1959 output doubled in value but the labour force was reduced from 15,000 to 14,800, an outstanding case of capital-intensive type of growth industry. The major investments at the oil refineries have also produced new jobs numbered only in a few hundreds.

The Northern chemical industry was less diverse than the national in 1958 (Table 29) but since then the gap has been closed somewhat, in mineral oil refining, detergents and artificial fibres; plastics and

Table 29

CHEMICAL INDUSTRY OF THE NORTHERN REGION. SALES AND
EMPLOYMENT AS A PERCENTAGE OF THE UK 1958

	Percentage sales		Percentage employment		Northern employment as a percentage of UK
	UK	Northern	UK	Northern	
Coke oven products	8·7	19·0	5·3	10·9	26·6
Mineral oil refining	16·8	—	4·4	—	—
Lub. oils and greases	3·0	0·5	2·1	0·5	3·3
Dyestuffs	2·4	—	4·0	—	—
Fertilisers	5·5	—	5·3	—	—
Coal tar products	1·7	1·6	1·4	1·4	13·3
Chemicals (general)	24·4	37·4	29·7	41·0	17·9
Pharmaceuticals	6·3	1·9	10·7	3·3	3·9
Toilet preparations	2·0	—	3·0	—	—
Explosives	2·2	—	6·9	—	—
Print and ink	6·9	4·9	10·3	6·5	8·1
Vegetable and mineral oils, fats	6·9	0·1	2·6	—	0·3
Soap, detergents, etc	5·4	5·7	5·0	4·9	12·4
Synthetic resins, plastics	6·0	17·0	6·9	16·3	31·0
Polishes	1·0	0·2	1·3	0·2	2·4
Gelatine, etc	0·7	0·5	1·1	0·4	—
Other products	12·1	11·2	19·2	14·6	—
All chemicals	100·0	100·0	100·0	100·0	12·9

(— No information)

Source: *Census of Production* 1958.

Note: The major chemical firm in the Northern region but outside the North East is Marchon Products Ltd at Whitehaven, producing sulphuric acid (anhydrite process), cement and raw materials for the detergents industry.

aromatics raw materials have bounded ahead, but processing of vegetable oils and fats is still under-represented.

Fig 20 shows the distribution of employment in the North East chemical industry in 1966. There is immediately a strong contrast between the industry on Teesside and in the immediate Tyneside hinterland. Teesside industry is much more concentrated in large plants and firms, dominated by the ICI Billingham–Wilton complex, with associated linkages; on Tyneside there is a profusion of medium-sized plants in much more diverse branches of chemicals more directly related to consumer industry markets. Outliers of each concentration usually relate to the exploitation of some natural resource since rationalisation of plants from earlier more dispersed phases of chemical manufacture has usually been carried out systematically. The most dispersed pattern is that of the NCB coke-ovens but this branch has very considerably declined since 1945, dramatically so since 1958.

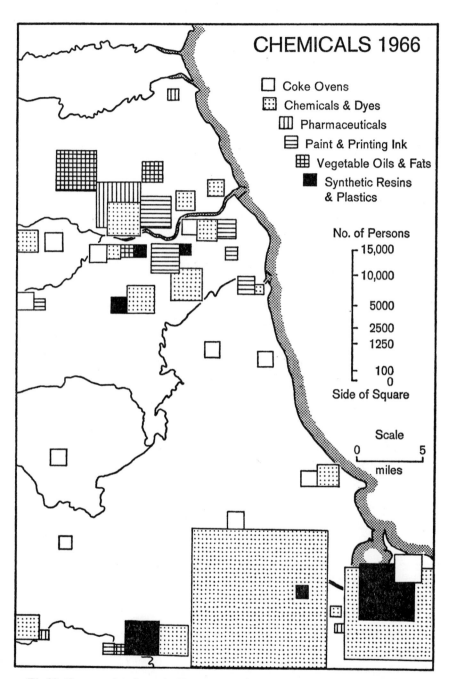

Fig 20. (Source: data from the Department of Employment & Productivity 1966.)

The Teesside Chemicals Complex

The ICI plants at Billingham and Wilton dominate Teesside chemicals and in their development, interrelationship by pipeline under the Tees, and changing character of major products, well illustrate national trends in the industry and the changing part played by chemicals in the regional economy. The essential links and bonds between ICI Teesside and other divisions of the company and with other chemical producers shed further light on the function and significance of the local chemical industry on the national and international scene.

It is necessarily a complex and sophisticated story which it is difficult to simplify or generalise from. In broad terms it is the history of a move from dependence on certain resources of the North East, such as coal, locally generated thermal power, or salt and anhydrite, to the increasing capitalisation of other local assets for large scale industry, eg availability of extensive tracts of level estuarine land, including the possibilty of reclamation, port facilities, and communication links of all types with other parts of Britain and the European mainland. In the shifting balance of locational advantages Teesside has consistently maintained its status as a major chemical location; indeed present trends indicate an enhanced importance.

Though Billingham and Wilton works in one sense indicate successive technological phases in the development of ICI the two major plant groupings have become increasingly interrelated in more recent years, with petroleum-derived raw materials of universal importance to both.

Billingham was the first site to be developed, on the north bank of the Tees, on or near salt and anhydrite deposits and in proximity to the Durham coalfield. From the late 1920s it grew as an orthodox heavy inorganic chemical plant producing staple products based on acids and alkalis. Manufacture of petrol from coal was a somewhat exotic process, fostered by fears of wartime shortage, but continued from the mid-1930s until closure in 1958, by which time 750 million gallons of petrol had been produced.

Since 1945 Billingham has had a great increase in the output of staple products: acids and fertilisers, urea, cement and plasterboard among others. Rising demand led to decisions to duplicate some forms of production including fertilisers and plasterboard at the Severnside complex of ICI. The chemistry and technology of making basic products has undergone vast transformations in scale and chemical routing. For example the introduction of the light distillate oil process, in pressure reforming plant, produces ammonia, methanol, and fertilisers at prices often less than the cost of labour and raw materials by the earlier coal-based process. During 1967 the increasing scale of the ammonia process increased capacity to 900,000 tons per annum, whereas even a few years ago a unit of 10,000 tons capacity would have been considered economic.

New developments at Billingham have been the rapid expansion of alkylamines and the production of hydrogen from light oil rather than from coal. The Billingham plant is now one of the largest world producers of methylamines and ethylamines. In association with the refinery on the north bank one of the largest aromatics complexes yet seen is being developed, shared with Wilton across the river.

ICI Wilton, on the south bank of the Tees adjacent to the Dorman Long steel complex, has been the major British example of a large estuarine integrated chemical plant, based on petroleum feedstock as a raw material but not operated by a petroleum company. More than 600 acres of the 2,000 acre site have been covered by plants since 1945. The Wilton works is really a giant chemical trading estate based on the working up of the raw materials produced from olefine cracking plants into a wide and proliferating product range.

Ethylene capacity is the key to the fastest-growing part of the petro-chemicals industry, with a technology and scale of production that is probably the most rapidly changing of any at the present time. The three olefine cracking plants (two of 60,000 and one of 30,000 tons capacity) were replaced by one of 200,000 tons capacity, and a 450,000 ton cracking plant is already on stream on Teesside. The problems of growth in ethylene and the risks to any one company of excessive capacity led to the construction of an inter-connected ethylene pipeline system, completed in 1968, linking the ICI and Shell plants on Merseyside and in Manchester with Teesside. The pipeline linkage within ICI is supplemented by a regular flow and interchange of products by rail, eg between Teesside and Severnside.

From the cracking plants a tremendous range and volume of materials leaves, at various stages of processing, to form the base of synthesised products. Polythene is a general purpose plastic for which demand is escalating (1953 UK market demand 3,000 tons; 1963, 100,000 tons) and in which ICI is already the largest producer in Europe; propathene is another striking growth product. Terylene and nylon polymer (both polymer 66 and 6) have been other fast rising growth lines, prompting ICI to take an interest in financing outlets in the man-made fibre textile industry.

To indicate some of the vast and intricate range of ICI production on Teesside further major capacity increases have either recently been made or are shortly to be undertaken in: terylene, maleic anhydride, polypropylene, perspex acrylic sheet, methyl methacrylate, hydrogen synthesis, vinyl chloride, acetone, and in methylamine and ethylamine production.

The ICI Teesside plants are thus leader plants in a leader firm in a leader industry. Their linkages within the North East's economy include farming, building, the paint industry, pharmaceuticals and road transport, to mention only a few sectors, but there is no close identity with dominant trends in the local economy. Because the ICI market is national and international the plants are free-standing, usually prosperous when traditional elements of the regional economy are depressed. This and their immense capacity for further growth and change make them virtually unique elements in North East industry, though employment figures which have changed but little in recent years would not conventionally identify them as parts of a growth industry—a clear indication of the limitations of using insured employment by itself.

There is a rising momentum of industrialisation on the Tees estuary with the likelihood of further chemical plants agglomerating near the refinery sites. A recent example is the Monsanto Chemicals' intended development of 100 acres on reclaimed land in the Seal Sands for the production of acrylonitrile (a chemical used for acrilan fibre) from propylene and ammonia. The plant is expected to be producing by 1970.

The chemical product range, its technology, and the rate of change in the ICI heart of the Teesside chemicals complex is difficult to resolve simply, and this is also true for the range and character of other chemical plants in the Teesside hinterland. For convenience they may be classified into broad categories. Firms exploiting local natural resources include the few processing coal for derived chemical by-products, now generally in decline in the face of competition from petroleum-based products; the salt industry of the north Tees lowland; and the manufacture of furnace linings and magnesia insulation products using local limestone and elements extracted from sea water at Hartlepool. The magnesia insulation industry is an important North East specialisation, found at plants on or near the magnesian limestone outcrop near Darlington, Stillington and at Washington.

Manufacture of industrial gases relates not only to symbiosis with the basic chemical industry but also, in oxygen production, increasingly

Page 143: (above) *Wear gorge in central Sunderland*; (below) *Peterlee town centre looking south-east.*

Page 144: (above) *Peterlee industrial estate*; (below) *site of Cramlington and south-east Northumberland plain.*

to the needs of the local steel plants for tonnage oxygen. The manufacture of titanium oxide and pigments at Billingham represents the
largest site of such production in the Commonwealth and is organisa-
tionally closely linked with the paint manufacturers and ICI. The latter
firm is currently increasing its output of titanium metal.

The major chemical plant on an industrial estate site on Teesside is
at Aycliffe, where a subsidiary of Union Carbide is producing plastic
materials, together with laminated and plastic sheets. Small plastics
fabricating firms, often with short life and high turnover have been
another feature of post-war developments on North Eastern industrial
estates.

Chemicals on Tyneside

The Tyneside chemical industry is not only more varied in character
and different in balance but its firms are independent of those of Teesside, with very limited interrelationships. Laminated plastics, Formica
Ltd at North Chirton, Commercial Plastics at Wallsend and the
product Fablon, are well established manufactures on the industrial
estates and represent an industry which has grown substantially since
1945. Recently the Dominion Tar & Chemical Company of Montreal
has joined the plastics complex to manufacture 'Arborite' at West
Chirton.

The manufacture of paints and pigments is one of two important
survivors of traditional Tyneside chemical production. The paint
industry was at one time vertically linked with shipbuilding but is now
large and diversified at sites in Newcastle and Felling on Tyne, producing for the national and international markets. In recent years the
paint industry has seen many mergers for the benefits of larger scale
production, affecting all the Tyneside firms, but there have as yet been
no proposals for closures or run-down in local plants. A second survivor
is the soap industry, now producing mainly detergents, a traditional
industry in east Newcastle before the local firm of Thomas Hedley
was taken over by the American-based corporation of Proctor &
Gamble Ltd. The formerly local market is now world-wide.

Illustration of the range of Tyneside chemicals' manufacture
includes: industrial gases at Birtley, a growth industry serving many
types of manufacturing establishments; melamine plastic, vandyke
emulsions and polyvinyl pyrrolidone for the paint, plastics and
cosmetics industry at Chester-le-Street; and the magnesia insulation,
brick and tile industry at Washington. A recent closure is the former

I

ICI plant at Prudhoe, in the Tyne valley west of Newcastle. This was a wartime strategic dispersed site which changed to post-war ammonium sulphate fertilisers but eventually fell victim to the demands of very large-scale production concentrated on Teesside.

Long-Term Prospects

The chemical industry in the North East has substantial long-term growth prospects. A blend of traditional lines is likely to progress roughly in proportion to industrial and general economic expansion at home with fast-rising momentum and dramatic growth potential in the mammoth petro-chemical plants on the lower Tees. Nevertheless the growth of world petro-chemicals is itself gigantic and risk of over-production from vast plants involving very high capital investment in a short-term technological working life remains something of a spectre. Hitherto interruptions in the momentum of growth have been short-lived, but the present closer association of major petro-chemicals producers in Britain, typified by the shared ethylene grid, indicates both the scale of operation and the sensitivity of the industry. The developing links between ICI Teesside and that firm's plant at Rozenburg near Europoort in the Netherlands seems a particularly promising prospect within the Common Market.

Electrical Machinery and Goods

Commercially electricity is a child of the twentieth century, creating a major supply and distribution industry affecting virtually every factory and home, proliferating also into a telecommunications industry of increasing sophistication, with other uses in rail transport, docks and the like. From an earlier dispersed location pattern the machinery industry developed into large plants and firms but still kept some representation in most economic regions, in touch with the then regional basis of generation and supply. The goods industry has always had very large firms but also, at the point of the multifarious and frequent innovations, small firms growing in some cases very dramatically. These trends towards monolithic organisation on the one hand and extreme diversity on the other have been powerfully reinforced recently, citing the AEI–GEC merger and the fragmented nature of the electronics industry as evidence from both ends of the scale.

Trends, and location of plants, in the machinery and goods sectors have been in a measure independent and are thus worthy of separate treatment. In the North East the machinery industry is indigenous and concentrated, with little relation to government industrial-location policy. The goods industry is, contrastingly, alien, and remarkably tied to government industrial estates sites; indeed growth in the goods sector is the most dramatic single development on the estates since the war. Table 30 shows that in terms of employment afforded the goods industry has grown rapidly on a rising crescendo, particularly in telegraph and telephone equipment, whilst the machinery sector has grown but more slowly and steadily. Once again, as in chemicals, the measurement of growth solely in employment terms is somewhat inadequate since the value of products is high. Jobs are a more reliable indicator in the goods sector, much of which is of an assembly character with a fairly high labour input.

Table 30

THE NORTH EAST. ELECTRICAL MACHINERY AND GOODS, PERCENTAGE EMPLOYMENT BY SECTOR 1921–66

	1921		1931		1951		1960		1966		UK per cent structure 1958
	number (1,000s)	per cent	number (1,000s)	per cent	number (1,000s)	per cent	number (1,000s)	per cent	number (1,000s)	per cent	
Machinery	0·6	19·7	1·3	24·4	13·6	50·9	17·1	44·0	19·5	36·9	30·2
Cables and wire	0·2	7·5	0·5	9·2	1·6	6·2	1·8	4·9	3·1	5·9	7·0
Accumulators, etc	—	—	0·05	1·0	1·6	6·0	—	—	—	—	—
Telegraph and Telephones	—	—	0·02	0·5	2·8	10·8	4·6	12·0	13·0	24·6	11·9
Radio and Television	—	—	0·2	4·1	2·6	10·0 ⎫	9·1	23·5	9·5	17·8	26·9
Lamps and valves	0·04	1·3	0·1	2·2	2·1	8·0 ⎭					
Domestic appliances	—	—	—	—	—	—	2·8	7·4	2·7	5·1	7·1
Other electrical	2·2	71·5	3·1	58·6	2·1	8·1	3·1	8·2	5·0	9·7	16·9
All electricals	3·1*	100·0	5·4*	100·0	26·7*	100·0	38·9*	100·0	53·1*	100·0	100·0

(* includes undistributed fractions)

Sources: 1921, 1931, 1951 Industry tables of the *Census*. 1931 excludes unemployed. 1958 *Census of Production*. 1960 and 1966 Department of Employment & Productivity returns.

Electrical machinery manufacture occupies rather more than one-third of those employed in the industry, producing mainly heavy equipment such as transformers, generators and switchgear of all types, and serving particularly public utility companies at home and overseas. This branch is dominated by the recently merged Tyneside firms of C. A. Parsons and A. Reyrolle, with almost nine-tenths of the machinery labour force.

Electrical goods cover a rapidly developing diverse range of lighter branches with almost two-thirds of the electricals labour force, 57 per cent of whom are women and girls. The siting of plants within daily travelling distance from mining settlements and near areas of heavy local unemployment has tapped a substantial female labour supply and often contributed a valuable second wage packet to the family in areas where opportunities for women to work have been notoriously few. In machinery manufacture, by contrast, 80 per cent of the jobs are for men. The main branches in electrical goods, in terms of employment and growth status are: telegraph and telephone apparatus, radio and television, cables and wire, and domestic appliances. In all branches large-scale organisation has become increasingly the case: in telegraph and telephone apparatus, AEI–GEC and Plessey; in radio and television, AEI and Thorn; in cables and wire AEI; and in domestic appliances Thorn once again. The spread of AEI interests in the North East since 1960 has been one of the most valuable in terms of employment offered.

Electrical machinery has been a growth industry since its commercial inception earlier in the twentieth century. It successfully avoided unemployment even in the darkest days of the early 1930s since it was then working almost to capacity on the supply of equipment for the developing power grid with its associated supply stations. Numbers employed remained modest until the Second World War, for a few years after which boom development took place under the steadily rising national and international demand for electricity supply and distribution (Table 30). Later steadier but progressive growth in employment took place. Similarly the goods industry, many of whose larger plants first started on industrial estates in the years 1946–9, expanded rapidly but with great contrast in timing. Telegraph and telephone apparatus has had its most rapid growth since 1960; radio and television in the period 1951–60. Today virtually all electrical goods employment is on industrial estates or in government-sponsored factories.

Apart from telegraph and telephone apparatus, produced on contract for government departments or utility companies abroad, electrical goods mostly serve a direct consumption market rather than other industries. The sector has thus proved sensitive to the booms and depressions of consumer spending or credit restrictions imposed by governments. Furthermore the pace of technological change has been rapid and in itself a cause of instability in some firms; for instance the post-war period covers the commercial development of television and the invention of transistors, to mention only two examples of change. There have consequently been shifts within the structure of the goods industry, especially decline in radio set and valve manufacture and shifts in consumer demand for electrical appliances. With such trends in innovation, and the rising scale of production, the working arrangements between firms and the emergence of very large firms by merger have been perfectly logical.

Table 31

COMPARISON OF THE ELECTRICAL INDUSTRY OF THE NORTHERN
REGION WITH THAT OF THE UK 1958

	Sales £m	as a percentage of UK	Employment as a percentage of UK
Electrical machinery	19·9	5·1	5·9
Telegraph and telephones	8·7	8·4	8·1
Radio and other electronic	7·9	2·5	3·5
Miscellaneous	7·4	3·7	4·0

Source: Census of Production 1958.

In 1958 the structural correspondence between the North East, in which all the electrical industry of the Northern region then lay, and nation in the electrical industry was fairly close (Table 31), but this region ranked in national production status behind Greater London, Lancashire/Cheshire, and the west Midlands. Since then the significance of telegraph and telephone manufacture has probably risen to over 10 per cent of national employment in that branch.

Fig 21 shows the distribution of branches of the industry within the North East. More than two-thirds of the jobs are concentrated on Tyneside and Wearside, with smaller centres on the Spennymoor industrial estate, and at Hartlepool, St Helen Auckland, Aycliffe and Middlesbrough. There is some sub-regional specialisation: Tyneside shows great variety in types of production and size of plant; telephone equipment and valves characterise Wearside; the Spennymoor estate produces electrical cookers, lighting equipment and fluorescent gears; on Teesside and at Aycliffe the telecommunications industry is dominant.

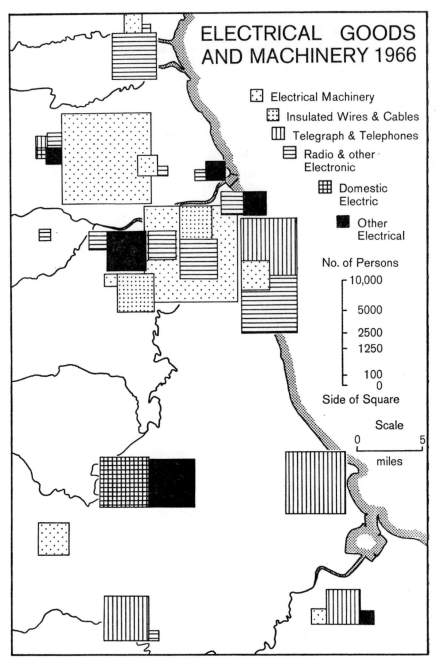

Fig 21. (Source: data from the Department of Employment & Productivity 1966.)

Electrical Machinery Location

The two major production units on Tyneside are complementary in character. At Heaton in east Newcastle there is manufacture of steam turbines and electrical machinery, surface condensing and feed heating plant, turbo-blowers and compressors, turbo-electric propulsion units for ships and electric transformers and generating sets. At Hebburn, on the south bank, there is specialised production of all forms of switchgear. Originally two independent firms, working arrangements since the war became increasingly close, with some participation also by AEI, culminating in merger.

The Heaton unit has traditionally been diversified outside the electrical industry, retaining close touch with shipbuilding and marine engineering. The Hebburn unit on the other hand has diversified only within its specialised switchgear range, with a more marked dependence on public authority markets. Both units were initially located with regard to the availability of coal and steel and the early regional market. Quality production and specialisation have underpinned the early locational advantages.

Prospects for heavy branches of the machinery industry depend upon the continuing rates of electrification in Britain and overseas, and also on the degree of competitive status with German, Japanese and US manufacturers. Steady rather than spectacular growth may be envisaged with occasional slow-downs linked to the sensitive changes in rates of capital investment in the public sector.

Electrical Goods Location

The story of growth in the goods sector is complex but fascinating in the light it sheds on the organisation of the industry and the influence of government location policy. Growth since 1945 in the North East has been the regional counterpart of rapid national growth and territorial diffusion of the industry. Products are high in value, usually low in bulk, and require considerable manual dexterity in handling and assembly; female workers have proved remarkably adaptable and successful in such work. Transport charges do not play a decisive rôle in the final cost of the product or in the location of the points of manufacture. For many of the smaller firms, particularly those in the electronics sector, an available factory, sufficient labour, and capital to start production were foundation needs; location as such was of negligible importance. With such locational flexibility, and in an industry with labour-intensive characteristics, a development area site in a government-sponsored factory had many attractions, particularly so since the post-war boom found many firms unable to expand their premises on the congested original sites, and with shortages of labour. For these reasons the inducements of development areas proved particularly effective.

Though expanding generally the structure and balance within products has changed frequently, a process well illustrated by the history of AEI in the North East. The earliest development by AEI was a radio and television valve factory at Pallion, Sunderland; a second factory there later made cathode ray tubes. At the Spennymoor industrial estate a Siemens factory, later absorbed by AEI, manufactured batteries and telephones whilst AEI also set up a factory for telephones and tele-communications material at Hartlepool. The decline in the radio industry, following large-scale introduction of television, led to closure of valve manufacture at Pallion and concentration of AEI radio interests at the major plant at Rochester on the Medway. In 1961 AEI battery interests at Spennymoor were sold to Ever Ready Ltd who closed the plant; the telephone plant was closed and production transferred to Hartlepool, whilst the manufacture of fluorescent fittings were trans-ferred to a larger AEI group factory at Hereford.

Other AEI–GEC products from the North East include cables (Birtley), motor and control gear (West Chirton), and the firm is also associated indirectly with production of resistors at Bedlington and electrical machinery at Newcastle. The incorporation of Metropolitan-Vickers locomotive works on Teesside was short-lived with closure of the plant. Since the AEI–GEC merger the telephone apparatus and telephone exchange equipment plant at Middlesbrough, glassware manufacture at Lemington, and lamps at Team Valley have increased the range of products under common industrial organisation.

This illustration brings out the scale and variety of the operations of a single major firm operating a pattern of diverse plants located in the North East mainly on the government industrial estates. A second example of flexibility and change may be illustrated from the operations of Thorn Electrical Industries Ltd, also at Spennymoor industrial estate, a substantial development employing around 3,000. In 1951 Thorn took over an empty factory, which had previously made domestic switches and control gear, and developed manufacture of radio sets, the firm's Enfield factory concentrating on the rapidly rising demand for television sets. The manufacture of fluorescent lighting equipment was shortly afterwards transferred from the company's factory on the Welsh industrial estate at Hirwaun. In 1961 the manufacture of radios and radiograms ceased at Spennymoor and the work was transferred to group factories in the London area. On the other hand the manufacture of domestic cookers expanded rapidly, production being concentrated from a plant which had formerly made refrigerators at Uxbridge.

Undoubtedly the growth in telecommunications equipment manufacture in the 1960s has been, and prospectively remains, quite outstanding. The AEI–GEC plant at Hartlepool, from employing 47 workers in 1947 today employs about 4,000, three-quarters of them women. The Plessey telecommunications group with a sizeable plant at Sunderland is building a 350 acre factory on the Tees industrial estate to employ ultimately 3,500, one-third of whom will be men. The AEI–GEC plant at Aycliffe, transferred from Coventry to a development area, is a further recent development of significance. Telecommunications tends to sell its equipment in 'protected' markets, strongly influenced at home by centralised government buying; for example, AEI–GEC supplies 20 per cent of GPO telephone requirements. The export market is also substantial, 25 per cent for AEI–GEC, 40 per cent for Plessey telephone equipment.

The successful transplantation of varied branches of the electrical goods industry into the North East since the war has thus been firmly established and on a substantial scale. It is confirmed by the case of specialised manufacture of resistors at Bedlington and at Bede industrial estate, Jarrow. In both cases the firms originated elsewhere, respectively in Welwyn and Battersea, the latter also with factories at Nuneaton and near Worcester. The most interesting fact is that both firms have now closed their southern factories and centralised all operations within the North East.

Progress since the war has not been without its casualties, including a transistor and television set manufacturer at Sunderland, but the failures appear to have been due to international competition, particularly from the Japanese, and not to any inherent disadvantages of siting within the North East. The net range of new jobs provided, some 13,000 in the past six years, is the clearest indication of the electrical goods industry's momentum and prospects.

As a spearhead of innovation, the electronics end of the industry[5] has perhaps had less than its reasonable quota of investment within the North East. Firms such as Westool at St Helen Auckland, Burgess Products at Gateshead, Joyce Loebl at Team Valley are well-established but there is a feeling in the industry that the region has not received its fair share of firms in industrial electronics or of the granting of adequate government contracts. The main reason postulated is the assumed locational advantage of the Greater London area, in close daily personal contact with ministries and research organisations. Furthermore the financial structure of the developing electronics field has favoured location close to the major centres of finance and near established firms, perpetuating the concentration on Greater London. An adoption of the United States practice of dispersing government electronics sub-contracts to smaller firms throughout the USA might well be followed here to help counteract the psychological orientation of electronics towards the Greater London area.

Other Growth Industries

Two of the other industry groups, vehicles and paper with packaging, have had high national growth rates since the war (Fig 22). It clearly cannot follow either that such growth is to be seen in all regions or indeed that in industrial relocation policies by government such growth industries may readily and universally be transplanted as an instrument of fostering growth in development areas. As it happens the motor vehicle industry has been so guided and the major large new plants on Merseyside and in the Scottish central lowlands indicate the regional benefits accruing from such a policy of steering additional capacity away from the Midlands and the South East. In the paper industry the major plant at Fort William in the Highlands brought a much needed harvest of new jobs and stimulus to the local economy. It remains to be seen how far the North East has benefited from its representation in these national growth industries or how it might so benefit by attracting such plants and firms.

Vehicles

The vehicles industry group illustrates well the dangers in generalising trends, for in the North East dramatic decline in some sectors since the war has been paralleled by more modest growth in others. Besides this some of the more intriguing changes have been indirect, ie in the manufacture and supply of component parts to national branches of industry, notably the motor vehicles industry.

The most important vehicles sector for more than a century in the North East has been the manufacture of railway locomotives, wagons

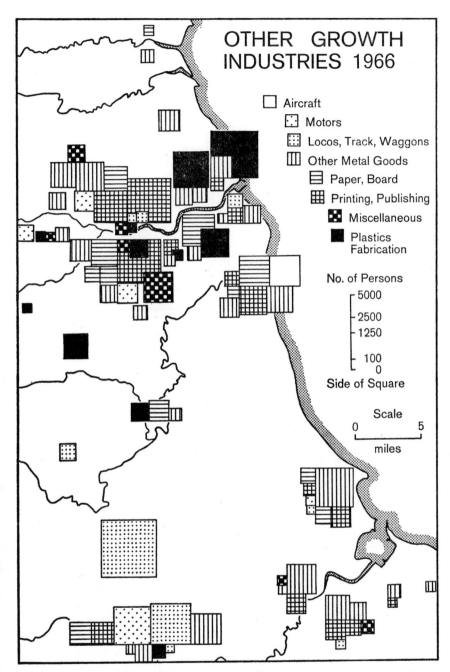

Fig 22. (Source: data from the Department of Employment & Productivity 1966.)

and track; indeed this area was one of the earliest hearths of these manufactures in the world. In 1921 in an era before the motor vehicle industry had abandoned its many early dispersed sites of manufacture to concentrate in the Midlands, manufacture of rail locos and trams was a slightly lower source of employment than that for self-propelled motor vehicles (Table 32).

Table 32

THE NORTH EAST. EMPLOYMENT IN THE VEHICLE INDUSTRY 1921–66

| | 1921 | | 1931 | |
	(1,000s)	per cent	(1,000s)	per cent
Rail and tram locos and stock	3·0	40·8	2·5	40·8
Road vehicles (self propelled)	3·3	44·9	2·7	43·8
Coach and car bodies	0·6	9·3	0·6	11·0
Carts, Lorries, etc	0·3	4·2	0·1	2·5
Other vehicles	0·05	0·8	0·1	1·9
Aircraft	—	—	—	—
Total	7·5*	100·0	6·3*	100·0

| | 1951 | | 1961 | | 1966 | |
	(1,000s)	per cent	(1,000s)	per cent	(1,000s)	per cent
Railway locos	6·5	48·0	4·8	36·6	0·3	3·7
Railway wagons	4·5	32·8	4·9	37·6	4·0	40·0
Motor cars and cycles	1·6	12·0	1·8	13·8	4·6	45·8
Coach and car bodies	—	—	—	—	—	—
Other vehicles	0·3	2·7	0·04	0·4	0·05	0·5
Aircraft	0·6	4·5	1·5	11·6	1·0	10·0
Total	13·7*	100·0	13·1*	100·0	9·9	100·0

(* includes undistributed fractions)

Sources: 1921, 1931, 1951 *Census of Industry* tables; 1931 excludes unemployed. 1961 and 1966 Department of Employment & Productivity data.

The vehicles industry of the North East had changed but little by the time of the 1930s depression, but thereafter locomotive and wagon manufacture and repair increased considerably, culminating in a peak of employment at the end of the Second World War. Since then this branch has declined, with gathering downward momentum during the past few years, from almost 5,000 workers in locomotive manufacture in 1961 to less than 400 today. The wagon manufacture and repair side has maintained its employment more effectively, concentrated at Shildon (British Rail) in south-west Durham. Between 1960 and 1965 one of the North East's most distinctive industries was thus virtually eliminated, with particularly heavy impact on the economy of the Darlington area, an area which had been among the most prosperous throughout the twentieth century. The closure of British Rail's North Road works in 1965 took away virtually 4,000 male jobs, following the loss of 1,000 with the local closure of the works of Robert Stephenson, whilst other loco works closed on the Tyne and at Stockton.

Fortunately at the same time, and in the same Darlington area, growth was stimulated in specialised branches of the motor industry. The development was one of only a few in the North East inspired by American capital and established a plant for Cummins Ltd to manufacture medium-range lightweight V-diesel engines for tractors and tracks, intended to be marketed throughout Europe. Nearby an engine plant was built to produce components, both factories together employing about 1,200 in late 1967, mostly skilled and semi-skilled male engineering workers. The Darlington plants together with a heavy engine plant at Shotts in central Scotland represent the nearest the North East has yet come to gaining a major development in the postwar motor industry. Unfortunately the marketing of the engines has met setbacks in Europe and the British market has failed to absorb more than one-third of the output. The main representation in the motor vehicles body group is in production of electrical delivery vehicles at Team Valley, and in several scattered coach and caravan-building firms. A heavy earth-moving equipment firm flourished at the time of opencast coal mining and Caterpillar Tractor has a substantial plant at Birtley. On the other hand the Vickers tractor plant has closed and Aveling Barford have concentrated road-roller manufacture from Tyneside to Grantham.

The North East was a contender of one of the new motor vehicle assembly plants in the early 1960s, sites canvassed being at Washington and in south-east Northumberland. The plants went to other development areas, on Merseyside and in Scotland. Factors militating against a choice of the North East are thought to have included:

1 Distance from a major port with regular cargo-liner sailings and from existing car-production centres. Though Merseyside was more favoured in these respects the Scottish sites would seem to have been inferior to the North East.

2 Lack of supplies of sheet steel though Consett was prepared to request installation of a strip mill.

3 Risks of finding engineering labour scarce or of disrupting the labour force of existing industries by the higher wage-levels and generally better working conditions in the motor industry.

4 'Habitat' factors as viewed by potential executives and their families.

Though lacking a motor vehicle assembly plant the North East engineering industry is an important source of components, both traditionally and from newer plants on the industrial estates. Examples of this are the manufacture of crankshafts at Hartlepool, pistons and piston-rings at Sunderland, brake control equipment, gears and springs at Aycliffe, or gears and oil seals in Newcastle. A particularly interesting development, having regard to its site and the specialised nature of its products, is the Ransome & Marles' ball-bearing plant at Annfield Plain on the north-west Durham plateau, some seven miles west of the A1 and outside the 'growth zone' designated for a short time in 1963. Moreover it represents one of several examples in the components industry of a firm with organisational linkages along the east coast axis.

The aircraft industry of the North East has always been very limited in scale and linked to aero-engines at Pallion, or to specialised components from Darlington and Stillington. It would require a government industrial-location policy of dispersal for strategic reasons before the North East could expect additions to its token aircraft industry, a prospect which in the present state of the national aircraft industry seems extremely unlikely.

There is as yet no British counterpart to the American missile industry but the North East, with its growing tradition of fine engineering for car components allied to its electronic firms and a wide range of chemical manufacture, seems well-fitted to play some significant rôle in the space age.

Paper and Packaging

The national paper and board, and printing and publishing industry has had an impressive post-war growth record. Discounting printing and publishing which are markedly related to regional needs (Fig 22), paper and board are on a small scale in the North East. Nevertheless the trends are indicative of decline in employment in paper manufacture being more than compensated for by growth in packaging, and, more recently, in the making of speciality products (Table 33).

The paper mills are small to medium-sized, located at Sunderland (2), and Fourstones to the west of Hexham. The Hartlepool mill closed in 1966 in face of competition from Scandinavian partners in EFTA. The remaining mills produce special grades of paper or paper product to offset the disadvantages of small-scale manufacture and independent ownership; the Ford paper mill at Sunderland is in the Wiggins Teape

Table 33

THE NORTH EAST. EMPLOYMENT IN PAPER, BOARD AND PACKAGING
1931–66

| | 1931 | | 1951 | | 1961 | | 1966 | |
	(1,000s)	per cent	(1,000s)	per cent	(1,000s)	per cent	(1,000s)	per cent
Paper and board	1·4	65·9	1·3	43·6	1·6	31·5	1·2	21·5
Cardboard boxes, cartons	0·2	13·0	1·2	41·6	2·0	40·0	2·8	47·7
Other paper goods and stationery	0·4	21·1	0·4	14·8	1·4	28·5	1·8	30·8
Total	2·0	100·0	2·9	100·0	5·0	100·0	5·8	100·0

Growth index 1931=100, 1951=141, 1961=237

Sources: 1931 and 1951 *Census of Industry* tables; 1931 excludes unemployed.
1961 and 1966 Department of Employment & Productivity data.

group. The large supplies of timber in the Border forests are an attraction for pulp and paper makers; shortly a sulphite pulp mill is to be developed on the former ICI site at Prudhoe.

Packaging more clearly shows signs of substantial growth, being an industry with a very sizeable market as the use of packaging develops to American standards. New forms of packaging compete with old: plastic film and aerosols with glass, wood, paper and cardboard. Recently such competition has become very sophisticated: polypropylene competes with cellulose film, polyurethane competes with expanded polystyrene, and new lightweight glass bottles fight back against plastic or metal containers and cartons.

Though packing tends to be concentrated within the Tyneside conurbation, with outliers at Durham and Aycliffe, it is a fairly freely mobile industry with labour-intensive characteristics. As at Haltwhistle, plants can function effectively at some distance from markets and this kind of industry may also have a part to play in the development of jobs in market towns or at sites in the rural hinterland. In a different branch of the industry the manufacture of chipboard at Hexham, on a nodal site in the rural territory near the large-scale North Tyne forests, already provides welcome employment at the market towns.

The food and drink industry (Fig 23) illustrates a range of manufactures which refers in the first instance to the regional market. Some, such as beer or biscuits, often travel far afield but in most instances the scale of production relates to regional demand, not necessarily confined to the industrial North East discussed in this book but more often the general market of Northern England. The pattern of produc-

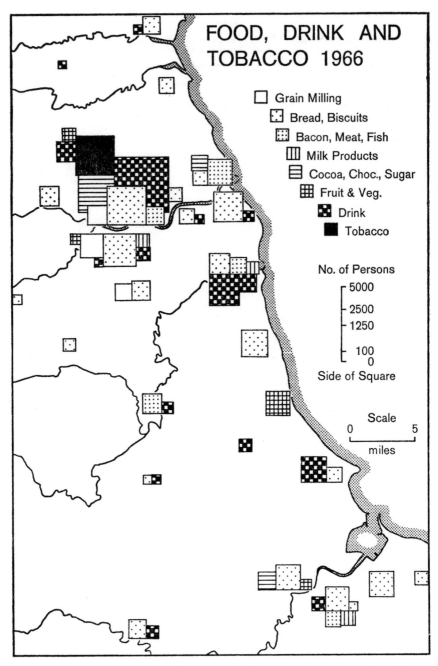

FOOD, DRINK AND
TOBACCO 1966

☐ Grain Milling
⊡ Bread, Biscuits
▦ Bacon, Meat, Fish
▥ Milk Products
▤ Cocoa, Choc., Sugar
▦ Fruit & Veg.
▨ Drink
■ Tobacco

No. of Persons

5000
2500
1250

100
0

Side of Square

Scale
0   5
miles

Fig 23 (Source: data from the Department of Employment & Productivity 1966.)

tion emphasises Tyneside, a traditional feature, with unusually little location on Teesside. The production of the staples of bread and drink is more dispersed than most. Growth in food and drink essentially rests in the first place on the size of the regional population and its purchasing power; apart from some change in habits the lack of both more people and wealthier people explains why the 1966 growth index for employment in food and drink remains obstinately at the level of 1959.

Any discussion of rapid growth industries in the North East since the war would be both incomplete and, to some extent, out of focus without some mention of the contribution by the service sector.[6] This is indeed a complex story, beyond the scope of this book, and only one or two salient points can be made here. Service industries can be divided into those which primarily relate to the regional population and the regional market and those which are more free-standing, with service to a wider region or the nation. Retailing, whole-saling, utilities, transport, insurance and banking, professional services and public administration are found in all major economic regions and several are under-represented in the North East, an indication of lesser purchasing power and a less sophisticated economy which at best serves its internal population with services. Free-standing services are illustrated by national government departments such as the Ministry of Social Security in Newcastle or the Post Office Savings Bank at Durham. Decentralisation of white collar jobs from Greater London can thus contribute to regional employment as part of government policy.

In the years 1959–66 the services to grow most rapidly in the North East were professional and scientific services, followed by construction, a general barometer of public and private investment, and then insurance and banking. Transport employment fell by 10 per cent and most other branches remained almost static. These trends probably mirror the national position and it is doubtful if much has been accomplished during recent years in remedying the dearth of top level posts not only in services but also in manufacturing in the North East.[7]

In regional policy the representation of rapid growth industries is a platform for employment boost in the short-term. Alternatively implantation of growth industries offers the best prospect for dramatic and early improvements. As Table 2 in Chapter 1 showed, the Northern region may lag behind the nation in fast growth sectors, services included, but one-half those in insured employment in 1966 in the North were in the fast growth sector; the seeds have been sown by introduction of fast growth as in the electrical goods industry since

K

the war. These are praiseworthy but the problem regionally is to see that growth in employment over the next few critical years matches the undoubted and large-scale redundancy certain to occur in the declining industries.

References to this chapter are on page 242.

8

Traditional Industries in Change

THE PREVIOUS chapter looked at the representation of some of the major national growth industries in the North East. To balance the picture it is now appropriate to review the significance and status in the region of those national manufactures which, like coal in the fuel industry, have been undergoing considerable structural change and decline in this century, most markedly so in recent times. Equally as in the case of growth industries it would be inadequate to review change entirely in employment terms, yet the loss of jobs in the course of transformation in some of these industries lies at the heart of the North East's problems over the next decade or so.

At the head of any list of transformation and decline, at least in employment terms, stands shipbuilding and repairing, with marine engineering—manufactures with a long, complex and fluctuating history. There has been a decline in jobs of as much as one-quarter in shipbuilding in the North East during the years 1959–66. At present these industries are in the earliest stages of a substantial reorganisation following early implementation of the *Geddes Report* of 1966.[1]

Less clearly identifiable, by virtue of its diverse categories and variable trends in different branches, engineering is as readily as shipbuilding linked in the public mind with the traditional industrial image of the North East. The national engineering growth groups of vehicles and the electrical machinery and goods industries have already been reviewed. In this chapter attention must be turned to the engineering staples: industrial plant and steelwork, metalworking machinery, mechanical handling equipment and contractors plant, to mention only the major fields of employment in North Eastern engineering. The story is very difficult to simplify and scarcely capable of generalisation, but with almost 70,000 employees in the region some overall assessment is required.

As dramatically as shipbuilding the textile industry, notably the cotton textile branches, has undergone profound change on the national scene during this century. Though textiles do not represent a large-scale indigenous industry in the North East certain branches have been implanted in the region since the war and well illustrate both the influence of government locational and regional policy upon a fairly mobile type of manufacture and also the contribution such an industrial growth in a development area can make to the solution of local unemployment problems.

Finally consideration is briefly given to a range of small traditional industries, mostly those using local natural resources or benefiting from a coastal location for imported raw material. Indicative of this group are bricks, pottery and glass on the one hand, timber and furniture on the other. The first exemplifies a relatively tied kind of location; the latter enjoys greater freedom of locational manoeuvre.

Shipbuilding, Shiprepairing and Marine Engineering

In its contribution to British shipbuilding the North East stands supreme. During the present century it has never built less than one-third of the annual national tonnage and that only during the depressed years between 1934 and 1937. In 1901 the North East launched 55 per cent and in 1966 51 per cent, thus giving the lie to the belief that the Clyde has been progressively taking over the leading rôle in British shipbuilding.[2] During the 1920s and 1950s the proportion of tonnage built in the North East varied between 41 and 47 per cent of the national. In terms of the value of ships launched the regional comparisons are not likely to be greatly changed, though the greater production of sophisticated ships, both merchant and naval, on the Tyne would probably underline the stature of the North East even more fully.

It has been the fate of the North East to lead the nation in an industry which more than all others, has been heavily affected by international competition, with almost no tariff protection and no permanently secure home market for its ships. The declining importance of Britain as a shipbuilding nation, from shipbuilder to the world in the 1890s when four-fifths of world tonnage was launched on British rivers, to a contributor of a mere 11 per cent of world launchings in 1965, has been dramatic and progressive. In 1901 55 per cent, in 1921 39 per cent, in 1960 15 per cent of world tonnage was built in British yards.

It is, however, important to realise that the reduced rôle of Britain is in relative terms, related that is to a great increase in world tonnage

Table 34

NORTH EAST COAST. ANNUAL TONNAGE OF MERCHANT SHIPS LAUNCHED 1901–66, IN THOUSAND GROSS TONS

	1901	per cent	1921	per cent	1938	per cent	1949	per cent	1953	per cent	1959	per cent	1966	per cent]
Tyne	292	33·6	354	53·4	157	37·0	202	37·9	221	35·3	225	36·3	210	36·2
Blyth							17	3·3	14	2·3	34	5·6	8	1·4
Wear	268	30·7	144	21·9	169	39·8	181	33·9	199	31·8	249	40·0	267	46·2
Tees	161	18·4	129	19·6	52	12·2	104	19·6	159	25·5	92	14·9	93	16·2
Hartlepool	150	17·3	34	5·1	47	11·0	28	5·3	32	5·1	20	3·2	0	nil
Total	871	100·0	661	100·0	425	100·0	532	100·0	625	100·0	620	100·0	578	100·0
Percentage of UK tonnage	55·0		43·0		41·0		41·0		47·0		45·0		51·0	

Source: Shipping Record and Shipbuilder, *Annual Reviews*.

Table 35

NORTH EAST COAST. EMPLOYMENT IN SHIPBUILDING AND SHIPREPAIRING, MARINE ENGINEERING, 1923–66
(In thousands)

	1923	1938	1948	1953	1959	1966
Shipbuilding and repairing	59·8	39·1	49·9	45·3	46·4	34·4
Marine engineering	25·6	16·8	20·2	16·9	17·6	8·4

Source: Department of Employment & Productivity data.

launched. The absolute figures of British tonnage launched have fluctuated violently during the present century but, eliminating the recurrent years of acute depression culminating in 1933–4 when scarcely 100,000 tons of ships were launched, the output in more normal times was upwards of 1·5 to 2 million tons until the depression of the 30s. Since the Second World War the output has been steadier at between 1·0 and 1·3 million tons; yet it should also be remembered that, with very considerable rise in the tonnage of the average ship launched, even a similar tonnage output means fewer ships at each succeeding stage.

The figures of shipbuilding tonnage for the North East (Table 34) reflect those of the nation, with a peak in output at the turn of the century, successive peaks and troughs until the mid-1930s, and a post-war output normally between 530,000 and 630,000 tons for each year since 1945. Exceptionally, however, the worst post-war depression from 1958–64 saw only 488,000 tons of shipping launched in the region in 1962.

More dramatically than the figures of tonnage launched the loss of jobs in shipbuilding and repairing underlines the social and economic problem posed in the North East (Table 35). Just as the region has the greatest national concentration of the industry so too it has very great local concentration on the lower reaches of the Tyne, Wear and Tees (Fig 24). These industries employed 1 in 10 of all those in manufacturing in the North East in 1966, but no less than 1 in 4 on Wearside, and 1 in 5 on the north bank of the Tyne. Abrupt changes in employment thus have both a highly localised impact and a very severe effect on local economies. The spectacular downturn in employment since 1959 highlights the scale of the present human problem.

Shipbuilding has had a centuries' long history, emerging from a craft into a modern highly-organised technological industry.[3] The transition has been complex, at times retarded, and with such an important historical perspective it is important to review first the influence of the past on the present, an influence widespread and subtle from its more obvious manifestations in the siting, layout and equipment of yards to the intricate management-labour and union-to-union relationships. The past has been a two-sided legacy, the traditional skills and concentration of shipbuilding facilities on an unparalleled scale during the latter half of the nineteenth century being an asset which, on the other side, is reflected in the difficulties of adapting the facilities to radically changing circumstances in more recent times and in the rigidity of demarcation among workers in the yards.

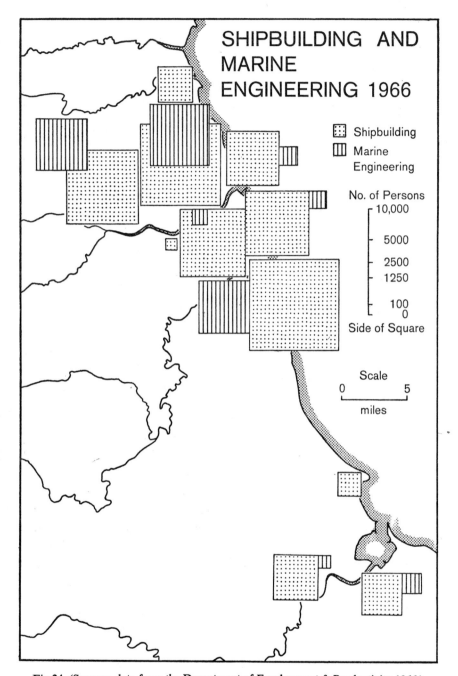

Fig 24. (Source: data from the Department of Employment & Productivity 1966.)

Historical Background

The requirements for shipbuilding were originally simple and wide-spread: a navigable river, preferably with gently sloping or flat banks and an unencumbered channel; supplies of wood either from local forests or as imports; and a national or regional market for the ships. It was not an industry which necessarily grew at the larger ports and indeed there the competition between quays and shipyards tended to drive out the latter. Through time the development of labour skills, the success of management and the specialisation in economic activity led to a greater concentration of the industry on fewer rivers. As the size of ships grew after the mid-nineteenth century, iron replaced wood as the raw material first of the structure, then of the hull; steam power replaced sail and shipbuilding developed close links with the heavier branches of the iron and steel industry and became more closely related to engineering. Furthermore the growing need for specialised components made shipbuilding increasingly an assembly industry, with perhaps only 20 per cent of the cost of the ship generated within the yard. These progressively developing requirements of the shipbuilder confirmed the locational advantages of the North East and greatly facilitated the transformation from a craft to a highly organised technological industry.

The earliest centre of commercial shipbuilding in the North East was on the Wear, one-third of the nation's ships being launched there as late as the 1830s.[4] The early history of the industry at Sunderland remains obscure but by the mid-seventeenth century several shipyards were active, with modest growth in numbers during the next 150 years. By the late eighteenth century wooden ships of about 150 tons average were being built, with a sharp boost to the industry during the Napoleonic Wars. The earliest of the firms still building on the Wear dates from this period: Laings formed in 1793.

The 1840s were a very formative period in shipbuilding in the North East even though this decade followed upon a period of profound depression in the industry. Contemporary with the establishment of ironworks there was a proliferation of new shipbuilding firms, though the use of this metal was not to become universal until many years later. Iron construction and steam propulsion arrived almost simultaneously on the Wear between 1845 and 1852 but the last wooden ship was not built there until 1880 and the last sailing ship in 1893.

On the Wear the major firms extant today were established early:

Austin on the North Sands in 1826, Bartrams at Hylton in 1838, Pickersgill at Southwick by 1851, Doxford at Ox Green in 1840 (moving to Pallion in 1870), J. L. Thompson on the North Sands from 1846, and finally Short at Claxheugh in 1850. These firms are the survivors of a much greater number which have flourished and died out in the past 100 years. Though shifts of siting of shipyards have taken place it is interesting that the present firms have been building on their present sites for around a century: Bartram moved to the South Docks in 1871. This stability of site, even though size of ships has grown and layout of yards has greatly altered, bears striking witness to the ingenuity of the firms and to their adaptability to changing conditions. In recent years however the physical limitations of site, both river frontage and hinterland, have posed more difficult aspects of this long-standing problem.

Also around the mid-nineteenth century the scattered shipbuilding industry on the Tyne began to grow, some of the early sites going back to the mid-eighteenth century.[5] Smith's, later Smith's Dock Co, bought the St Peter's yard in east Newcastle as early as 1810; Sir Charles Palmer established a shipyard at Hebburn in 1851, followed two years later by the shipyard of Andrew Leslie at Hebburn. In 1871 the St Peter's yard was transferred to R. and W. Hawthorn and was converted by them to an engineering works whilst Smith's moved their centre of operations to the Shields, establishing shipyard and ship-repair facilities on both banks. In the late 1860s the building of warships started at the Elswick works of Sir W. G. Armstrong, transferring to Walker in 1911 as the size of vessels had greatly increased. During the same period the firms which were to form Swan, Hunter & Wigham Richardson were beginning to develop.[6] In 1860 John Wigham Richardson bought the yard later to be named the Neptune yard at Wallsend, adding an engine works and in time enlarging the yard by take-over. In 1872 C. S. Swan & Hunter Ltd had established a shipyard at Wallsend and in 1903 the two firms amalgamated, the adjacent yards and shops of the new company then covering a total of 78 acres with a river frontage of 4,000 ft. Shortly afterwards the Wallsend Slipway & Engineering Co was taken over and in 1912 the company acquired Barclay Curle & Co Ltd of Glasgow.

The establishment of commercial shipbuilding on the Tyne thus came later than on the Wear, partly because the Tyne was under a navigation monopoly of the Newcastle Corporation and it was not until after 1850 that the navigability of the river could be radically improved. The Tyne had the advantage over the Wear in the closer association between shipbuilders and engineers, illustrated by the association between Hawthorn and Leslie, or Armstrong with Vickers and Whitworth.

Though the Tees had early shipyards at Stockton large-scale production came later than on Tyne or Wear: Wm Gray at Hartlepool in 1862; Smith's Dock at South Bank, Middlesbrough in 1909; and the Furness Shipbuilding Co at Haverton Hill in 1916. Like the Tyne and Wear the Tees yards have persisted at the same sites and, until recently, have adapted successfully to the changed siting and layout requirements of larger ships.

The brief review of the evolution of the major firms on Tyne, Wear and Tees stresses the indigenous nature of most firms, their localisation on one river in the North East (Smith's Dock Co Ltd the exception, with yards on Tyne and Tees), and their growing integration with the marine engineering industry. Early makers of ships engines emerged from general-engineering firms, as for example George Clark on the Wear, concentrating on marine work from 1854 onwards. In 1865 North East Marine Engineering Co developed at the South Docks, Sunderland, and in 1938 both firms amalgamated with Richardson Westgarth & Co Ltd, a Hartlepools firm. Thus was built up a specialised marine engineering firm with plants on Tyne, Wear and Tees.

An alternative growth was within the shipbuilding firms, witness the marine engine building starting at Wm Doxford, Sunderland, in 1878 and developing into a wide range of steam, turbine and later diesel main engine manufacture. The incorporation of Wallsend Slipway into Swan, Hunter & Wigham Richardson was a similar development, this time an addition to main engine capacity within a shipbuilding firm.

The last twenty years of the nineteenth century were years of unparalleled supremacy for British shipbuilding, continuing little changed to the First World War. Ships grew in size, in sophistication, and in specialised characteristics, yet the base load of demand continued to be for tramp shipping and dry cargo tonnage, requiring simple and cheap construction in large volume. This the yards of the North East were well-equipped to meet, such ships requiring little yard modernisation or re-equipment. On the other hand notable technical achievements and innovations were made. For example between 1893 and 1911 Doxfords launched no less than 178 of the novel turret-deck steamers, representing more than 1 million tons of shipping. On the Tyne there was some specialisation in both passenger and cargo-liners and in warships, in addition to a substantial output of tramp ships and the earliest oil tankers. The launching of the *Mauretania* on the Tyne in 1907 was a hallmark of then contemporary achievement.

The twentieth century has already been described as one of major readjustment for British shipbuilders, faced with mounting international competition and enduring almost catastrophic fluctuations in demand for ships. Table 34 showed the output of ships from the North East between 1901 and 1966 and Table 35 carried the implications of the changes in terms of jobs lost or gained.

Until the Second World War shipbuilding in the North East was plagued by recurrent crises.[7] The firms and yards hardest hit were those producing tramp steamers or those attempting to build too wide a variety of 'once-off' ships. Nevertheless specialisation by yards made only limited progress since when orders were scarce builders would rather accept any kind of ship than face empty berths and unemployed workers. It seems probable, however, that there was less specialisation than was desirable and funds were limited for the essential re-equipment of yards. At the Hartlepools, it is true, one firm built only cargo vessels and did not tender for liners or tankers, whilst one Tyneside firm concentrated on passenger liners, oil tankers and floating docks. Most yards, however, prided themselves on being able to tackle anything offered.

The growing demand for tanker tonnage also involved simpler types of construction. Between 1924 and 1930 almost 1 million tons of tankers were built in the North East, some 159 ships, which represented almost two-thirds of those built in the United Kingdom and virtually one-third of the world tanker output. This is a specialisation which has developed massively since 1945, colouring tonnage outputs from all three North Eastern rivers.

In the inter-war period the building of warships, a specialisation of the Tyne, fell away to only about one-eighth the level of the rearmament years 1907–13. This situation improved after 1937 on the approach of the Second World War in which, as in the 1914–18 war, the shipyards performed prodigies of output and repair work.

Prior to 1938 there had been a shift in the general balance of tonnage launched as between Tyne, Wear and Tees. The decline at the Hartlepools is the most striking feature. In 1890 the Wm Gray yard had topped the world shipbuilders with an output of 64,000 tons from eleven berths employing 4,000 men, and in 1901 nearly 1 ton in every 5 built in the North East came from the Hartlepools. The proportion fell to 5 per cent in the early 1920s and only rose fortuitously in 1938. The Tees had greater stability in its proportion of tonnage launched but the Tyne and Wear disputed the leadership of North Eastern shipbuilding.

A further product of the depression of the 1930s was the enforced rationalisation of yards which took place under the National Shipbuilders' Security Ltd. In 1931 alone seven yards, with forty-five berths, were closed in the North East, a process which continued with a further twelve yards and fifty-nine berths by 1939. The most dramatic of these closures was that of Palmers at Hebburn and Jarrow in 1935. Fortunately the Hebburn yard with dry dock and repair works, was taken over by a new company, now a subsidiary of the Vickers group, and during the Second World War the dry dock at Jarrow was brought back into service. Most of the yards closed, however, became derelict land, some of which has still not been brought back into use.

Post 1945

The problems endemic to British shipbuilding were slow to reveal themselves after the war. Shipyards had been working near to capacity through the war and there had been little time for reorganisation and modernisation; consequently the risk was that there would be surplus capacity and a generally inadequate level of modern technology and layout of yards (Fig 25).

The post-war changes occurred in well-marked phases. In the immediate post-war years, to the end of 1951, replacement of world tonnage lost in wartime and a phenomenal demand for tanker tonnage ensured steady order books and foreign competition had not effectively set in. Until 1950 orders for export remained significant but began to fall away perceptibly after that. In 1949, for example, forty ships totalling 226,500 tons were launched in the North East for foreign owners; only three of these, however, were from the Tyne where the pre-war specialisation seemed to have returned with the building of fourteen liners, five cargo vessels and one cable ship. The export orders were very varied at this time with Scandinavian owners prominent in ordering tankers averaging 10,000 to 15,000 tons. Some yards, notably Wm Gray at Hartlepool, devoted an entire annual output to launchings for export.

Tanker tonnage figured increasingly in order books but the average size of each vessel ordered grew with striking speed only after 1959. Until then the largest tankers launched in the North East were: 1949, 15,000 tons (Furness); 1953, 22,000 tons (Furness); 1959, 27,585 tons (Swan, Hunter). Pre-fabrication and welding techniques developed on

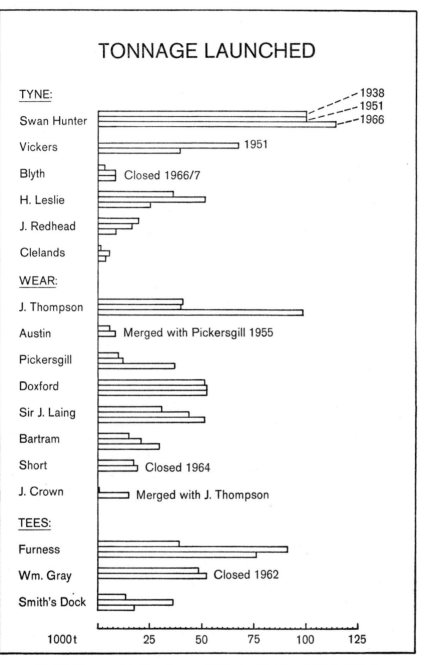

TONNAGE LAUNCHED

TYNE:

Swan Hunter — 1938 / 1951 / 1966

Vickers — 1951

Blyth — Closed 1966/7

H. Leslie

J. Redhead

Clelands

WEAR:

J. Thompson

Austin — Merged with Pickersgill 1955

Pickersgill

Doxford

Sir J. Laing

Bartram

Short — Closed 1964

J. Crown — Merged with J. Thompson

TEES:

Furness

Wm. Gray — Closed 1962

Smith's Dock

1000t   25   50   75   100   125

Fig 25. (Source: data from issues of *Shipping World and Shipbuilding*.)

a large scale, and the improvement of dry dock facilities was set in train.

Warship building remained on a small scale and in 1949 only one naval vessel left the stocks on the Tyne, a 2,600 ton destroyer, though it was also decided to resume work on the uncompleted aircraft carrier *Albion*. The complaint of the lack of orders for naval building or re-fitting has recurred at intervals ever since, but related principally to the specialised yards of the Warship group on the Tyne.

From 1952 to 1957 the situation deteriorated on several counts. Order books remained fairly full but new contracts began to decline and orders for foreign owners fell away sharply towards the end of the period. In the early 1950s the shortage of steel limited shipbuilding output, later its cost rose and this was partly responsible for pricing British shipyards out of foreign contracts. As late as 1957 steel shortages, especially of sections, were said to be keeping shipbuilding some 10 per cent below its possible output. The loss of foreign orders was also to be related to the lack of firm delivery dates and to serious labour stoppages, particularly in 1956 and 1957. Nevertheless 1956 recorded 646,000 tons launched, a post-war record for the North East. As an example of the decline in tonnage launched for foreign owners the Wear supplied fourteen ships of 88,380 tons in 1949; only four of 15,500 tons in 1953.

During the mid-fifties the trend towards building larger ships seemed to have been temporarily arrested, fewer tankers were being con-structed (with exception of the Tees) and there was greater emphasis on dry cargo tonnage. For example, on the Wear during 1956 twenty-two of the twenty-nine ships launched were of this variety. Yards on the Tyne were beginning to plan for the 100,000 ton super tankers then on the horizon, and the building of ore carriers began to be a feature.

The shiprepairing industry had also enjoyed steady work since the war, at first on peacetime reconversion jobs, then on the changeover of ships from coal to oil-burning and progressively on the refitting of tankers of an increasing size. To accommodate the larger ships an extensive programme of dry dock construction was undertaken on the Wear (Greenwell 1952), and Tyne (Brigham & Cowan 1956, Smith's 1965). In 1955 a major reconstruction of the Swan, Hunter Wallsend yard was undertaken, reducing berths from seven to five, with new dry dock facilities.

The years 1958–64 were the most difficult known in North East shipbuilding since the 1930s, depression in world shipping coinciding with intensive competition from Japanese and European yards. Just as in the steel industry the depression of demand took place just as the effects of heavy investment in modernisation were beginning to be felt, an unfortunate conjunction of circumstances. Order books declined catastrophically and in 1962 only five bulk carriers, twenty-six cargo vessels and six tankers were launched in the North East.

The financial effects were severe on some yards and led to closures, a process which has not yet run its full course. The shipyard of Wm Gray at Hartlepool closed in 1962, having turned a year earlier fully onto repair work; the Central Marine Engine works failed at the same time, even though it had sought to diversify outside marine work. A specialised builder of tugs and barges, T. Mitchison of Gateshead, closed in 1963, and in the following year Short Bros Ltd of Pallion, Sunderland closed, their fitting-out berth being acquired by Bartrams. The Shorts' closure was said to be due to lack of financial resources to build larger berths and also to the fact that the minimum size of ships to be built under the government shipbuilding credit scheme was too large to be built at Pallion.[8] Closures have since taken place at Blyth (1966-7) and were temporarily threatened for the Furness yard on the Tees (early 1969) until that yard was taken into the Swan Hunter & Tyne group.

The average size of ships built grew substantially during the early 1960s. This was particularly due to the escalating size of ocean-going

Table 36

NORTH EAST COAST. AVERAGE SIZE OF SHIP LAUNCHED, 1938–66, BY SHIP BUILDING AREA

(Thousand tons)

	1938	1949	1953	1959	1966
Tyne (with Blyth)	4·1	6·7	8·1	10·3*	11·0*
Wear	4·8	4·9	7·2	8·9	15·7
Tees (with Hartlepool)	3·4	4·5	10·1	11·2	13·3

* Excluding small yards at Gateshead and Berwick.

Source: Various.

oil tankers, the two largest launched in the North East being 27,585 tons in 1959, 90,000 tons in 1965. In 1968 the first 100,000 ton tankers were under construction and 200,000 ton tankers were being planned on the Tyne. Indeed no upper limit is presently envisaged beyond that where physical limitations of launching space would inhibit further progress.

The government shipbuilding credit scheme of 1964 is generally reckoned to have benefited the North East dramatically. It is estimated that without such credit advanced to British shipowners to build in British yards probably only 100,000 tons would have been launched on the Wear instead of the 234,000 tons put into the water.[8] Indeed at that time the Wear yards were estimated to be working only to two-thirds of capacity.

Since 1964 there has been some recovery and a good deal of forward-thinking about the reorganisation and prospects of the industry, stimulated in part by the *Geddes Report*.[1] The difficulties of the situation are illustrated by the state of affairs at the Furness ship-building yard at Haverton Hill on the Tees. In spite of its distance from traditional shipbuilding centres on Wear and Tyne the Furness yard has developed steadily since its inception in 1916. It was acquired by the Charles Clore interests in the 1950s and has been extensively modernised and equipped, with a highly successful tradition of building tankers. During the early 1960s, in particular, the yard was equipped with two berths to enable 150,000 deadweight ton tankers to be built, but profitability has fallen and the yard, in spite of its up to date layout and equipment, was scheduled for closure early in 1969, with the prospective loss of some 3,000 male jobs. It has now been taken into the Tyne-based shipbuilding consortium.

During 1966 Swan, Hunter & Wigham Richardson merged with Smith's Dock Co Ltd and the Doxford group at Sunderland was reorganised and rationalised: Doxford's yard to build specialised vessels, Sir John Laing's to concentrate on bulk carriers up to 46,000 tons, and J. L. Thompson to build bulk carriers and tankers. In 1968 all Tyne shipyards became part of the Swan Hunter & Tyne Ship-builders Ltd, the kind of merger strongly advocated in the *Geddes Report*. The new group had a 1967 launching tonnage of 242,000 tons, still some way from the 0·5 million ton threshold advocated by Geddes for reorganised groups. Under the Tyne merger each shipyard will maintain its identity but there may be greater specialisation than hitherto, one yard probably being set aside for naval construction. The Hawthorn Leslie engine works at St Peter's and the Vickers Hebburn repair yard have remained outside the merger. Continuing the merger process, in August 1968 Austin & Pickersgill (themselves merged in 1955) became one with Bartrams, confirming the close working relation-ships over recent years and the successful involvement of both in the building of the *SD 14*—a 14,200 ton standard cargo ship designed as a Liberty-ship replacement.

During recent years the marine engineering industry has also been structurally changed. The demise of a marine engine works at Hartlepool has already been mentioned. In 1967 the firm of George Clark & North East Marine closed at Sunderland in order to concentrate production at Wallsend, and in the same year Swan Hunter determined to cease marine engine manufacture on the Tyne. The era of large diesels and steam turbines has been giving place to the high demand for geared medium-sized diesel engines, often built under licence from abroad. The Doxford group, on the other hand, illustrates a continuing tradition of building marine engines both for their own and other ships; the revolutionary J-type engine is presently ahead in its field.

At this time the shipbuilding industry of the North East is at a critical stage, modernised and almost completely reorganised. It remains to comment briefly on the relevant findings of the *Geddes Report* on the future of British shipbuilding. Published in 1966 some of its main recommendations are already being implemented in the region. The proposal for two shipbuilding groups in the North East, each with 8,000 to 10,000 workers and aiming at between 400,000 and 500,000 gross tons of launchings per annum in the longer term, will take time to realise but the Swan Hunter & Tyne Shipbuilders group is a major step forward. The second group, not necessarily Wear-based, but most likely so, may take longer to achieve. Both yards on the Tees are now within the Tyne consortium.

Some progress has been made in regrouping main engine building but the four main national groups still seem far away and evidence from within the North East shows difference of opinion on the merits of building as well as installing main engines within a shipbuilding firm. The recommendations on labour practices and union organisation are being tackled constructively on both sides of the industry, but there still seems far to go in this critical field.

Final comment on shipbuilding in the North East may with advantage be made from general statements in the *Geddes Report* about British shipbuilding in general. There are no natural or geographical obstacles to a competitive shipbuilding industry and its problems are neither peculiar nor unsurmountable. The recent history of full order books but profitless prosperity for firms may well be beginning to pass and the industry in the North East, by its century-long tradition, facilities, skills and recent reorganisation, is well placed to lead in proving once again that shipbuilding in Britain is one of the best indicators of our general industrial competitiveness.

L

General Engineering

One of the most polygamous of industries, and one with deep roots throughout the process of industrialisation, engineering defies clear delimitation and escapes simple categorisation. Because it has been identified with all stages of economic growth its structure at any one phase, and increasingly at the present time, is a complex mixture of growth and decline sectors, of historically important with techno-logically novel, of large combines in a multifarious range of changing products standing side by side with nascent 'one-man' firms starting in some new line of manufacture. Its range of products sounds like a catalogue involving all British industry, a tribute to its linkages ramifying into most manufacturing sectors. Indeed there is a wide but broken spectrum ranging from firms which are in essence first-stage re-rollers of semi-finished steel with added individual products through firms which concentrate on a particular product range such as machine tools, mechanical handling equipment or industrial plant and steel-work, to firms, often with large-scale organisation, which cater for most requirements and also sell 'know-how' and patent processes. Other firms manufacture but also supply services in machining, and process work on a commission basis. Categorisation of such a multi-product, multi-function industrial group must be to some degree arbitrary and changeable, often within a short space of time.

Of the importance of the engineering industry in the process of economic growth there can be no possible doubt, either in past, present or future. Because of its central status the branches of engineering taken together are the most useful general barometer of economic progress and prospects. This is all the more so in that the heavy sector, ie machinery, industrial plant and steelwork, is directly linked to the investment cycles of capital goods industries, themselves an indicator of national economic development.

Additionally, there is a general belief, partly a misconception, that 'light' engineering is universally a growth sector and that it comprises firms and a product range relatively 'footloose' in modern times and thus freer to locate new plant. If this is true 'light' engineering should prove an effective indicator of government location policies for steering industry towards development areas, should be widely represented on the industrial estates and should be the means of diversifying the traditional heavy engineering sector. Indeed many go further and view the prospect of dispersing individual 'light' engineering plants as a kind of universal panacea for mining and market towns or even the remoter countryside. The evidence already cited in Chapter 7 on the electrical goods industry or the motor vehicle components sector comes nearest to justifying the benefits envisaged by the fanatics for 'light' engineering.

The chief difficulty in an effective consideration of engineering is the intricacy of the firms and products, their complex linkages both vertical and horizontal, and the lack of published data other than in the broadest general terms. It is particularly difficult, for once, to compare growth and decline sectors in employment terms since the minimum list headings are rarely consistent for long and perimeter groups pass into and out of the engineering classification.

Engineering in the North East

The electrical and vehicles industrial groups have already been examined in their guise as national growth industries. Attention here is focused on general, constructional and specialised branches of engineering. Until perhaps the post-war period the terms general and structural covered a greater part of the industry's output in the North East than today. The 1932 Board of Trade survey[7] was able to argue that the general structure of engineering had changed little in general outline since the British Association survey of Tyne, Wear and Tees as far back as 1863.[9] The growth of the electrical branches and of naval and ordnance work covers, of course, outstanding exceptions of industries growing subsequently.

The earliest engineering firms, using iron, were in three manufactures: locomotives for the early railways, colliery gear and machinery, and manufactures connected with shipbuilding.[10] In 1823 Robert Stephenson opened the Forth Banks loco works at Newcastle, followed on an adjacent site in 1831 by the works of R. and W. Hawthorn, the early start to an industry which has died out during the 1960s. The 1840s were productive of new firms: in 1840 Head Wrightson were first established in foundry and general engineering at Thornaby on Tees; in 1847 William George Armstrong started the Elswick works, later to become one of the largest engineering firms in Britain.[11]

All these early starts were in lines destined to become staples of heavy engineering and all were the beginnings of the substantial firms of indigenous origin which characterise the North East. By the 1860s, following on the railway age, the improvement of the Tyne, and the rapid development of the coalfield of Northumberland and Durham, and the establishment of large-scale iron and steel manufacture and the building of iron ships, further and substantial developments in engineering were required. In 1864 Messrs Clarke Chapman established a business in Gateshead to make colliery winding gear and auxiliary appliances for the marine trade, sectors still represented in their production. The 1860s were also the years in which ordnance manufacture grew at Elswick, at first for the British government but shortly thereafter on a world-wide scale. From 1867 W. G. Armstrong & Co were warship builders as well, in association with the Mitchell shipyard at Low Walker.

During the last two decades of the nineteenth century and until the 1930s heavy engineering developed in both the general and constructional fields, sharing the prosperity and suffering the depressions of the important client industries of coal mining, shipbuilding and marine engineering, locomotive and wagon making, and the setting up of factories and public buildings in the rapidly growing cities of the late nineteenth century. Manufacture of armaments remained little affected by regional conditions but for most branches the North East provided the base demand in the market for staple engineering products. Firms tended to grow from within their own resources, remaining locally based in most instances; the severe depression of the early 1930s, however, forced many firms into liquidation, others into mergers. The most famous of these was in 1927 between Armstrong's and Vickers, originally a Sheffield firm, producing an industrial combine with interests in iron and steel, shipbuilding, armaments and general heavy engineering, later in aircraft and submarines.

By 1931 there had crystallised out a sub-regional specialisation within engineering in the North East, a distinction broadly represented even today. General engineering (machine and mill work; stationary and steam engineering and loco manufacture) was concentrated on Tyneside, exceptions being loco making at Darlington and iron and steel founding at Stockton and Middlesbrough. Constructional engineering, on the other hand, was already a specialisation of Teesside, whilst the smaller metal-working trades were found only on the lower Tyne: other branches, such as stove, grate, pipe and general iron-founding were widely dispersed through the North East. Fig 26 shows that in 1966 these basic elements of distribution are still present.

The early post-war years saw some decline in general engineering and an increase in more specialised lines, whilst constructional engineering was itself becoming internally specialised. The small-scale machine-tool industry employed around 1,500, but there were few growth lines

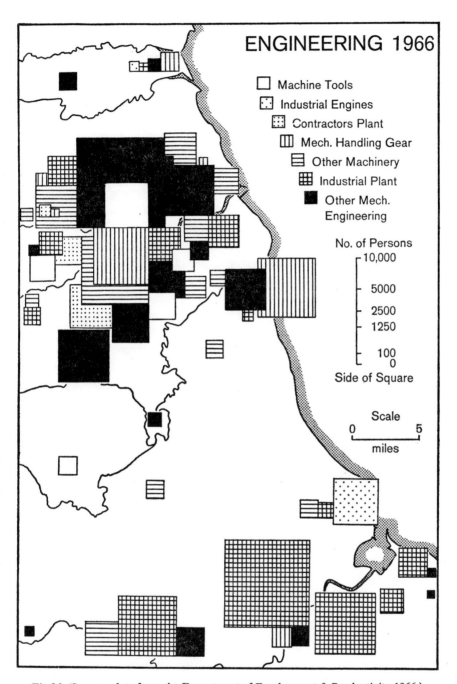

ENGINEERING 1966

Machine Tools
Industrial Engines
Contractors Plant
Mech. Handling Gear
Other Machinery
Industrial Plant
Other Mech. Engineering

No. of Persons
10,000
5000
2500
1250
100
0
Side of Square

Scale
0   5
miles

Fig 26. (Source: data from the Department of Employment & Productivity 1966.)

not related to the major capital goods industries of the North Eastern economy. The effect of the war had been to reinforce traditional products, even to narrow the range.

By 1966 the structure of engineering had become diversified both within the larger traditional firms, who were moving into new markets, widening their raw materials from conventional iron and steel and adopting new processes and technologies, and also by the introduction of new firms or the rapid growth of firms already in the North East but with a range of new specialities. In order of employment importance in engineering (100 per cent) the following branches were significant: industrial plant and steelwork (almost 18 per cent), mechanical handling gear (11 per cent), machine tools (5 per cent) and contractors' plant (4 per cent). Some of these are widely defined groups but it is in the 'other machinery' and 'ordnance and other mechanical' groups that the infinite variety of the term engineering is really disguised.

The contemporary engineering industry of the North East still has strong indigenous firms but the newcomers, sometimes settling on the industrial estates, sometimes arriving by industrial take-over, have introduced London or Birmingham based decision taking into the region. As yet there is no widespread ownership from abroad. At the same time there is less dependence on any North Eastern market and much greater relation to other parts of Britain and to overseas, both in traditional and in new types of engineering product.

Clear evidence exists that many types of firm have been following policies of diversification, particularly with a view to deliberately lessening dependence on declining markets in the local or national coal industry, steel, the railways or shipbuilding. All these major traditional clients had led to the growth of firms specialised in serving them, keyed in closely to the investment cycles of each industry, many of these cycles coinciding in that of national capital goods investment. For example a firm at Heaton, Newcastle, traditionally engaged since 1908 in the manufacture of colliery surface and coalshipping plants has specialised instead since 1945 on plate fabrication, machining and plant removal and erection. A firm manufacturing mining equipment at Team Valley has developed new markets for its conveyor belts in gas, quarrying, cement and food processing. Teesside firms specialising in blast furnace equipment have moved into more varied products and reduced capacity in order to meet a long-term lower market demand. The rationalisation in marine engineering has been mentioned earlier in this chapter, whilst an example of a change relating to the decline in demand for rolling stock is a Darlington firm which has moved from wagons wholly onto structural steelwork, profile cutting and the manufacture of tin bars. The loco and railway plant firms which have gone out of business since the war were referred to in Chapter 7.

Industrial plant and steelwork covers a wide range of firms and great flexibility of products. Fig 26 shows their concentration on Teesside though there are more numerous, smaller firms on the Tyne. Four main categories of product-mix and industrial organisation can be identified. The first group comprises the structural steelwork erection firms, including the offshoots of the steel manufacturers, for example Redpath Brown from Dorman Long. Others are specialised bridge-builders such as Cleveland Bridge & Engineering, but there are many smaller firms offering a complete engineering service from structural steelwork to the installation of plant of a wide variety. Some are developments from welding firms, or from foundry and forge plants or re-rollers of steel; increasingly the smaller firms are using aluminium and alloy steels and either compete effectively on special contracts or sub-contract for the larger firms.

The second group covers the post-war diversification of marine engineering firms, such as Hawthorn Leslie on the Tyne or Richardson Westgarth at the Hartlepools and on Tyneside, into wider ranges of boilers, pressure vessels, heat exchangers and pipework, in some measure as conventional marine engineering has declined. Richardson Westgarth indeed closed the south works at Hartlepool in 1967 as part of a policy of concentrating on condensing and feed-heating plant. Indicative of a new technology in heavy engineering the firm has been participating as a partner in a nuclear power equipment consortium.

Three firms, Whessoe Ltd of Darlington, Head Wrightson & Co Ltd of Thornaby, and the Power Gas Corporation of the Davy Ashmore Group at Stockton, represent the most substantial firms in the highly capitalised industrial-equipment group. Whessoe designs, produces and markets process plant, particularly for the gas, chemical, petroleum and petro-chemicals fields, and is also involved in the advanced technology for nuclear power station construction. Head Wrightson has attempted to develop a pattern of sales to selected industries whose capital investment cycles dovetail to some extent: steel, transport, mining, electrical supply, chemicals, oil and petro-chemicals. In particular, the non-ferrous metal industries market has been developed since its investment cycle for re-equipment rarely coincides with that of steel. Power Gas is a process-engineering company, designing and constructing plants, mostly for the chemical, petroleum and non-ferrous metal industries.

International in their connections these large firms also sell the 'know-how' of design and process throughout the world.

Fourthly there is a great variety of firms, especially on Tyneside, making component parts, sometimes specialised as ships' davits, windlasses, instrumentation and control systems, or general purpose products such as tanks, pipework, chimneys or chutes. The identification of Teesside with the supply of pipes and all equipment to the nuclear power industry, oilfields, petro-chemicals or natural gas fields is a strongly rising phenomenon of the 1960s.

Manufacture of mechanical handling equipment has traditionally been related to coal mining, port operation, intra-plant movement of goods and sand or quarrying equipment. Vickers Ltd, Engineering Group, at Scotswood, produce dock and harbour machinery, including cranes of all types in perhaps the most comprehensive product range of any North East engineering firm: a range which includes printing machinery and newspaper presses; power presses; pressure vessels; marine equipment; gearing; plastic moulding machines.

Most firms, however, are smaller and more specialised: mobile cranes at Sunderland; lifts and lifting tackle in east Newcastle; trailers, trucks and lorries at Framwellgate Moor. This is a growth sector in engineering particularly in the production of conveyors for varied industries.

The manufacture of 'other machinery' tends to be much more specialised, less flexible, and the North East clearly lacks adequate representation of the full national spectrum. On the Team Valley industrial estate there is manufacture of printing machinery and news-paper conveyors (R. W. Crabtree), and packaging machinery (Adams Powel). The diversity represented by soil compaction machines (Armstrong Whitworth) at Gateshead, washing and washing drying machinery (Powley & Sons) at Sunderland, or laundry, and food machines (Baker Perkins) at Hebburn, underlines firmly that though the North East has novel and promising growth elements in machine manufacture it lacks adequate coverage in the sector as a whole. By tradition machinery manufacture has tended to be market-orientated but, since it needs machine-skilled labour and is a product high in value, encouragement should be given to machinery firms to settle in the North East. A straw in the wind is the settlement of Bonas Bros, Weavamatic loom manufacturers, on the Pallion industrial estate at Sunderland.

Other growth sectors in North East engineering include the production of pumps, gear machines, and ventilation and air conditioning equipment. Pump manufacture goes back to the early days of colliery dewatering but also was important in the equipment of ships, both associated with staple regional industries. This branch is concentrated on the south bank of the Tyne and at Sunderland, with outliers at Framwellgate Moor and Morpeth. Clarke Chapman and Armstrong Whitworth illustrate traditional pump manufacturers but within general-engineering firms. Sigmund Pulsometer Pumps Ltd, Team Valley, represents a specialised manufacturer, developing since 1938 into a wide range of centrifugal pumps and pumping equipment for industries as diverse as refineries, waterworks, power stations and sewage installations.

Gears and gear machines represent a specialised and sophisticated branch of engineering, traditional in heavy-engineering districts but with very wide application today. Almost without exception the firms manufacturing gears or gear machines are on industrial estates, one of the largest, Churchill Gear Machines Ltd, coming to the North East in 1946; others are on the Pallion and Aycliffe estates with a further firm at Darlington.

Finally, and illustrative of growth elements, the manufacture of heating, ventilating and air conditioning equipment has been developing in the region since 1945. Apart from unit air conditioners and de-humidifiers as a subsidiary line at Westool Ltd, Bishop Auckland, there are four firms at Newcastle and one at Sunderland, variously sheet metal works which have specialised or marine firms which are converting to a landward market.

There is no doubt that engineering in its many forms will continue to be a staple industry in the North East for the foreseeable future, or that it will continue to exploit its flexibility of jobbing operations and will shift its dependence on particular types of market. Versatility of product and process for some; for others the benefits of a narrow specialisation. One thing is certain, it is no longer possible, as it was in 1932, to see little basic structural change in the previous seventy years. Since 1945 there have been profound changes in the traditional structure and also, particularly on the industrial estates, the introduction of novel and promising growth elements. The transplant of an all-purpose engineering works to Hartlepool from Surrey in 1965 underlines the advantages of the North East, particularly in local skilled engineering labour, whilst the arrival of Black & Decker Ltd, tool manufacturers, at Spennymoor illustrates the particular merit of novel introductions to diversify further the region's engineering structure.

Other Traditional Industries

Shipbuilding and engineering are leader industries in the North East and in them the region enjoys both a national and an international reputation. In assessing the prospects for further economic growth it is now relevant to look briefly at the development and status of other industries, which may not be within the conventional growth groups reviewed in Chapter 7, but which are nevertheless usefully represented in the region's industrial spectrum. Some, like textiles, are major growth industries of the past, others may be labour-intensive and, on that account alone, seemingly attractive to the North East, at least in the short-term. In the case of a further group, manufacturing may be based on local raw materials and justifiable on that account, as in bricks or clay products. Finally there are industries benefiting from a coastal location and imported raw materials, such as timber, or industries primarily serving the regional market.

Textiles

On two counts, total number of jobs and rate of employment growth in the North East, the textile industries merit close consideration (Table 37). No less important is their close and sensitive relationship to government industrial-location policies and the state of the national, rather than international, consumer market. No one is likely to think of these industries as leading in a new industrial revolution but their labour-intensive characteristics, on the face of it, make them attractive newcomers to job-scarce development areas. At first sight it seems illogical that some textile branches should be represented in the North East when they may be in decline nationally in their traditional hearths. Perhaps it seems even more illogical that forms of production should have moved out of their traditional areas to set up new capacity in areas like the North East since the war.

Table 37

THE NORTH EAST. EMPLOYMENT IN TEXTILES AND CLOTHING, 1938–66
(In thousands)

	1938	1948	1953	1959	1966
Textiles	4·2	5·9	10·3	12·3	15·2
Clothing	10·8	20·5	26·7	24·5	27·4

Source: Department of Employment & Productivity data.

Though there had long been dispersed sites of woollen manufacture on a small scale in the Pennine dales or on the flanks of the Cheviots and though Darlington had an early reputation in woollens, lasting through the nineteenth-century Industrial Revolution, it remains true to say that textiles were always on a small scale in the North East before the 1930s and never amounted to more than the woollen industry in scope. By 1938 the 4,000 workers included employees of at least one firm, in furnishing and weaving fabrics, attracted to the Team Valley industrial estate. In the early post-war years there was something of a short-run national boom in textiles, even in cotton, and labour was sufficiently scarce in traditional areas to encourage firms to look closely at development-area incentives and the possibility of setting up new capacity at reasonable cost in localities where an assured female labour supply was believed to exist. This was a period when branch factories flourished, with the possibility of bringing new production quickly into effect but, less fortunately, of closing down equally rapidly in times of recession without an immense commitment of immobile investment resources.

There has been much discussion in the North East on the merits and drawbacks of branch factories. The case in favour rests on the advantage of attracting a plant of a firm already established in production elsewhere, with likelihood of greater stability, introduction of known expertise, nucleus of skilled workers and a young, probably ambitious management. With such advantages the branch plant might be expected to make a quicker and more substantial contribution to the region in the short term. Although on the positive side there is some evidence of branch plants which outlived depressions a high mortality rate is a less favourable confirmation of their demerits. These are argued to be the proneness of head office to exploit branch factories, using them as safety valves for changes in pressure of demand, and closing them first as recession sets in. The lack of independent stature of the branch factory, usually only a production unit with limited decision-taking responsibilities for its management, is also usually seen as a less commendable feature. The turnover in management again illustrates a difficulty for the North East in retaining and building up mature management talent in certain of its developing industries. The tendency of the young manager to look on service in a provincial branch factory as a necessary evil on the way back to head office has often been reported.

In the early 1950s about one-third of all textile jobs in the North East were on industrial estates with, additionally, the large independent site of Patons & Baldwins Ltd making knitting wools and man-made fibres east of Darlington. The Tees area at that time had about half the total regional employment in textiles and was particularly affected by the closure of firms and general textile recession following on the ending of the Korean war. Other early post-war centres of textile manufacture were on Tyneside and at Sunderland. Carpet making at Durham city was a long-standing craft industry.

By 1959 the weighting of textiles towards Teesside was more pronounced, with almost two-thirds of jobs in the North East located there, due to the steady growth of Patons & Baldwins and to the introduction of new textiles products on the east Middlesbrough and North Tees estates coupled with the closure of celanese plants on south Tyneside. The distribution of jobs in branches of the textile industry in 1966 is seen on Fig 27. Patons & Baldwins, in a specialised line of woollen and acrylic yarn textiles, afford the largest single source of employment. This firm moved production to Darlington in 1947 from Halifax, Leicester and Melton Mowbray, with availability of female labour seen as a major advantage in coming to the North East. With increasing scale of production workers have had to be sought in a wider hinterland and production facilities for acrylic yarn have been set up at Bede, Jarrow, and Crook in south-west Durham. The latter development is particularly interesting in that it is in an advance factory and employs some men, many of them redundant miners.

Teesside with Darlington has maintained its 60 per cent of North East textile jobs but Tyneside has developed as the second most important sub-centre and there is a continuing tendency to disperse new production facilities. For example an advance factory was taken over in 1964 to spin nylon yarn at Crook, a second example of the impact of textiles offering some employment to former miners in south-west Durham, whilst Courtaulds Ltd are in process of establishing a worsted spinning factory at Spennymoor.

The textile industry in the North East is marked by its diversity of product, including for example acrylic yarn, silk and rayon weaving, stretch yarn and crimplene, wool and worsted spinning. The accent is on specialisation and there is an absence of the cotton branches which, though represented by branch plants in the North East during the early post-war years, have since been undergoing sharp contraction and rationalisation in the homeland of Lancashire. A further significant feature is the high proportion of firms with roots and traditions in other textile areas. Apart from the dramatic example of Patons &

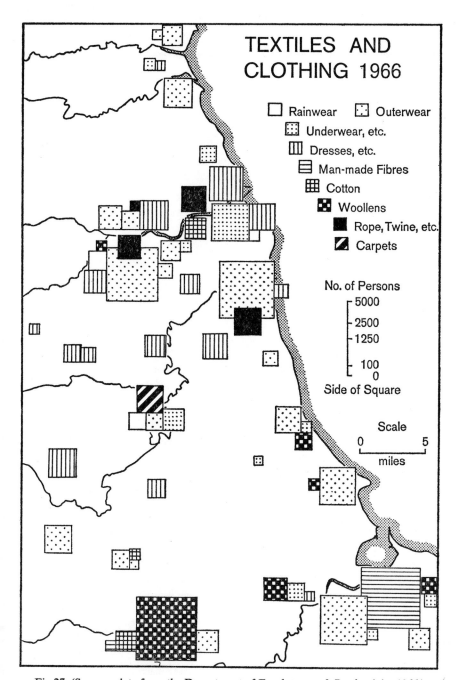

Fig 27. (Source: data from the Department of Employment & Productivity 1966.)

Baldwins Ltd it is too early to speak of substantial North East centred firms. The emphasis is still on links with established centres elsewhere.

Clothing

Manufacture of clothing is a more substantial source of employment than textiles in the North East, and is distinguished most of all perhaps by the fact that almost nine-tenths of its jobs are for women (textiles one-half). Clothing and textiles together offer almost as many jobs as chemicals in the North East and, unlike capital-intensive chemicals, labour-intensive textiles and clothing continue to grow in job provision. The number of jobs in these two latter industries is now almost at the level of employment in shipbuilding and marine engineering, so that, with 1 in 10 of all jobs in manufacturing and 3 in 10 of all female industrial jobs, clothing and textiles have already passed beyond the stage of interesting but unimportant sources of economic diversification.

As in textiles the accent in clothing manufacture in the North East is and always has been on variety of product, less markedly on tendency to locate on the government industrial estates. Early firms which are still in production in the region include Alfred Morris (Furs) Ltd at Shildon (1948) and John Barron Ltd making suits and overcoats at Team Valley (1938). There was a sharp rise in employment in the early post-war years and by 1952 about 40 per cent of the 26,000 jobs were on industrial estates. There was very strong emphasis on heavy clothing, four-fifths of the employment, particularly on men's and boys' outerwear. By 1966 numbers employed just topped the figure for 1953, since the industry had been hit by the consumer goods recession of the early 1960s; there had also been a change in structure of products. In 1966 only two-thirds of all jobs were in heavy clothing (four-fifths of these were in men's and boys' outerwear) whilst of the one-third in light clothing no less than two-thirds of the jobs were in dresses, lingerie and children's wear.

As an illustration of a firm in men's and boys' outerwear Hepworth's Ltd of Leeds set up two production units at Pallion, Sunderland, in 1949, part of a post-war rationalisation programme, and were attracted to the North East by availability of labour. In 1964 a further production unit was set up on the North Seaton estate. The management claims that the location in the North East is a perfectly rational one when serving a market dispersed from the Orkneys to Penzance, but sees no likelihood of the national centres of the clothing industry moving from the Leeds area or London.[12]

Fig 27 shows the distribution of the branches of the clothing industry. Though there is some concentration in production of outer-wear at Gateshead and Sunderland there are many dispersed sites of manufacture. On the other hand the making of ladies' dresses and lingerie is focused on Tyneside and at several localities in west Durham, with almost no representation on Teesside or at Darlington. This is almost a reverse image of the manufacture of woollens, little found north of a line from Darlington to Peterlee.

The clothing industry has potential for further development in the North East. Features of strength lie in the representation of at least three major multiple tailoring firms, in the numerous indigenous firms with specialised lines of product based upon the North East, and in the very diversification of the product range itself. Some thirty firms have establishments in the region today compared to thirty-six in 1954, but the present firms employ more, are larger and better consolidated. Though the industry is in constant change, and some firms may flourish whilst others decline, the representation of the industry in the North East is overall a source of strength. The only uncertainty lies in the labour-intensive characteristics of many branches and the very high ratio of female to male jobs. On the other hand this very feature has commended the industry to parts of the coalfield where work for women has been traditionally scarce.

Other Industries

Fig 28 shows a miscellaneous group of traditional industries, illustrating clearly the focus of most of these on Tyne and Wear, where they add usefully to the diversity of employment. Both the bricks and clay category, which also includes fireclay and cement, and the timber and furniture groups are modest in employment size and in scale of recent development, having together grown around 15 per cent in terms of jobs between 1959 and 1966.

Brick and fireclay works are raw-material orientated, none beyond local scale and many are small in comparison with national standards. The production of high-quality bricks is scarce. The pottery industry, flourishing in many parts of Tyneside and at Sunderland in the eighteenth century has entirely died out, but glass manufacture, another traditional industry since the same period, has maintained a specialised reputation at Sunderland and on Tyneside at Lemington and Wallsend.

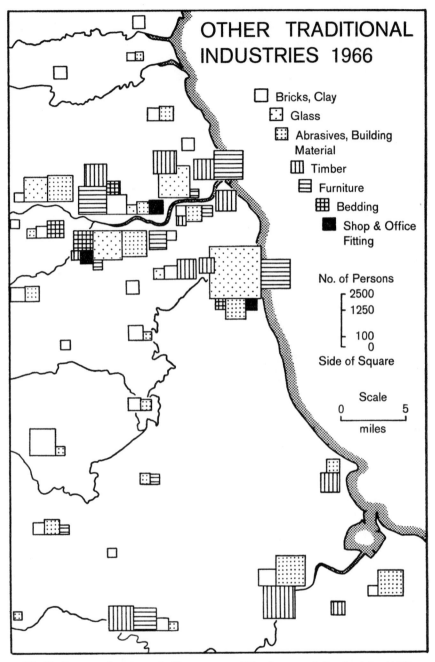

OTHER TRADITIONAL INDUSTRIES 1966

☐ Bricks, Clay
⬚ Glass
▦ Abrasives, Building Material
▥ Timber
▤ Furniture
⊞ Bedding
■ Shop & Office Fitting

No. of Persons
— 2500
— 1250

— 100
— 0
Side of Square

Scale
0 _____ 5
miles

Fig 28. (Source: data from the Department of Employment & Productivity 1966.)

The timber industry with its products illustrates characteristic port-orientation around the timber yards and timber ponds. On the other hand, the furniture industry has located and prospered on the government industrial estates, whilst manufacture of bedding and office and shop fittings adds modestly to the variety of jobs on Tyneside and at Sunderland.

Summing Up

The entire range of manufacturing industry in the North East has now been surveyed, with broad categorisation into sectors of rapid growth (Chapter 7) and traditional industries in change (Chapter 8). These groupings hold broad truths and are especially relevant in making any comparison of the regional with the national scene. Within each category there is considerable variety of trend and prospect and the categories themselves are not necessarily immutable in the longer term. In the short run however, for better or worse, they do contain the seeds of change, for closures or for new plants, for more jobs or fewer, for male jobs or female jobs. The interpretation attempts to show that it is inappropriate to make over-general statements on either the nature or the prospects of the North East's industrial economy, and least of all acceptable to look too much over the shoulder at the past. A balanced assessment demands equal consideration of the nature and composition of growth and of the intricate changes in readjustment or refashioning in those industries ceasing to be competitive in their old forms. The North East emerges from the examination as having an industrial economy with valuable post-war diversification and a useful range of growth industries, but overshadowing all is the certainty of sharp declines in others, setting a most serious problem of rapid and radical redeployment of men over the next critical fifteen years.

References to this chapter are on pages 242 and 243.

M

9

Industrial Districts

EMPLOYMENT STRUCTURE and changing job provision in the industrial sub-regions of the North East were the concern of Chapter 5. It is now time to turn to the contrasting industrial landscapes of the major industrial districts, their land-use characteristics and problems, set within the matrix of planning policies and the administrative framework. The point has already been made that none of the industrial sub-regions is 'free-standing' in its economy, but that there is limited interrelationship between Tyne, Wear and Tees and each has a distinctive blending in its employment composition. This latter is partly the result of contrasting environmental characteristics of coastline and land surface, hinterland and its accessibility, but is also intimately connected with the course of past economic development, its phases and their landscape impact. Once established, industrial sites, housing, port facilities, road and rail layouts, and street patterns tend to influence the course, shape, layout and interrelationships of land-use categories at future dates. Among these categories the persistence of land in industrial use, even though there may be intervals of 'fallow' or dereliction, is perhaps the most fixed point in the land-use pattern of those industrial districts whose main lineaments date from the nineteenth-century Industrial Revolution.

During the past thirty years the influence of comprehensive planning legislation has established guide-lines for land-use change, in terms of land allocation by zoning, area and plot. During the same period the course of industrial change in the North East, though still emphasising the heavy industries, has seen the introduction of new manufactures, or technological revolutions in some of the older industries. These changes have often led to new kinds of siting or land-using requirements, sometimes more free-working and thus susceptible to guidance through the statutory planning process. In particular, the land demands of most types of industrial establishments have tended to grow with the increasing scale of industrial organisation and processing. Traditional industrial sites on the river frontage or embedded in the urban fabric have been able to adapt to increasing land requirements in varying measure, but often only with difficulty. Some industries, notably shipbuilding, have necessarily been tied to the river frontage, being often sharply bounded by a nineteenth-century built-up area on the landward side. Redevelopment of sites has often had to await takeover of other strips of frontage land or the slum clearance of the immediate hinterland. At the other end of the industrial spectrum the government-sponsored industrial estates, with possible exception of those which took over wartime ordnance factories, have been established on 'greenfield' sites where estate services could be provided at the outset and a modern layout of sites and communication arteries offered.

The processes of industrial siting changes are thus intricate and vary between Tyne, Wear and Tees. Changes on the Tees have been perhaps the most dramatic in land-using terms, with the abandonment of sites in older industrial locations and a massive development of downstream estuarine land since the war. Within central Middlesbrough considerable urban renewal is taking place. On the Tyne and Wear the growth of peripheral industrial estates has been striking and redevelopment of land under urban renewal has opened up new sites. In both areas, but more particularly on Tyneside, there remains the problem of the most effective utilisation, even reclamation from dereliction, of riverside frontage land, some of it abandoned for decades.

Teesside

The first difficulty in looking at Teesside is to know which area any particular evidence refers to. Three definitions are currently in use:

(1) Sub-region of the Northern Economic Planning Region, population 556,000 (1964). This is the definition used in this book and it includes Hartlepool and Cleveland.

(2) County borough established for the conurbation on 1 April 1968, population at that time estimated at 393,000. This is the narrowest of the three conventional definitions, comprising mainly the previous immediate riverside administrative units, but excluding Hartlepool and, of course, Cleveland.

(3) Planning area of *Teesplan*, a consultants' land use-transporta-

tion planning study, population 478,000 in 1966. This is virtually the
economic planning sub-region, but excludes Hartlepool.

Data for all three definitions of Teesside continues to be produced
without clear attribution in many cases. To an impartial observer the
economic sub-region definition seems the most satisfactory: even for
any individual administrative purpose the exclusion of Hartlepool is
hard to justify, whilst Cleveland is a problem area whose planning
relates to Teesside rather than southwards to the National Park or the
rural North Riding. Indeed it may be argued with good reason that
the economic sub-region definition itself needs enlarging to include the
Darlington area which, in its location on the major north–south road
and rail arteries and in its industrial composition, is an integral part
of a realistic definition of a Teesside economy. The freight flows seen
in Fig 1 provide some useful support for this assertion.

Characteristics and Functions

At first sight the irregular 'open plan' conurbation of Teesside,
with its distinctive nodes at Middlesbrough, Thornaby, Stockton,
Billingham, Hartlepool and Redcar, seems to be an odd outcome of
situation and siting on an open trias-floored lowland which presumably
gave freedom for settlement to develop in a more coherent way.[1] The
reasons for the incoherence are two-fold: first, the lowland is diversified in its superficial deposits, so that siting conditions vary locally and
in some places were unsatisfactory in early days and, secondly, the
individual nodes developed differently at various stages in the economic
evolution of Teesside. This differential development and the continuance of independent urban traditions has militated against strong
centralisation of functions in Middlesbrough and, given the economic
and social dividing link the lower Tees continues to represent, poses
a subtle problem to those wishing to integrate the conurbation into a
more coherent structure. It is an interesting side-light that the new
county borough has, in its early stages, continued its quasi-federal
origins by a division of administrative functions, each centralised for
a time in one of the former component towns.

The Tees lowland, though floored by triassic sediments which contain at depth the salt and anhydrite important for establishment of
the heavy inorganic chemical industry, rests in terms of the modern
land surface on glacial and post-glacial deposits.[2] The most characteristic is the reddish boulder clay, which itself varies considerably over
a short distance in both thickness and composition. Sand and gravel

patches create locally better-drained sites; conversely, lenses of peat are poorly-drained and, without preparation, were unsuited to building in earlier periods. Add to this diversity the character of the Tees bed and those of its tributaries, all of which have broad, shallow valleys, liable to flooding in the natural state—a hazard present extensively in the estuarine tract—and the selectivity of settlement sites becomes more intelligible.

A general distinction, though blurred with time and building replacement, may be drawn between the traditional rural and market town structure, eg Darlington, Stockton, Thornaby, Hartlepool, and the 'new towns' developing in response to the urgent demands of industry, Middlesbrough and the south-bank towns, or West Hartlepool in the nineteenth and Billingham in the twentieth century. Linear development away from the river at the bridge-crossing in Stockton–Thornaby or the compact peninsular growth of Hartlepool may be contrasted with the attempts at Middlesbrough, South Bank or West Hartlepool to produce a planned town with regular grid-iron layout. These distinctions, based on the origins of the towns, became less clear-cut during the latter half of the nineteenth century as the momentum of building reached a crescendo and the monotonous red-brick terraces proliferated in all the Teesside towns. They nevertheless help to explain the situation of industrial sites in the urban fabric and are very relevant to consideration of present-day central-area problems. Developed earlier, on smaller and irregular plot sites, with a discordant superimposition of nineteenth-century development, the older market centres have been faced with the need for draconian measures in order to redevelop extensively whilst preserving the best of town character from the past personified, for example, in the central area of Stockton. In Middlesbrough and to the east the regularity and homogeneity of housing-development areas, the earliest of which have either been cleared or are nearing redevelopment, offers the prospect of considerable land-use change in a broad belt extending southward from the river, and a unique opportunity to redefine the sites for industrial land.[3]

In general the housing development of the past thirty-five years has been on the periphery of the Teesside towns away from the river and the congested central areas with their admixture of industry and low-quality housing. This is nowhere more clearly seen than southwards from Middlesbrough in a broad zone of geometrical housing estates and intervening open spaces stretching towards the foot of the Cleveland escarpment. The entire town of Billingham is essentially a phenomenon of the past forty years, whilst the westward spread of both West Hartlepool and Darlington indicates other examples of suburban development.

The pressures for development and the mechanism of the Teesside urban system are not easily defined or related to particular land-using requirements. Distribution of urban functions within the conurbation is one general-purpose indicator, journey-to-work patterns another. The lack of a single predominant urban focus has already been commented upon. Middlesbrough and Stockton are two centres of major status, roughly comparable in range of function and services, Middlesbrough distinguished by being somewhat larger. Billingham and Redcar act as district centres, whilst Hartlepool and Darlington are detached and for many services virtually self-contained. In general, it is true that facilities of regional metropolitan character, fitting to an area with 500,000 population, are lacking and must be met at Newcastle or at Leeds.

The length of journeys to work on Teesside has been increasing since 1945 as a product of progressive urban renewal removing the workers from housing immediately around the factories to outlying estates, and of the tendency for traditional industries to move eastwards and redevelop on sites flanking the estuary, whilst the industrial estates have also been situated on open spaces outside the main urban centres. The growth of car ownership has reinforced the tendency to increased distance between residence and workplace.

The chief journey-to-work flow is[4] eastwards along the line of the river on the south bank, between the older residential centres of Stockton, Thornaby and Middlesbrough and the newer centres of industry at South Bank, Lackenby, Wilton and Redcar. Another group of movements converges on the industrial areas of central Teesside, Hartlepool and Darlington; the chemical works at Billingham form the major focus of journeys to work on the north bank of the Tees. Though many of these movements are tangential to the river the crossings are points of traffic congestion as the following vehicle per day densities (1966) illustrate: Victoria Bridge, Stockton 29,000; Newport Bridge, Middlesbrough 27,000; Transporter Bridge, Middlesbrough 2,000.

Industrial Sites

Fig 29 shows the industrial sites of central and estuarine Teesside. The first strong impression is that of large-scale industrial-land

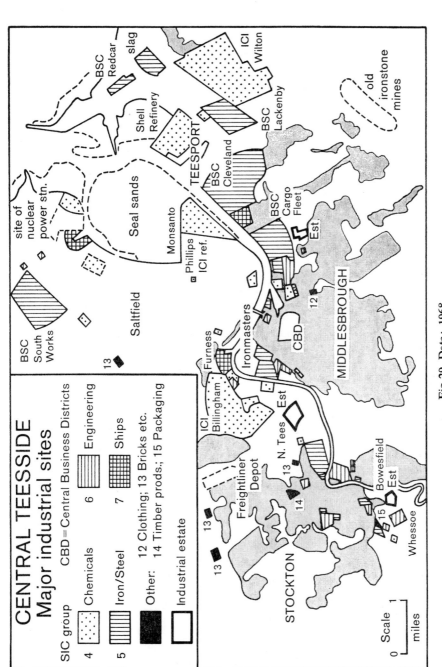

Fig 29. Date: 1968.

occupancy in contrast to the rash of generally smaller sites in the Tyneside conurbation; the second is the contrast between the larger more spacious estuarine sites and the more congested pattern of establishments in the Stockton, Thornaby, Middlesbrough areas. The contrast is also in type of industry upstream and downstream and, furthermore, in the balance of growth and decline prospects. The diagram shows only the more important sites and is not capable of showing the full variety of smaller plants within the built-up areas. A further general feature is the tactical location of the government industrial estates, generally small in comparison with those of Tyneside: North Tees, on open land between Stockton and Billingham; Middlesbrough, south of the Cargo Fleet steelworks. The reverse of the trend to small industrial estates in the post-war boom area of Teesside is the present construction of the large Yarm Road estate at Thornaby; a further more limited example is the development of the Bowesfield estate at Stockton.

A brief account of five contrasting sub-districts brings out the diversity in structure and siting of industry.

(1) In the west, Stockton has a well-preserved distribution of traditional sites embedded in the built-up area and, by contrast, developing industrial grouped sites to the south and in the direction of Billingham. Within the town individual iron foundries and steel-fabricating plants grew along the railway and on the outskirts of the eighteenth-century built-up area flanking the High Street; to the north of the High Street lies a joinery and plastic works. The southern industrial area includes foundries and the engineering plants of the Power Gas Corporation and Whessoe Ltd, together with the Bowesfield industrial estate. To the east of Stockton on the Billingham road, the Malleable works and pipe-works of BSC (South Durham) dominate the industrial scene, as do the engineering works of Head Wrightson Ltd immediately to the south at Thornaby within the bend of the Tees.

(2) At Billingham the later development of industry permitted clear segregation between industrial and residential land uses. The Billingham works of ICI Ltd, British Titan, Davy United and the Furness shipyard are the major components, with the town of Billingham sited to the north and the minimum of residual settlement downwind of the heavy industrial pollution spreading eastwards. North-eastwards the low-lying, ill-drained plain of Salt Holme stretches towards the reclamation area of the Seal Sands.

(3) Middlesbrough industrial sites were, from the early days of

the town, grouped in two areas: the Ironmasters' district within the northward bend of the Tees, and, secondly, the riverside group extending eastwards from Middlesbrough dock to include the Cargo Fleet steelworks and Smith's Dock Ltd. In both these areas there has been considerable industrial change during their long history and dereliction in patches is something of a present-day problem. With the development of major new steel plants at Cleveland–Lackenby since the war the Ironmasters' district has been abandoned piecemeal. Today almost half the 400 acres are derelict, the remaining plants being a steel mill, a steel works, a steel foundry and a steel-fabricating plant. Some of these may be expected to close within the next decade, offering a great opportunity for redevelopment within the very heart of Teesside and closely adjacent to the Middlesbrough central area. The future of Middlesbrough dock is itself uncertain, with the major port facilities likely to be increasingly focused downstream at Teesport. To the east of the dock lie chemical works, the Teesside Bridge & Engineering Works Ltd, the Cargo Fleet steel plant and Smith's Dock shipbuilding yard, with, as already mentioned, a modest government industrial estate to the south of Cargo Fleet.

(4) & (5) The remaining two sub-districts flank the north and south respectively of the bell-shaped estuary. Their common characteristic is that developments are large in land-using scale and relatively modern; indeed the use of land on the shores of the estuary has been transformed since 1945. On the south side the iron and steel works at Cleveland and Lackenby rival the vast organic chemical 'trading estate' of ICI Wilton in status but only Cleveland has direct access to the waterfront. The Teesport dock is flanked to the east by the Shell refinery whence unreclaimed land, the Bran Sands, extends to the Redcar jetty which serves the Dorman Long Redcar steel plant. The post-war erection of large industrial plants on lower-south Teesside has led to an almost continuous industrial strip from south Stockton to the river mouth.

The northern, 'open', flank of the estuary is not as yet fully allocated for industry. It is a less well-drained area and off the main routeways linking Teesside to the national economy; the most direct access, by the transporter bridge from Middlesbrough, has very limited capacity. Industrial sites can be classified into those on the outer-northern arc flanking Greatham creek, few of which have as yet been developed, and those on the peninsula of land in the south, already reclaimed from the Seal Sands. The former include the small repair yard of Smith's Dock (until 1961 Gray's of Hartlepool), the site of the Seaton Carew nuclear power station, and a chemical plant to the north of which the south works of BSC (South Durham) occupy the site of the former Greatham airfield. A small new industrial grouping of metal industries is growing close by. At the base of Seal Sands the Phillips-ICI refinery has been developed and Monsanto will occupy a site nearby for an acrylonitrile works.

Planning problems and Prospects

There are three time-levels of significance in the strategy of planning for Teesside: the setting-to-rights of the unfavourable features in the legacy from the past,[5] the response to the dynamic trends in the present economy; and, finally, the planning of Teesside within a regional, indeed a national, strategy. These are clearly and closely interdependent issues, an amalgam of physical, social and economic problems.

Since the war the development of statutory planning under the 1947 Town and Country Planning Act has led to detailed land-use plan formulation but, unfortunately, to little co-ordination among the four borough and county authorities in the preparation of a coherent plan for Teesside as a whole. In 1965 the Teesside Survey and Plan (Teesplan) group started work on a land use-transportation study, concerned with putting forward a planning strategy and an urban-structure plan for the conurbation. In April 1968 the inauguration of the Teesside County Borough gave administrative reality to a coherent conurbation though, as has already been said, for a different area from that studied by Teesplan.

In *Challenge of the Changing North* the Northern Economic Planning Council followed the policy for promoting the economic growth of Teesside which had been outlined in the 1963 Government White Paper and strongly recommended designation of Teesside as a national growth area. The *Teesplan* study was within a frame of reference that Teesside would be a growth area and would attract a substantial in-migrant population by the end of the century. In the short-term the government has deferred judgement on accepting Teesside as a national growth area and the economic planning council has not as yet formulated its more detailed sub-regional strategy for the North.

The legacy from the past concerns particularly the congested, poor-quality housing inherited from the nineteenth century, its location overclose to the noxious atmosphere of industry and the need for very substantial urban renewal programmes requiring extensive rehousing and relocation. A new territorial definition is required for the relationship of residence and workplace during an age of greater mobility and infinitely higher housing standards.

Air pollution[6] is heavy in localised concentrations on Teesside, especially over Billingham and in the Cleveland–Wilton areas of south Teesside. The 200 ton solid deposit per mile per annum line includes the greater part of the new county-borough area. The prevailing south-west winds draw the peaks of pollution away from their centres of emission and towards the north-east so that more recent residential development has been on the north, west and south periphery of the nineteenth-century built-up area and scarcely at all downwind from the major industrial areas.

Land has not been a scarce factor in the post-war development of Teesside. Indeed in its availability of land, for both industrial and residential purposes, Teesside has been among the most favoured of all British estuarine regions. There are possibilities of further substantial reclamation in the estuary mouth and the unused land in the lower reaches has already permitted considerable relocation of industry in the past twenty-five years. The major concentrations of new housing lie between the towns of south Teesside and the foot of the Cleveland hills, shortening journeys to work and at the same time limiting the sterilisation of good quality farmland to the west and north of Teesside.

The future shape, functional distribution, and composition of Teesside form the hub of the Teesplan recommendations. These will in part necessarily be shaped by commitments already entered into by the statutory planning authorities, but the major decisions to be reached are clear. The controlling framework is population size, employment structure, and social composition; the basis for strategy within Teesside is the relationship of journeys from residence to work, shopping facilities, entertainment, and so forth. A particular feature arising from the growth of Teesside around several centres is the need to decide upon either a further centralisation policy, featuring Middlesbrough as the 'capital' it has never hitherto unambiguously succeeded in becoming, or a continuance of something of the federal structure from the past.

The Teesplan recommendations[7] envisage, firstly, a regional centre for Teesside at Middlesbrough, with Stockton acting as a lesser, secondary centre, secondly, a development strategy emphasising the merits of adding future development as closely as possible to the existing or already committed built-up area, rather than the provision of some new network of linear or stellar distribution or the designation of 'new' towns on free-standing sites.

Given the locational pulls on Teesside from the major growth areas of the British economy to the south, and the likelihood that further major industrial-estate projects are going to be sited in the south and west sectors of Teesside, it seems logical to recommend that major growth in the conurbation should be in that direction and away from the traditional focus on the river. The major industrial sites in the estuarine area will continue to be served with labour from nearby towns but also by growing journey-to-work flows along the prospective west-east Teesside Parkway. The closer integration of Hartlepool into the Teesside economy remains an open question, with mutual advantage seemingly on the side of closer association.

The place of Teesside in a prospective strategy for the North East is more fully discussed in the final chapter.

Tyneside

Tyneside is larger, more compact and less ambiguous in definition than Teesside, yet the sense of town pride is such that, unlike on Teesside, there has as yet been no administrative unification. The Maud Commission on Local Government has recommended a Tyneside city region, taking in most of the commuting hinterland. Tyneside has a more lengthy industrial history than Teesside in all its principal settlements, and, in contrast to that urban upstart Middlesbrough, Newcastle has always been the premier city of Tyneside and indeed can justly lay claim to status as the capital of the North East whatever the stronger spirits of Teesside may say.

To some degree Tyneside, both as a census conurbation or as a statutory economic sub-region, is a statistical abstraction woven around the fairly continuous built-up area focused upon the river, its suburbs driving up into the flanking plateaus and out onto the coast lowlands of south-east Northumberland. The census definition of the Tyneside conurbation has no administrative significance and is a narrow one, even in terms of the contemporary built-up area. Blaydon, Ryton and Boldon Urban Districts are not included, although they contain important post-war housing estates. As an economic sub-region of the North East Tyneside is variously defined: in *Challenge of the Changing North* it is widely construed, being virtually the journey-to-work hinterland from near Morpeth in the north, Prudhoe to the west, and Houghton le Spring to the south. For the purposes of this book the definition in economic terms more closely approximates to the conurbation boundary (Fig 8).

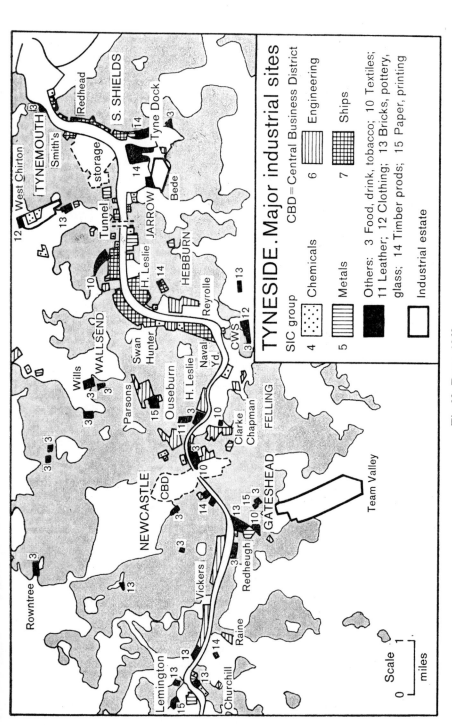

Fig 30. Date: 1968.

A further territorial definition, likely to become administratively significant in the near future, is that of the Special Review Area of the 1963 Local Government Commission for Tyneside.[8] The area of a proposed new Tyneside county authority was in one sense slightly less than the conurbation definition by the subtraction of small parts of existing administrative components, but larger in that it included the three urban districts in County Durham mentioned above as omitted from the conurbation. As well as advocating a county authority the commission further proposed that it should comprise four boroughs based on Newcastle, Tynemouth, South Shields and Gateshead.

Currently notions of 'city regions' are widespread and it may be that a combined 'Tyne–Wear' city region should be the logical outcome of administrative rationalisation. At the moment, even though the *Challenge of the Changing North* includes Sunderland within its Tyneside definition, it is more realistic to consider Wearside as having its own distinctive sub-economy and special variant of common planning problems.

Physical Characteristics and Evolution

Land forms and surface levels are more varied than on Teesside. The Tyne flows through a succession of low sandstone plateaus, cloaked with glacial deposits, and its deep trough is thickly floored with alluvium. Above the junction with the Team the main valley is broad, with extensive 'haughs', from which slopes rise steeply on the north covered by the westward suburban extensions of Newcastle, and which to the south pass up onto the rural with mining country of the northwest Durham plateau. Probably a former course of the Tyne, the Team valley trends south, its once marshy floor now occupied by the largest industrial estate in the North East (Fig 30). Downstream from Dunston the Tyne enters a well-marked gorge tract, with firm land on whose shoulders early roads ran down to the bridging point at Newcastle,[9] aided in their courses up the steep northern bank by the incised streamlets cutting into the plateau edge. In eastern Newcastle the deeply-trenched Ouseburn limited the spread of the commercial town but also provided, in its lower reaches, land for a diversity of congested industrial sites, a characteristic feature until very recent times. Below Bill Quay the Tyne sweeps north and it is the west bank which for the first time offers the wider stretch of gently sloping land on which some of the major shipyards have been developed. A further characteristic entrenched valley or 'dene' comes in at Wallsend, below

which the south bank is backed by the shallow plains to the east of
Jarrow. Towards the mouth the banks steepen again but there are
narrow shelves on the immediate shore and these have permitted the
growth of industrial sites.

Unlike the lower Tees, the difficulties of marshland and poor drainage have been insignificant in comparison with steep slopes, and, later,
derelict or unstable industrial land, as impediments to the development
of the river frontage. In 1800 the main settlements were on the sites
of the present-day four county boroughs, ie, at the Newcastle–Gateshead crossing and at either side of the mouth of the river. Newcastle
in particular has an urban history dating from Roman times, was a
later fortress town in the Norman period and then a medieval walled
city. By then the rivalry between the riverside towns was already acute,
with the Shields resisting the encroachment of the authority of Newcastle, not altogether successfully. Traditional industries flourished:[10]
salt from pans at the mouth of the river, glass using local coal and
sand brought in ballast by the empty colliers returning from the
Thames, and a scattering of small shipyards throughout the course of
the lower Tyne.

During the early nineteenth century the coal industry spread outwards from the river banks as improved technology permitted mining
at increased depths and under more difficult conditions. The developing pattern of wagonways fed growing volumes of coal to the 'staiths',
or shipping-points, on the river. Coal in its turn fuelled the rising industrialisation of the banks, with their heavy inorganic chemicals and
pottery and glass manufactures. Industrial sites congregated on the
river frontage but also penetrated the lower reaches of the deeply-
entrenched side valleys.

The establishment of the Tyne Improvement Commission in 1850
led to greatly improved navigability and port accommodation, and
strengthened the pressures for further development of the river frontage. From the mid-century the pattern of major shipyards began to
emerge, with a focus on the middle and lower reaches of the river.
Sites were sought between the older industrial areas of Newcastle and
the Shields towns, on ground partly won from the river and on drained
tidal flats. Towns for the workers spread rapidly behind the shipyards;
Walker and Wallsend on the north bank and Hebburn and Jarrow on
the south.

The acid and alkali industry prospered throughout the nineteenth
century seeking large undeveloped sites away from the main settlement
areas. The strip between Gateshead and Felling became the centre for

an industry using vast quantities of imported pyrites, sulphur and limestone, combined with local salt in the early days, and drawing in coal from nearby collieries. The development of the Solvay alkali process gave a competitive advantage to the Cheshire saltfield, however, and the Tyneside works declined, indeed decayed in many cases by the end of the century. The last works closed in the 1920s, completing the dereliction of a considerable zone on the south bank with unstable, chemically-impregnated land.

By the end of the nineteenth century riverside frontage had been fully occupied, with most industrial sites hemmed in by congested built-up areas. Shipyards had been consolidated from scattered sites into the central reaches of the river; and the industries serving the yards, marine engineering, roperies and so forth, congregated as closely as possible nearby. On the other hand newer industries such as heavy constructional engineering, or electrical machinery and switchgear, grew on sites outside the main built-up zones, on the plateaus, ie, on the outskirts of the towns from which most of the workers came. The trading (industrial estates) of the 30s and 40s followed the same trend, locating on open land at Team valley, Bede (Jarrow), and West Chirton.

The intimate association of settlement and workplace infilled the spaces between the older towns and led directly to the more or less continuous urban mass of Tyneside flanking the river banks for a distance of almost 18 miles from the river mouth. Meantime the central area of Newcastle crystallised as a shopping, entertainment and administrative hub for the entire conurbation.

Functional Relationships

The early existence of four nuclei on Tyneside led to separate, and in a measure self-contained, reproduction of urban facilities and service to a divided hinterland away from the river banks. The late nineteenth-century boom growth immediately around the industrial sites produced workers' towns which were deficient in many urban assets and almost single-class communities in contrast to the social balance in the older towns. Spread of the tramways permitted social segregation within the suburbs and the development of the characteristic Northern city, territorially stratified in its community and journey-to-work habits. Added to historical tradition, and distinctiveness in kinds of employment, there was a further decisive feature—class consciousness.[11]

Journey-to-work patterns have changed considerably over the years, mostly becoming longer and more complex. In 1968 the traditional inward movement to Newcastle was very strongly represented, with striking two-way flows on the Tyne crossings, about 37,000 vehicles in each direction every day. The most substantial volume of other movement was along the north bank in both directions, from the out-lying estates on the coast, and at Longbenton north-east of Newcastle; the lateral movement along the south bank was smaller in scale. The most prominent feature, and an important one in the persistence of community feelings of separateness on north and south banks, was the lack of significant cross-river movement below Newcastle. The open-ing of the Tyne Tunnel in 1967 now permits much freer interchange than the previous ferry crossings.

Overall the greater scale of inter-urban flow has increased the co-hesiveness of the conurbation and, on balance, the importance of the central-area functions at Newcastle.

Industrial Sites

Fig 30 shows the distribution of industrial plants in relation to the built-up area. For a fuller total land-use pattern of Tyneside sheet 815 of the Second Land Utilisation of Britain (1960) should be consulted. First impressions are of the persistently-marked linear orientation along the river, with greater land occupancy of riverside plots in depth below Walker. Yet there has been nothing of the transplantation of major industries downriver seen on lower Teesside; the accent on the Tyne has rather been on growth and redevelopment *in situ* or on the use and re-use of industrial sites as old industries declined and others grew. The prominence of small clusters of major plants away from the river, and the normal scatter of individual factory sites in the outer zones of the built-up area, are other features for comment.

Some seven sub-districts, clusters or nodes of plants can be dis-cerned:

(1) From upstream the first district extends from Ryton–Newburn to Swalwell–Low Elswick. In this section the most prominent features are the Vickers Engineering group plants lining the north bank, facing the Dunston power station; in the mouth of the Derwent valley on the south bank lie long-established metal-working plants. Upstream, on Newburn 'haughs', a new industrial zone has developed since the war, including the Stella power stations, the Anglo–Great Lakes graphite plant and the Lemington glassworks, the latter an old-established in-dustry now pioneering in the fields of specialised glassware. A small industrial estate at Newburn includes plants decentralised from Tyne-

N

side, whilst in contrast on the opposite bank, at Blaydon, sanitary ware and engineering represent a traditional nucleus.

(2)   The Team valley shows an interesting internal contrast: in its mouth a congested group of steel-rolling mills, a ropery, paper mill site (closed 1967) and glassworks, have long been traditional; in its upper reaches stands the planned government Team Valley industrial estate, with its rectangular pattern of a highly diversified range of manufacturing and storage establishments. These include representatives of most growth industries and a high proportion of the firms were attracted to the North East by government policies. The very varied industries include mining-equipment manufacture, ladies' dresses, banknotes, cork tiling, printing presses or packaging—almost a catalogue in fact of growth lines in contemporary industry. The estate lies on a 'greenfield' site, developed in the late 1930s, its spaciousness and green patches a striking contrast to the gorge tract between Newcastle and Gateshead.

(3)   The gorge tract illustrates the traditional problem of making use of steep slopes. Port facilities are cramped along narrow quays, and access, particularly by rail, has always been difficult. Apart from timber, scrap metal yards and warehousing the most substantial industrial sites are the flour mills where the gorge begins to open out. Otherwise industrial plants have sought either the side valley of the Ouseburn, plateau sites, or have been scattered in the outer built-up area. The lower Ouseburn (Fig 30) lay outside the medieval city of Newcastle and already in the seventeenth and eighteenth centuries was congested by bottle and glassworks, potteries, corn mills and a miscellany of industries. In more recent times, with the decay of these industries, the ratio of warehousing and derelict land has risen sharply. Today the Ouseburn is a subject for landscaping under the city development plan.

(4)   East of the Newcastle CBD (Central business district) lie paintworks, the soap and detergent plant of Proctor & Gamble Ltd and the oil-seal works of George Angus Ltd; along the rail tracks at Heaton the extensive complex of Parsons–Reyrolle making electric generators and specialised optical ware, is paralleled by the switchgear plant of the same firm in Hebburn across the river. Elsewhere in the Newcastle built-up area the food industry is represented by a scatter of plants.

(5)   On the plateau in east Gateshead is a concentration of engineering plants, including Clarke Chapman Ltd and Armstrong Whitworth, a complex which is spreading on cleared land towards the river. Closer to the bank and at a lower level lies the ropery of British Ropes Ltd,

originally an ancillary industry to shipping and shipbuilding but today with a stake in many alternative markets.

(6)   Between Gateshead and Hebburn lies the most extensive tract of dereliction flanking the river, the site of early chemical plants. Reclamation and landscaping is now in progress but industrial sites are few apart from chemical plants and a paintworks at Heworth Shore and Bill Quay. The Friar's Goose shipyard of T. Mitchison, closed in 1963, had been the last example of a once common feature, the small specialised yard, building, in their case, tugs and barges. On the north bank facing the site of Mitchison's yard lies the engineering works of H. Leslie, once the site of a shipyard building elegant East Indiamen.

The great sweep of the river below Bill Quay is flanked by the major shipyards, now Swan Hunter & Tyne Shipbuilding Ltd, lining both banks of the river, though the south bank has more derelict open spaces on the riverfront and a more varied industrial structure in the immediate hinterland: switchgear, gear-works, electrical cables and paints. Jarrow is today a strong contrast to the company town of Palmers (Hebburn) which it once was. Chemicals, foundry work, rolling mills (Consett) and engineering compete for labour with steel construction and paintworks, whilst the Bede industrial estate closely to the east has a varied range of lighter industries, including cigarette filters, transformers and electrical resistors (Morganite Ltd). The location of the estate, between Jarrow and South Shields, makes it readily accessible from a wide labour-hinterland.

(7)   Below the Tyne Tunnel crossing there is an extensive area used mainly for storage purposes and there, in earlier times, were the main coal shipping staiths both at Whitehall on the north bank and Tyne dock on the south. The Scandinavian sailings are concentrated at Tyne Commission Quay with roll-on roll-off facilities; on the south side lies the iron-ore quay, which serves the Consett plant in north-west Durham.

Within the boroughs of Tynemouth and South Shields the water-front sites are constricted by the dense housing areas but there is a concentration of shiprepairing, especially on the South Shields bank which also accommodates the John Redhead yard of the Swan Hunter group. The fish quay and food factory on the North Shields side and the battery works at Burndept Ltd on the south complete the brief survey of industrial use on the river frontage. Away from the river the West Chirton industrial estate, flanking the Coast Road at Tyne-mouth, is a 'greenfield' development rather like Team Valley but with a different industrial structure: plastics and plastic sheeting, pressure die castings, ladies' dresses, aircraft components giving some idea of the diversity. The estate is also notable for its balance between male and female employment.

The Problems of Tyneside

Perhaps the greatest problem is the definition of the economic rôle of Tyneside within the strategy of the Northern region and also the relationship between growth prospects of the Tyne *vis-à-vis* Teesside. These matters are considered in the next and final chapter.

As on Teesside, the pressing problems of today in one sense concern the setting to rights of the physical legacy from the past, but just as important and immediate is the need for increased efficiency in the working of the complex and interrelated economic system which the conurbation represents. It seems inevitable that, if the system is to be better ordered and work to the advantage of all its constituent parts, there must be a more co-ordinated administrative mechanism. The liaison between the existing six statutory planning authorities has worked hitherto in somewhat piecemeal fashion.

The devising of an acceptable form of Tyneside local administration has proved notoriously difficult. As early as 1935 a Royal Commission[12] recommended unification of the urbanised areas on both banks of the Tyne and their incorporation with Northumberland into a regional council. The view was then expressed that the river was 'not so much a barrier as a spinal cord from which the social and industrial life of a wide area radiates'. No action followed, nor did it from the report of the Local Government Boundary Commission (1945) which proposed independent status for Newcastle, incorporation of the rest of the north bank into Northumberland and of the south bank into Durham.

As already mentioned, the 1963 report, under the Local Government Commission,[8] came down in favour of a new continuous county authority for Tyneside, divided into four boroughs based respectively on Newcastle, Gateshead, Tynemouth and South Shields. Furthermore there was to be division of functions, those for highways, housing, sewerage and town and country planning to be shared between the council and its boroughs. This 'judgement of Solomon' had all the essentials of a compromise, designed to achieve the merits of co-ordination whilst respecting the minimum sovereignty at a quadrant level— a compromise between absolute unity and the present-day fragmented pattern. The population of each 'quadrant' borough would be near the

200,000 level fashionably regarded a few years ago as the minimum for financial efficiency and availability of all necessary technical skills in government. The Newcastle quadrant would have had about 330,000 but would not be in any position to dominate the county authority, allaying some of the fears of other constituents. The counties of Northumberland and Durham would lose population under the proposal but the commission felt that neither would suffer inordinately, though Northumberland might be the more seriously affected. A final decision on Tyneside local government may emerge from the Maud Commission proposal for a unified city region, clear recognition that a wider journey-to-work hinterland should be the proper base for urban planning. The problems of life and work continue to grow and solutions must be attempted for the present within the existing administrative framework.

As on Teesside the basis of urban planning rests on understanding and manipulating land use and transportation. A study of these issues was started in 1968 and a Teesplan-type document should emerge in due course. The issues involved are many and complex. In the first place urban renewal is active, many slums have been cleared, but one-third of the remaining housing stock on Tyneside was declared obsolescent in 1963 and much remains to be done. A vital decision concerns the rehousing of those displaced by urban renewal, either in new housing on the same sites or by relocation of designated overspill in suburban or out-of-town estates. Elements of both policies have been followed, but overspill has tended to be directed with some degree of rigidity within existing administrative units. Some of the most impressive rehousing *in situ* may be seen in the Scotswood Road redevelopment area and in central Gateshead. Building land within the Tyneside urban area is scarce and, furthermore, public open space is both inadequate and often badly situated. Since the existing housing densities in the nineteenth-century heart of Tyneside are among the highest in the nation the pressures on peripheral extension of the built-up area or for the development of high-rise tower blocks are necessarily great.

Allocation of land for industrial development and its relation to the new housing areas again depends for its efficiency on both the transport network and on the effective working together of the six local authorities on Tyneside. Away from the river front the location of post-war industrial sites, apart from the government industrial estates, shows some evidence of the lack of co-ordination among the responsible authorities.

Ultimately the transport pattern, in an era of increasing mobility, may be the key to urban development. The recent establishment of a Passenger Transport Authority permits the co-ordination of existing transport media. The urban motorway proposals for Newcastle as part of a fundamental central-area redevelopment,[13] the south bank spine road, the coast motorway and the Tyne Tunnel are all integral parts of major transport programming for the conurbation.

With these developments it becomes increasingly doubtful if the river today is 'the spinal cord' it was alleged to be in the 1935 Royal Commission report. Indeed several question-marks hang over its future. Unification of the Port of Tyne under a single administration in 1968 is certainly a step forward, but the longer-term development of the port remains to some extent under the cloud cast by the Rochdale Report and the National Ports Council, which made no recommendation for major developments on the Tyne. The coastal coal trade continues to decline (total shipments 1966 were just under 4 million tons), there is absence of oil-refinery proposals, and the uncertain future of the Consett steel plant may affect the iron-ore trade. Cargo liner routes on regular sailings remain limited. Further rationalisation of shipbuilding facilities may release riverside land but the main problem at present is to make the most effective use of land now derelict. Proposals for landscaping the gorge section must await considerable clearance but offer an exciting prospect. The largest stretch of dereliction, between Gateshead and Hebburn, is already undergoing some reclamation.

Sunderland

Unlike the conurbations of Tyneside and Teesside Sunderland is a unitary compact city, one of the largest county boroughs in Britain with a population of almost 250,000. Within its urban boundaries the land has been intensively developed; indeed congestion and lack of further building land has created particular problems and pressures for internal redevelopment or peripheral expansion. Although only some 7 miles from South Shields and the Tyne, and with only a token green belt between itself and Washington New Town, Sunderland has kept a strong town character and individuality. As already noted the dependence of the local economy on shipbuilding and repairing has traditionally been greater than on Tyne or Tees. For this reason the recurrent instability of her staple industry has made the economy of Sunderland more sensitive and the problem of diversification has been more sharply defined, provoking a vigorous and, in a measure, successful programme of attracting and settling-in new forms of manufacture in post-war years. In some respects overshadowed by Newcastle as a regional service centre and capital, Sunderland is more strikingly a Northern industrial town, with many of the legacies of industrialism writ large in its townscape—a townscape now changing rapidly under urban renewal and central-area redevelopment. Sunderland portrays many of the problems of the industrial North East and, because it is a substantial town, the impact is the more dramatic.

Site and Configuration

The site of Sunderland offered many difficulties, fewer opportunities. Though the Wear is an axial river of County Durham it offers no easy access inland from the coast, breaching as it does the permian (magnesian limestone) scarp in a deep and sometimes sinuous gorge. Abreast of central Sunderland, at the site of the Wearmouth Bridge, the gorge rises 100 ft steeply from the bank, giving onto the plateau presently occupied by the central business district of the town. Upstream from the Wearmouth Bridge the gorge follows a great loop, with a flattish 'haugh' land on the south shore, the site of Sir John Laing's shipyard. Above the Queen Alexandra Bridge the gorge slopes more gradually and evenly, and there is better access to the narrowish strips of land along the river banks. The plateau in western Sunderland rises to over 300 ft sloping eastwards, at first fairly steeply down to 150 ft, thereafter very gently through nineteenth-century Sunderland towards the main dockland.

Below the Wearmouth Bridge the gorge funnels out into a small bell-shaped estuary with shelves of land flanked by rising ground. The docks were added to the coastline by reclamation in the mid-nineteenth century and thus Sunderland early offered a protected haven and dry plateau land close to the Wear. On the other hand its site lay eccentric to the axial routeway of the North East from Tees to Tyne and the problem of bridging and intercommunication between north and south banks of the Wear has been a constant problem in the life of the town.

Development

By the mid-eighteenth century Sunderland had already had a long history as a seaport, coal mining and exporting town and was perhaps the premier shipbuilding centre of Britain.[14] There were three distinct and separate settlement nuclei which later fused into the industrial revolution town: the first two were ecclesiastical in origin, ie Monkwearmouth on the north and Bishopwearmouth on the south shore; the third was the port and settlement of Sunderland proper which flanked the south shore below the site of the present Wearmouth Bridge. The shipyards and industries were all small in scale and concentrated in the one settlement of Sunderland; in the lower estuary the shores were sandy, marshy and undeveloped.

One hundred years later Sunderland and Bishopwearmouth had merged into a continuous town. The rash of geometrical terraced cottages, such a distinctive feature of Sunderland's townscape to this day, had spread out towards Hendon and westwards towards Millfield; the iron founding and glass-making plants on the western fringe of the town had been developed. The wet docks had been completed and substantial coaling points were established there and upstream from the site of the Wearmouth Bridge. On the north bank, however, Monkwearmouth developed much less, in spite of its link by an early nineteenth-century bridge to Bishopwearmouth.

As on Tyne and Tees there was an accelerated momentum of town growth and industrial development from the 1870s onwards.[15] The railway which for long had terminated at Monkwearmouth from the Tyne, and at Sunderland from Durham, finally passed over the river; shipyards spread upstream to Pallion and Southwick. In contrast to the scatter of early industry through the old town, the glass and pottery industries, engineering, and iron and steel foundries grew on the plateau close to the river in the western part of the built-up area. Around the factories and in close proximity to the shipyards the workers' terraces spread and coalesced to form the densely settled late nineteenth-century town fabric. In the twentieth century recurrent crises in shipbuilding and some decline in other traditional industries led to stagnation and locally to decay, but since the Second World War Sunderland has become one of the most transformed of the North East's major settlements.

Industrial Sites

Fig 31 shows the distribution of industrial sites in early 1968. Broad distinctions may be drawn between dockland or river-frontage sites, scattered sites within the built-up area, and slope or plateau sites. The shipyards have been grouped into two concerns but the siting of yards within each lacks convenience. The nature of the narrower, more sinuous Wear poses problems both of launching increasingly large ships and extending the storage and prefabrication areas of the

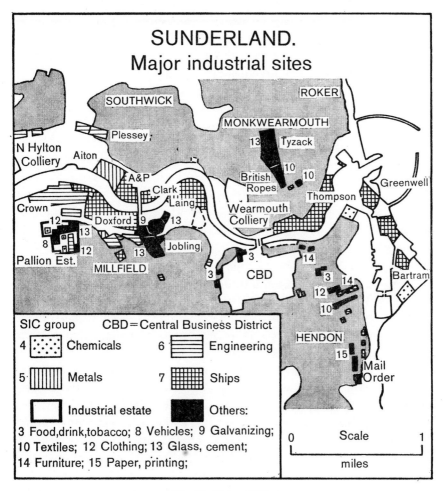

SUNDERLAND.
Major industrial sites

SOUTHWICK

ROKER

Plessey

MONKWEARMOUTH

N Hylton Colliery

Aiton

A&P

Clark

Laing

Crown

Doxford 9

13

13

12

8

12

13

Pallion Est.

MILLFIELD

Jobling

13 Tyzack

10

British Ropes

10

Thompson

Greenwell

Wearmouth Colliery

3

14

3

CBD

3 14

Bartram

12

10

HENDON

15

Mail Order

SIC group   CBD = Central Business District

4	Chemicals	6	Engineering
5	Metals	7	Ships
	Industrial estate		Others:

3 Food,drink,tobacco; 8 Vehicles; 9 Galvanizing;
10 Textiles; 12 Clothing; 13 Glass, cement;
14 Furniture; 15 Paper, printing;

0   Scale   1

miles

Fig 31. Date: 1968.

yards within the built-up area or onto rising slopes. The Austin & Pickersgill group has its major yard furthest upstream but also launches virtually direct into the sea from the Bartram yard in the South Docks. The Thompson yard, on the north shore in Monkwearmouth, launches at an angle oblique to the river and has been able to spread into slum-clearance land immediately behind the berths. Laing's yard on the inner arc of a sinuous bend, and the Doxford yard facing Austin & Pickersgill on the upstream side of the Queen Alexandra Bridge, also use the curves of the river to maximum advantage in launching; the former Short's yard at Pallion is today a fitting out quay for the Doxford yard.

At Pallion the Crown engineering works occupies an extensive site sloping down to the river; on the opposite shore lies the Aiton pipe-works. On the plateau at Pallion there are two distinct and contrasting works groupings: firstly the industrial estate; secondly, an engineering, metal working, glass-manufacturing nucleus at Millfield. The Pallion estate, which has been established substantially since 1945, has a varied industrial balance: aero-engines, clothing, industrial gas cutting and welding equipment, glass resistors, and gears. The Millfield nucleus contains the glassworks of J. Jobling, iron and steel foundries, a substantial galvanizing plant, and the engineering works of T. & S. Forster.

In Southwick across the river a new industrial estate is well-developed, with the telephone works of Plessey, piston manufacture, butterfly valves and engineering contractors; in Monkwearmouth the British Ropes plant and a concrete product works are the main industrial establishments. Within the central business district of Sunderland there has been a traditional scatter of consumer industries; breweries, bakeries, furniture works, paint works and printing establishments. Some of these have closed, others have been resited in the Hendon area, but there is still an intimate intermingling of factory, shop and housing along some streets.

South-west of the docks there is a new industrial zone in active formation from Woodbine Street southwards to Hendon. Parts of an older era are still represented in the roperies adjacent to the port, but the accent is on modern factories and new industries: clothing, pumps and compressors, springs, furniture. In Hendon the mail-order business, machine tools, printing and scaffolding illustrate the evolving industrial estate.

Within the dockland, ship repairing, shipbuilding, marine engineering, oil and timber storage, and coaling staiths are characteristic uses.

Urban Development

During the past few years the face of traditional Sunderland has been changing markedly. Three tall towers rise from the developing new central shopping precinct. In the formerly congested slums of the East End an action area plan[16] is in active implementation, with high-rise and lower terrace blocks situated within traffic-free precincts and segregated from the newly forming industrial zones. Across the river a similar project has taken shape and, in the zones of still service-able housing as at Southwick,[17] a comprehensive programme of housing clearance and revitalisation is in progress with the industrial estate already mentioned closely linking residence with workplace.

The problem of river crossings bedevils all Tyne, Wear and Tees towns. In Sunderland six traffic lanes are available at present river crossings, four on the Wearmouth Bridge. It is estimated that a capacity of twenty lanes across the river will be ultimately required; in the near future the conversion of the upper (former railway) deck of the Queen Alexandra Bridge would add two further lanes, with an additional two lanes if the two decks were each used two-way. The construction of new bridge crossings would be complicated by the depth and width of the gorge, the need to keep most of the river free for movement of substantial ships from as far upstream as the building yards at Pallion–Southwick, and the difficulty of finding suitable bridge approach roads.

Sunderland's economic problems are particular variants of those of all North Eastern industry. Though the town authorities have achieved much since the war, and industrial diversification is a term with real meaning there, the process has further to go before excessive dependence on shipbuilding and repairing has been reduced to stable proportions. With the designation and growth of Washington New Town closely to the west, the effects of the reduction in coal mining in the Wear hinterland, and the need to define a functional relationship to the Tyne conurbation to the north, Sunderland's future must surely be seen increasingly in the context of a broadly-defined Tyne–Wear city region, rather than as a 'free-standing' industrial town however traditional and well-founded its character.

The New Towns

A full consideration of industrial sites would logically go on to the character and distribution of plants and firms in the coalfield towns, in the market towns, and on dispersed sites throughout the industrial and rural North East. These points will be taken up in the final chapter on strategy for the area and, for the moment, discussion will be limited to the rôle and status of the New Towns of the region. Both in concept and practice a New Town should contribute something distinctive, contemporary, and forward-looking to the present economy. By their nature New Towns are potential growth points and the medium for introducing the most dramatic aspects of the new 'living environment' about which so much has been said so often.

The New Towns of the North (Fig 8 on page 56), as designated

under the New Towns Act, are, strictly speaking, three in number:
Newton Aycliffe (1947), Peterlee (1948) and Washington (1964). To
these must be added in practice the Northumberland County Council's
New Towns of Killingworth and Cramlington, the former coming near
to the notion of a 'city in the suburbs' so close is its location to the
built-up perimeter of Tyneside. Each town has been designed for a
particular purpose and is being custom-built on individual lines; the
first-mentioned three towns are shown in Fig 32. It is premature to
think of a co-ordinated New Town strategy on the Greater London
model but equally clear that the New Town concept is being modified
in a measure to suit regional conditions. At times the accommodation
of local cultural aspirations into individual design features reaches
towards the bizarre but it remains exciting.

The desirable target figure for New Town populations has steadily
been adjusted upwards in the South East, partly in response to demand
for provision for a rapidly expanding national population, partly as a
result of adjustment of general planning norms in the context of new
concepts of urban economics and the viable size of administrative
entities. The New Towns of the North East have not yet suffered from
this escalation-of-scale thinking but it may not be far off. Target
populations at present (1967 population in brackets) are; Newton
Aycliffe 45,000 (18,000), Peterlee 30,000 (19,800), Washington 80,000
(23,500). The Newton Aycliffe target has been raised in recent years,
compelling structural rethinking of the plan. At Washington, unlike
the other two, there has been a substantial existing urbanisation to
be incorporated in the designated New Town area, posing a rehabilitation and reconversion problem. In all five cases the provision of
grouped industrial sites means that the New Town is most decidedly a
working, as well as a residential, concept.

Newton Aycliffe

In concept Newton Aycliffe broke with the traditions being
formulated in the late 1940s for the Greater London New Towns in
several ways. It was initially to be small with 10,000 population but
was subsequently revised upwards first to 20,000 and then to 45,000.
At its initial target, and located within a few miles of the large industrial
town of Darlington, it could scarcely have been either self-contained
or a viable proposition as an urban community. Its 'raison d'être'
seems to have been two-fold: first as a residential area directly adjacent
to the wartime royal ordnance factory converted to a peace-time

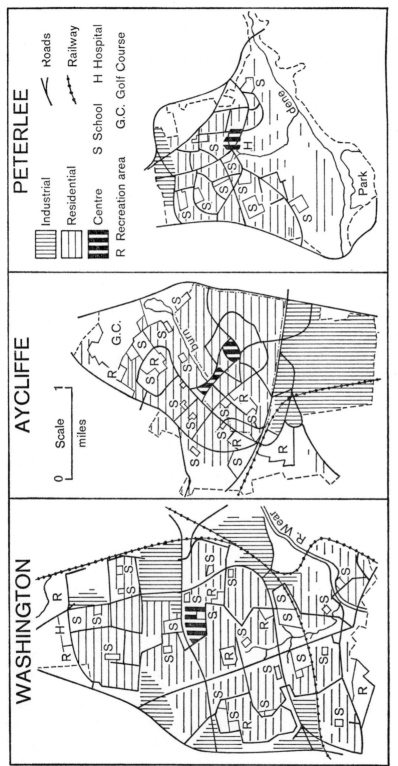

Fig 32.

industrial trading estate; secondly, as a concentration area for populations displaced from the declining sub-regional economy of south-west
Durham or as a place of work for those prepared to commute from
the decaying mining towns and villages. Since the New Town was as
integrally linked with the growth of its industrial estate as was the
free-enterprise case of Slough in Greater London, and since Darlington
was readily within commuting range, Newton Aycliffe grew within a
clear-cut, almost rigid framework.

The industrial estate, closely adjacent to the major through road-rail
links and located towards the southern end of the Tyne–Tees axial
zone, has proved attractive to industry. In early 1968 some 8,500 were
employed on the estate and, a very favourable even unique feature, no
less than 70 per cent were men. The estate has a strong representation
of growth industries, including industrial chemicals, motor-vehicle
components (gears and springs), telecommunications equipment, and
paints, among many others. There is ample land for expansion and
the initially difficult process of converting the ROF buildings and land
has been largely completed.

The successive upward adjustments of Newton Aycliffe's target
population are the result of government concept of the town as a
'growth point' in the North East economy. The proposed expansion
from 20,000 to 45,000 (1964) created problems of urban design inherent
in growth from a virtually complete town with central area, community
facilities and road pattern established for the lower target figure.[18]
The master plan now envisages a compact plan form extending the
existing town on the north-west; main shopping provision is to remain
within the central area but shopping points will be distributed through
the residential areas.

Peterlee

The Peterlee concept is rather different. The site lies on the coastal
tract of the magnesian limestone plateau of east Durham, deeply
trenched by Castle Eden 'dene'. The local economy is traditionally coal
mining and one major purpose of the New Town was to allow for regrouping of mining households 'living in badly serviced and congested
settlements too close to the pit heads'.[19] A further purpose was to 'provide for the first time the recreational and shopping centre . . . to give
the district as a whole a greater degree of cohesion and self-sufficiency'.
The notion of a balanced community with industrial development for
both men and women was also considered important, and a social

purpose, that of 'bringing to an end, if possible, the migration from the Easington area', was given pride of place in the master-plan report.

In the early stages there were problems in phasing the development of the town, having regard to the need to permit maximum extraction of the 30 million tons of coal underlying the site with minimum interference with surface stability and the most harmonious spread of the town. This problem of co-ordination imposed severe limitations on the pattern of land use and the flexibility of architectural design.

By early 1968 one-half of the residential development had been completed and the town-centre development advanced, central facilities being ultimately envisaged for a population of 100,000 within 5 miles around. As in housing there was a slow take-off in industrial development but recently the tempo has accelerated and employment figures for 1968 showed 906 males and 1,649 females in work. There is strong concentration on consumer-goods industries, i.e. wool spinning, clothing, potato crisps and household sections, but there are also car components.

The sharp acceleration of mine closures in the surrounding hinterland increases the scale of new job provision required at Peterlee if its original objectives are to be fully realised. In the meantime the closer approach of the Durham Motorway to the west, and the improvements on the A19, Sunderland–Teesside trunk road, promise to improve substantially the accessibility of Peterlee, early on thought by many to be one of the deficiencies in the situation of the town.

Washington

Washington New Town is the latest to be designated (1964), again with novel concepts.[20] The designated area, 5,300 acres, was more than double that of either Aycliffe or Peterlee and the purpose was defined as: 'to provide dwellings to cater for the need arising from population growth in south Tyneside and north-east Durham; to provide industrial sites to help to satisfy the industrial land shortage and to diversify the regional economy'. A third objective related to stimulating faster progress in raising the quality of the region's urban environment.

Situated on the southern fringe of the Tyneside conurbation and only 6 miles west of Sunderland this New Town has a problem of territorial identity within a narrow surrounding green zone. Its planners consider that such close proximity to major industrial and urban concentrations will enable the New Town to contribute more effectively to the expansion of the economy of a wide area around; in particular, there will be a complex and substantial journey-to-work movement both into and out of the New Town. The location of Washington at the head of the Durham Motorway and on the approaches to the Tyne Tunnel is clearly advantageous.

With a present population of about 23,000 living in mining villages, around the chemical works, and in some rural settlements, there is a problem of successfully dovetailing new with old investment. The prime concepts of the New Town layout relate to road networks, social organisation and the land-use pattern. The primary road network is based on a 1 mile grid of dual-carriageway roads with midway connections for the distributor network of secondary roads. Residential development will be divided into units, to be called villages, each accommodating about 4,500 people. Each village will have its own social provision and will be 'pedestrian-orientated'. Unusually, land uses are to be distributed throughout the town, eg there will be smaller groups of industrial sites rather than the conventional concentrated estate. Several major firms, including Tube Products Ltd, have already established factories, whilst small, unobtrusive and clean industries may be incorporated in some of the village centres.

NCC New Towns

The two county-council sponsored New Towns, at Killingworth[21] and Cramlington[22] in south-east Northumberland, form part of the sub-regional strategy for that area. Of the two the Cramlington proposal is the larger, with a target population of just under 50,000 compared with the 16,000 forecast for the North Killingworth Comprehensive Development Area. The purpose of both towns relates to the distribution of overspill population from the Tyneside conurbation, Killingworth is virtually an integral part of the conurbation perimeter, Cramlington is on a site some 8 miles north of the centre of Newcastle. A second prime purpose at Cramlington is to provide much needed new employment and activity to replace the decline of mining and, by introducing a new living environment, to transform the traditional appearance of this part of the south-east Northumberland coalfield. The accelerated programme of mine closures has added an urgency to this rôle. Both New Towns have been tactically situated with reference to the approach route to the Tyne Tunnel from the north. At Killingworth some 57 acres of land is zoned for industrial use; at Cramlington the figure is about 520 acres and it is hoped to attract substantial employers of male labour. Each New Town has benefited from the attractions of the new living environment and industrial arrivals have been prompt and adequate.

The New Towns in the North East have a lead rôle to play in transforming the regional image; their longer-term place within a regional strategy is referred to in the next chapter.

References to this chapter are on pages 243–4 and 249–50.

o

10

North East 2000

Stocktaking

NOT FOR the first time in its long economic history the industrial North East finds itself poised at a critical stage in its progress. Looking back through the twentieth century the scale of basic transformation has already been dramatic, from a lead rôle in the zenith of Britain's heavy industry, steel-making and coal mining shortly before the First World War to the trough of deep economic depression and male unemployment in the early 1930s. During the past thirty years or so covered by this book, there has been the fashioning, at times fitfully, never in a comprehensive or co-ordinated way, of the basis for a changed, modernised, streamlined industrial structure in the region, a metamorphosis still actively taking place. In this process of change governments of the day have fairly consistently been agents, sometimes seized by the urgency of economic and social 'first aid' measures, at other times almost inert observers of the changing scene.

It is difficult to assess the effectiveness of succeeding government policies for industrial areas like the North East, both cumulatively and at the level of the completion of each policy phase. In general terms judgment may be passed in the light of the declared objectives, more specifically in the assessment of objective criteria of economic growth, notably new job provision or new factory space occupied. Objectives have not always been clearly spelled out but the ruling concepts have fairly consistently related to one or more of the following. Firstly relief of unemployment, *in situ* whenever possible, but more recently rather more within daily travelling distance of residence. Secondly diversification, or reduction in the region's dependence upon an unduly narrow range of industrial employment, a policy proceeding mainly by the attraction to the North East of industries hitherto little represented in its employment structure, such industries to be of a 'growth' character with initial impact of new jobs and later, hopefully, some kind of agglomerating effect or multiplier rôle in the local economy. Balance is a third and more recent concept, national in its implications, referring essentially to a better regional distribution of national employment, a line of thinking going back to the 1940 *Barlow Report* of the Commission on Distribution of the Industrial Population. There are also more local and specific side objectives but those mentioned in differing blend cover the years since the middle 1930s.

The most formative phases of government policy in the North East were probably under the Distribution of Industry Act in the years 1945–9 and, very recently, in the early phases of regional thinking and planning since 1964.[1] Before the Second World War policies were being formulated in a 'pilot-stage' and through the 1950s the Distribution of Industry Act was applied with decreasing consistency and effectiveness. The early 1960s, under the Local Employment Act legislation, were a phase of piecemeal and often unsatisfactory application at a time when the economic downturns of 1958–9 and 1962–3 ushered in a more difficult phase of economic adjustment and faltering progress in the North East.

The relative merits of criteria for assessing economic growth and change in the North East as the result of successive government policies were considered in Chapter 4, whilst the impact of changes at the level of sub-region and landscape were the substance of Chapter 5. Certainly the scale of new job provision in the region since the war owes much to government industrial-location policy and to effectiveness of the mixture of controls and inducements used to persuade industrialists to set up new plants in development areas or development districts. Certainly too the function of the government-sponsored industrial estate, with its grouped sites and centralised services, has been an outstandingly successful one, more so perhaps at the larger sites than at the remoter individual ones to which the 'work to the worker' policy, in its more extreme forms, attempted to push the often reluctant industrialist. Certainly too the rapid growth of industrial jobs for women in the post-war years has introduced the two-job family to the North East on a noticeable scale and at the same time has increased female activity rates in the region. Furthermore, there has been a useful scale of diversification in the range of industrial employment, though without as yet changing the essential lineaments of the region's heavy-industrial character. Care must be taken in this respect for the decline

of some basic industries has reduced their predominance, at times
perhaps seeming to exaggerate the impact of new types of varied
industry coming in, but in purely statistical terms.

The overall verdict on the years since 1945 must then be that significant progress has been made in increasing the fundamental stability in
employment structure and in establishing the base of new industrial
growths which should further contribute to the prosperity of the North
East in the future. Without selective government aid it is unlikely that
much of the new industrial growth would have been implanted and
very probable that the scale of out-migration from the North East in
search of employment in the more affluent areas of Britain would have
been on a grander and more debilitating scale.

Yet disquieting features still remain and regional policies for basic
transformation of the regional economy still have far to go. The unemployment rate in the North East remains obstinately at a level double
the national average, national economic recessions hit the development
areas earlier and more severely, and economic take-off on the upward
turn of the trade cycle, or when 'go' replaces 'stop', tends to be more
sluggish in the development areas than elsewhere in Britain. Moreover
the deep pockets of localised unemployment, the problem areas of the
North East, persist in marginal rural, mining and industrial areas. The
current 'special development areas' of the coalfield of Northumberland and Durham are but the latest manifestation of this highly concentrated locality problem within the regional problem. In this sense
there has always been a dualism in governmental policies in that relief
in situ at the level of village or town has been combined with general
revival in the more logical 'growth points' or 'growth areas' from which
the benefits of more readily achieved prosperity would radiate outwards to the advantage of depressed marginal districts. Setting a limit
to the effectiveness of any regional or industrial-location policy has
been the national economic climate in post-war years. With a basic
instability and a fluctuating but generally slow growth rate in the
national economy it is perhaps surprising that the scale of growth and
change in the development areas has been so great.

The North East White Paper of 1963[2] was the first policy statement
to formulate a 'growth zone' concept, (for outline of area designated
see Figure 11). Apart from stressing the need to adjust the regional
economy and to diversify its industrial structure the main emphasis
lay upon concentrating major growth in the Tyne–Tees axial zone and
'that part of County Durham which lies between the Great North
Road and the coast'. However the 'growth zone' concept never became

a part of legislation and the proposal came to mean no more than a very significant pointer to future strategy for the North East. The regional planning document *Challenge of the Changing North*[3] emphasised the major growth prospects for Teesside, advancing a case not yet accepted by the government for its designation as a national growth area. On the case for a co-ordinated growth policy, spelled out in sub-regional detail for the Northern region, no arguments were put forward, the document contenting itself with fundamental stress on the need for 'encouraging technological development', as the key to realising the benefits of a more diversified economy.

The Way Ahead

The major problems of the North East remain what they always have been, those of continuing the stages of setting up a balanced, diversified industrial economy with stronger representation of growth elements and rising in new job provision at least as fast as the ever-present accelerating rundown in employment in certain basic industries, notably coalmining, iron and steel manufacture, shipbuilding and certain branches of heavy engineering. Allied with this is a general policy of improving the total living environment of the North East, or, in the initial stages, of certain parts of it, to encourage more people to stay in the area, indeed to come in and settle from elsewhere to live and work.

In looking ahead to the end of the century and in seeking to formulate some kind of policy or strategy for the North East for the next three decades the initial impression is of the difficulties of setting a properly meaningful national context. It is clear from *Challenge of the Changing North* that the regional population will be significantly larger than it is today, even allowing for continuing out-migration. Indeed the policy of the economic planning council is to reduce the level of out-migration, aiming at achieving a migration balance by 1981. It now seems that the expected regional population born and growing up in the North East between now and the end of the century may well be rather less than forecast in the *Challenge* but, on the other hand, it may be too optimistic to envisage balancing migration flows into and out of the region by 1981—this balance may have to be deferred towards the end of the century.

A further uncertainty which must bedevil regional economic planning and forecasting is the likely shape of government support policies for areas like the North East, presently designated development areas

and receiving considerable direct and indirect financial aid at the level
of the firm, the local authority and the regional investment programmes of central government departments. The Hunt Commission
considering the intermediate areas, the so-called 'grey areas' outside
the present development areas, reported in April 1969 and the Maud
Commission on Local Government put forward its proposals in June
1969. Such rethinking on the regions may change the form of policies
and the administrative areas within which they are applied, thus adding
further imponderables to existing uncertainties about the economic
future at the national level.

An interim verdict on the proposals of the Hunt Committee[4] and
their limited acceptance by the government suggests that development
areas, such as that including the North East have little to fear in the
short-term from the granting of qualified development assistance to
areas such as the Yorkshire coalfield, parts of Humberside or the main
industrial area of North East Lancashire east of the proposed New
Town. Such assistance will be at lower levels than in the development
areas and will be concentrated on areas with high unemployment,
high outward migration and real scope for industrial growth. Clearly
the development areas, with a severe redeployment of labour problem
over the next six years or so, as older industries continue to contract
sharply, will continue to have first priority in industrial location policy.
Nevertheless the North East may suffer from the probable cessation
of the movement of firms from the West Riding, moving north to enjoy
the development-area benefits. Between 1945 and 1965 no fewer than
fifty-one firms from Yorkshire and Humberside established plants in
the Northern Region (Table 12), the second most important source of
new plants after those from the South East.

Within the industries which have been discussed in this book profound structural changes have been detected and these frequently have
further to run. The general trend in most is towards job economy,
mechanisation and automation in processing. In certain branches there
is also a longer-term downward trend arising from closures, surplus
capacity and declining profitability. The combination of declining
demand and technological change makes certain a further substantial
male job loss in the North East, which means that in the short run
the region will have to combat a peculiarly severe downward trend,
likely to be most marked in the mining areas but also in steel-making
plants as the rationalisation of production releases manpower. Various
manpower estimates have been made, but all are periodically revised.
What remains certain is that the accelerating programme of colliery

closures will deprive many localities of their basic livelihood, a process likely to continue well into the 1970s.

Against the run-down in employment in many industries must be set the prospects of attracting new firms and lines of manufacture. Much will depend on inducements and the measure of industrial-location policy exercised by the central government. Improvement of the living environment will be important as an added attraction but the likely profitability of establishing and producing in a development area will remain the keynote. *Challenge of the Changing North* speaks of the need for the government to encourage the establishment and, where possible, the transfer of 'integrated industrial units', willing to bring their research and development departments with them. Such acts of faith have thus so far been few but the notion is sound. What certainly seems to be required is some definition of an industrial strategy which does more than simply judge the *ad hoc* merits of individual applications for industrial development certificates and considers them in relation to the contribution the plant or firm is likely to make, not only to gross job provision (the major test of importance hitherto), but also to the growth of an interrelated industrial complex. Side by side relationship of a miscellany of plants and firms whose major links in both the raw material and market directions are outside the North East is a poor substitute for related growths in associated industries, preferably grouped around the concept of a leader firm or leader industry. One of the shortcomings in the North East since the war has been that though leader firms have come in they have, all too often, had little multiplier effect on the local or regional economy.

Clearly the extent to which such a growth-orientated, co-ordinated industrial strategy is practicable depends in large measure upon the general economic growth climate. The major implantations of new firms in the development areas since the war have taken place with high annual growth rates in the national economy, with many firms and plants subsequently staying on to develop within the region. On the other hand some branch plants established in booms have been shorter-term unstable transients and have disappeared in subsequent depression. Only during a high and sustained national growth rate does selectivity and co-ordination of industrial introductions become remotely feasible and this has all too rarely been the case since the war.

Many kinds of manufacturing would be beneficial in the future industrial structure of the North East. There are virtually no branches not now represented in some fashion, but among the faster growth groups in recent years there is still no major motor-vehicle assembly plant between Doncaster and central Scotland. The pros and cons of establishing such a plant (or plants) were discussed in Chapter 7 where the limited contribution from within the North East to the space industry was also noted. Motor-vehicle assembly in the region would no doubt spark off further developments in components manufacture, already an important post-war growth in the development area. The strong traditions and skills of engineering labour in the North East could well be redeployed from declining branches of engineering and shipbuilding into new, flexible fields of machinery manufacture, machine-tool making or constructional engineering. Some of the largest engineering firms in the region have indeed achieved a measure of redeployment by changing the balance of operations within the firm; others remain traditionally-based. There is also a great variety of smaller growths for new products in engineering, eg tubes and pipes for air conditioning or refrigeration, pumps and compressors, butterfly valves, etc, which are characteristic of the needs of an affluent society and, in their diversity, indicate possible growth industries of the future.

The national and international chemical firms in the North East have greatly contributed to regional prosperity but in general have not as yet led to the growth of industrial complexes. It may be that the recent growth of regional oil refineries will provide a new starting point for consumer-orientated chemical industries, many of which presently congregate near the larger market centres in the country. Other major post-war growths in the North East have been in the telecommunications branches and in electrical goods generally. These clearly have further growth prospects but it remains to be seen what the regional impact will be of the massive rationalisation programme likely to follow the grouping of the national industry into a very few, very large groups.

Packaging is another new industry to be developed beyond the demands of the regional market, whilst clothing seems likely to continue as the fastest growing branch of textiles. Electrical goods and clothing manufacture employ large numbers of females and are within the group loosely-termed 'payroll' or 'labour-intensive'. They are extremely valuable in new job provision but they do not necessarily contribute to the central problem of more jobs for men to replace those being lost in mining and heavy industry.

Looking beyond 1981 at this stage may seem unreasonably speculative, but it is clear that during the last twenty years of the century there is almost certain to be an increase in population on a much greater scale than between now and 1981, requiring a rapidly accelerated job provision just when the full benefits of automation will probably be releasing an ever-increasing number of men. It may well be that a shorter working week, substitution of males for females in certain industries, more employment in service industries (particularly recreation and transport), will mitigate the employment problem. Fortunately, it is likely that the further growth of industries transplanted to the North East since the war will by then have contributed very considerably to further diversification and to a better representation of faster growth elements in the region.

Sub-Regional Allocation

The industrial population of the North East is unusually heavily concentrated on Tyneside, Teesside and at Sunderland and, unless there is a proposal for major 'greenfield' developments this weighting is likely to continue in general terms to the end of the century. The major 'greenfield' developments are likely to be limited to the continuing, perhaps priority, expansion of the five New Towns of the North East.

Economic growth pressures are likely to continue most strongly towards the southern border of the North East, most closely linked with the West Riding, the Midlands and the South East. There may even be detectable pressure stronger around Darlington, in south-west Teesside, and on the southern rim of the Tyneside conurbation. The pressure for growth along the improved major transportation arteries is also likely to become another strongly-felt feature.

It may be that response to such differential pressures for industrial growth may only be possible in any selective way if the total pressure for industrial sites is considerable and there are many claimants. Failing such high and sustained pressure it is likely that industrialists will seek to insist, even more fully than they have managed to do hitherto, upon rights to go to the best location and in any case never to any marginally-located site. If regional location policy is relaxed, inducements reduced, and controls lifted, it is even more likely that only the most accessible and best-equipped sites will be sought or utilised by new industry.

In this prospective situation it is the 'growth zone', 'growth pole' (or point) characteristics of the North East that will provide its competitive status. The 1963 White Paper definition of a 'growth zone' is still the most logical but there could be problems in determination of priorities for growth within it. At the northern end lies Tyneside and Sunderland whose short-term problems are considerable and whose longer-term prospects are something of an enigma but with interesting potentials. Both Tyne and Wear have difficult further adjustments to make in their heavy-industrial structure and the problem of redeployment of miners from the closing collieries falls within their hinterland rather than that of the Tees. Fortunately, and precisely because of the more deep-seated post-war industrial reconversion problem, Tyne and Wear have better short-term employment growth prospects arising from the 'new' and varied industrial base implanted since the war. It seems logical that major weighting should be given to further industrial growth at the northern end of the axis during the next fifteen years. The economic sub-region concept should be that of a widely-defined Tyne–Wear city region extending out to include the journey-to-work hinterland and the New Towns at Washington, Cramlington and Killingworth. Designation of the Tyne–Wear city region as a regional metropolis within the national context seems an excellent idea which might be borrowed from French regional-planning strategy.

Teesside has much stronger industrial growth momentum than the Tyne–Wear but, to a much greater extent, it is based on capital-intensive rather than labour-intensive industries. Designation of the Tees as a growth area should, in the period up to 1981, lead to a concentration on investment in basic infrastructure, communications, utilities, housing, shopping, educational facilities and so on, whilst the Tyne–Wear is allowed the major allocation of 'footloose' type industries. From 1981 onwards the Tyne–Wear should have self-sustaining economic momentum and Teesside would then be well equipped to expand economically as rapidly as circumstances required, and it might be very fast indeed. The Teesplan enquiry justifies the prospects for very substantial growth on the counts of position, port, land and layout. If the Tees expands too considerably in the short-run it may seriously damage the ability of Tyne–Wear to solve the mounting employment problems of the next decade. With Teesside, Darlington may prove the outstanding growth prospect for the latter decades of this century.

Growth cannot of course be channelled to either or both ends of the axial zone without affecting the prospects of the communities lying between Tyne and Tees. It is in this zone flanking the A1 (M)—Durham Motorway and the main east-coast railway, that the most serious problems of mining rundown will occur in the next ten years, particularly in the valleys to the west and on the east Durham plateau.

Difficult decisions will have to be taken here. The most logical growth points are at the New Towns of Peterlee and Aycliffe and these will serve as central places with a widely spread influence over mining settlements in south-east and south-west Durham. Other centres may be indicated for development but without doubt a great deal of decline must be envisaged. Category 'D' villages in County Durham are those where no further investment is intended beyond that needed to maintain existing facilities during a rundown period; much obsolete housing will be cleared and the population re-grouped elsewhere. The problems of north-west Durham may be partially solved by increased commuting to the Tyne–Wear city region, though if the Consett steelworks was to be closed the central prop would be taken out of the local economy. The likelihood remains that most growth outside the New Towns will be channelled into a growth corridor with nodes of development along the major north-south communications axis—a partial realisation of the concept of a Tyne–Tees linear city.

There remains the broad rural-hinterland zone from the Cheviots, through the Pennines to the Cleveland Hills. The rural population is thin and has been declining for many years. Locally there are more severe pockets of depopulation, in the hinterland of Berwick, in the more remote valleys of Weardale and upper Teesdale, and in Eskdale among the North York Moors. Industry was represented in great variety, but on a very small scale, in many of these areas during the first half of the nineteenth century but today there are only vestigial remnants and those are mostly confined to the market towns. These towns, with between 7,500 and 10,000 population, are irregularly spaced but share a common slow-growth characteristic, reflecting the barely stable economic and social situation within their hinterlands. Though the Hailsham strategy of 1963 envisaged the benefits of a successful 'growth zone' policy radiating in time to the most remote corners of the rural hinterland this seems less likely than an accelerated decline at the margins as the most logical counterpart of growth in the economic heart of the North East.

The market towns, or some of them, are likely to be the smallest units at which industrial growth of modest character might be implanted. On the coastal fringe the resort towns present special problems of dependence on a markedly seasonal industry. The basic strategy for the rural areas should be to select certain market towns for economic growth, recognising that not all of them are suitable and that the selection of industries likely to settle and prosper there will be from a narrow spectrum of the practicable. Commuting from a wide rural hinterland to the market towns will spread the benefit of increased employment out to the smaller settlements and farms. It is likely, however, that new industries moving to market towns will need to bring at least part of their labour force with them and in any case it is desirable to build up the total rural population.

In a sense development at the market towns would be something of a holding operation and a defensive element in regional strategy. It should be the means of holding more people in the countryside and thus underpinning the basic agricultural population, of keeping up the level of social provision and of community life, which is now, in many rural districts, at a critically low ebb.

The very fact that it is now fashionable to think in terms of a comprehensive regional strategy[5] shows that the traditional piecemeal approach of government policy-makers in the past is no longer appropriate. The North East will require a carefully chosen strategy if it is to overcome the impending difficult stage in its economic transformation and to progress to a balanced and more stable regional industrial structure before the turn of the century.

Finally, the 1969 publication of the Maud Commission on Local Government confirms the identity of the North East, by defining it as one of the eight provinces of an administratively-reorganised England. The boundaries proposed are similar to those of the area treated in this book, but excluding the southern part of the North Riding. Within the North East there will be five unitary authorities: an enlarged Teesside, Tyneside and, more controversially, Sunderland with East Durham and two 'rump' authorities from the former counties of Durham and Northumberland.

References to this chapter are on page 244.

Acknowledgments

MATERIAL for the book has been gathered from libraries, planning reports, a variety of research schemes from the past and also from many conversations with the people of the North East, industrialists in particular. I gratefully acknowledge all these sources, too numerous to mention individually, but wish to make especial mention of the regional office of the Department of Employment and Productivity, under whose generous sponsorship I have conducted a research investigation into migration and mobility in the Northern region during the past four years, a task which finally clarified to me the true dimensions of our regional problems.

My grateful thanks are due to Mr Eric Quenet and Mrs Olive Teasdale for kindly drawing the figures for reproduction and to Miss Margaret Bell and Mrs Mary Whitehouse for typing the manuscript.

References

CHAPTER 1

Region and System. Page 15

1 *Challenge of the Changing North.* Northern Economic Planning Council, HMSO, 1966.

2 *Abstract of Regional Statistics No 3* 1967. Central Statistical Office.

3 *Survey of Road Goods Transport 1962. Final Results. Geographical Analysis.* Statistical Paper 6, Ministry of Transport, 1966.
   The Reshaping of British Railways. British Railways Board, HMSO 1963.

4 *Survey of Transport Needs and Resources in the Tyneside Area.* Pt V. Goods Vehicle Survey, EIU, 1965.

5 *Digest of Port Statistics.* National Ports Council, 1967.

6 House, J. W. & Willis, K. G., 'Northern Region and Nation', *Papers on Migration and Mobility in Northern England*, No. 4, Apr 1967.

7 Elliott, N. R. 'The functional approach in port studies', *Northern Geographical Essays.* Newcastle, 1967, pp 102–18.

CHAPTER 2

Resources and Development. Page 38

1 Smailes, A. E. *North England.* Nelson, 1960.

2 *A Physical Land Classification of Northumberland and Durham and part of the North Riding of Yorkshire.* NEDA, 1950.

3 House, J. W. 'North-Eastern England. Population movements and the landscape since the early 19th century'. *King's College, University of Durham, Dept of Geography Research Series*, No 1, 1954.

4 Warren, K. 'The shaping of the Teesside Industrial Region'. *Advancement of Science*, Vol 25 (124), 1968, pp 185–99.

CHAPTER 3

People and Work. Page 49

1   House, J. W. & Willis, K. G. op cit, Plate 13, 1961.

2   See *Papers on Migration and Mobility in Northern England*, Nos 1–9, 1965–8, University of Newcastle upon Tyne.

3   Fullerton, B. 'The pattern of service industries in North-East England', *King's College, University of Durham, Dept of Geography Research Series* No 3, 1960.
    Fullerton, B. 'Geographical inertia in the service industries: an example from Northern England', *Northern Geographical Essays*, Newcastle 1967, pp 157–77.

CHAPTER 4

Development and Government Policy. Page 66

1   Allen, E., Odber, A. J. & Bowden, P. J. *Development Area policy in the North-East of England*, NEDA, 1957.
    The Northern Region, Publications 2–9, NEDA, 1946–61.

2   House, J. W. 'Recent economic growth in North-East England', *University of Newcastle upon Tyne, Dept of Geography Research Series*, No 4, 1964.

3   *The North East. A programme for regional development and growth*, Cmnd 2206, HMSO, 1963.

CHAPTER 5

Growth and change in Sub-Region and Landscape. Page 82

1   House, J. W. 'Margins in regional geography: an illustration from North East England', *Northern Geographical Essays*, Newcastle 1967, pp 139–56.

2   Daysh, G. H. J. & Symonds, J. S. *West Durham. A study of a problem area in North-Eastern England*. Basil Blackwell, 1963.

3   House, J. W. *Northumbrian Tweedside*. Rural Community Council, 1956.
    House, J. W. 'Rural North-East England 1951–61', *Papers on Migration and Mobility in North-East England*, No 1, 1965.

4   House, J. W. & Knight, E. M. 'People on the move: the South Tyne in the Sixties', *Papers on Migration and Mobility in North-East England*, No 3, 1966.

5 Daysh, G. H. J. (editor). *A Survey of Whitby and the surrounding area*. Shakespeare Head, 1958.

CHAPTER 6

Coal and Steel. Page 100

1 North East Industrial and Development Association. *North East Coast. A Survey of Industrial Facilities*. Andrew Reid, 1949, Chapters 1 and 2.
Scientific Survey of North-eastern England. British Association, 1949, pp 87–96.
Durham Coalfield. Regional Survey Report, HMSO, 1945.
Northumberland and Cumberland coalfields. Regional Survey Report, HMSO, 1945.

2 Smailes, A. E. 'The development of the Northumberland and Durham coalfield', *Scottish Geographical Magazine*, Vol 51, 1935, pp 201–14.
Smailes, A. E. 'Population changes in the colliery districts of Northumberland and Durham', *Geographical Journal*, Vol 91, 1938, pp 220–32.

3 *Plan for Coal*, NCB, 1950.

4 House, J. W. & Knight, E. M. 'Pit closure and the community', *Papers on Migration and Mobility in Northern England*, No 5, 1967.

5 *The steel industry. The Stage I report of the Development Co-ordinating Committee*. British Iron and Steel Federation, July 1966.

6 Carr, J. C. & Taplin, W. *History of the British Steel Industry*. Basil Blackwell, 1962.
Keeling, B. S. & Wright, A. E. G. *The development of the modern British steel industry*. Longmans, 1964.
Burn, D. 'Steel', Chapter VII in *The Structure of British Industry*, Vol I, Cambridge University Press, 1958, pp 260–308.
Roepke, H. G. *Movements of the British Iron and Steel Industry, 1720–1951*. University of Illinois Press, 1956.

7 Ridley, The Viscount, 'The development of the iron and steel industry in North West Durham', *Tyneside Geographical Society Lecture* 1961. University of Durham, King's College, Newcastle upon Tyne, 1961.
Wilson, C., 'Company histories 1. Dorman Long', *Steel Review*, Apr 1957, pp 11–23.
Willis, W. G. *Skinningrove Iron Company Ltd 1880–1968. A History*.
House, J. W. & Fullerton, B. *Teesside at midcentury*. Macmillan, 1960, Chapter 11, pp 195–213.

8 Warren, K. 'Iron and steel in North-East England: Regional implications of development in a basic industry', *Regional Studies*, Vol 3 (1), 1969, pp 49–60.

P

CHAPTER 7

Rapid Growth Industries. Page 133

1   House, J. W. 'Recent Economic Growth in North-East England', *University of Newcastle upon Tyne, Dept of Geography Research Series*, No 4, 1964.

2   House, J. W. & Fullerton, B. *Teesside at midcentury*, Macmillan, 1960, Chapter 10, pp 153–194.

3   Board of Trade. *An industrial survey of the North Coast area*. HMSO, 1932.

4   Association of British chemical manufacturers. *Reports on the chemical industry*, 1949 and 1953.
    Reddaway, W. B. 'The chemical industry', Chapter VI in *The Structure of British Industry*, Vol I, Cambridge University Press, 1958, pp 218–59.
    Imperial Chemical Industries Ltd. A survey by *The Times*. 1962.

5   Wilson, T. 'The electronics industry', Chapter XIII in Burn, D. *The Structure of British Industry*, Vol II, Cambridge University Press, 1958.

6   Fullerton, B. 'The Pattern of service industries in North-East England', *King's College, University of Durham, Dept of Geography Research Series*, No 3, 1960.
    Fullerton, B. 'Geographical inertia in the service industries: an example from Northern England,' *Northern Geographical Essays*, Newcastle, 1967, pp 157–77.

7   House, J. W., Ruddy, S. A., Thubron, I. M. & Storer, C. E. 'Mobility of the Northern business manager', *Papers on Migration and Mobility in Northern England*, No 8, 1968.

CHAPTER 8

Traditional Industries in Change. Page 163

1   *Shipbuilding Inquiry Committee 1965–1966 Report*. (Geddes Report). HMSO, Cmnd 2937, Mar 1966.

2   Smith, W. *An Economic Geography of Great Britain*. Methuen, 1949.

3   Parkinson, J. R. *The economics of shipbuilding in the United Kingdom. Cambridge University Press*, 1960.
    Dougan, D. *A History of North East shipbuilding*. George Allen & Unwin, 1968.

4   Smith, J. W. & Holden, T. S. *Where ships are born, Sunderland 1346–1946*. T. Reed, 1953.

5   Middlebrook, S. *Newcastle upon Tyne. Its growth and achievement*. Kemsley House, Newcastle upon Tyne, 1950, especially pp 237–47.

6 Swan Hunter & Wigham Richardson Ltd, *Launching Ways*, 1953.

7 Board of Trade. *An industrial survey of the North East Coast area.* HMSO, 1932, pp 222–95.

8 *Shipping World and Shipbuilding*, Feb 1964.

9 Armstrong, W. D. *Industrial resources of the three northern rivers, Tyne, Wear and Tees.* British Association, 1863.

10 Gibb, Sir. C. 'Mechanical engineering', *A Scientific Survey of North-Eastern England*, British Association, 1949, pp 133–41.

11 Scott, J. D. *Vickers. A history.* Wiedenfeld & Nicholson, 1962.

12 *Voice of North East Industry*, Aug 1968.

CHAPTER 9

Industrial Districts. Page 194

1 House, J. W. & Fullerton, B. *Teesside at midcentury*, Macmillan, 1960, Chapter 1, p 15.

2 Agar, R. 'Glacial and post-glacial geology of Middlesbrough and the Tees estuary', *Proceedings Yorkshire Geological Society*, Vol 29, 1954, pp 237–53.

3 Best, R. H. 'The urbanization of Teesside', *Planning Outlook*, Vol 5 (3), 1961, pp 15–36.

4 House, J. W. & Fullerton, B. op cit, Chapter 22, 'Accessibility', pp 361–74.

5 Op cit, Chapter 26, 'Problems and Prospects', pp 430–41.

6 Op cit, pp 56–7.

7 *Teesside Survey and Plan: Vol I: Policies and Prospects*, HMSO, 1969.

8 Local Government Commission for England, Report No 5. *Report and proposals for the Tyneside Special Review Area*, July 1963.

9 Conzen, M. R. G. 'Geographical setting of Newcastle', *A Scientific Survey of North-eastern England.* British Association, 1949, pp 191–7.

10 Smailes, A. E. 'Early industrial settlement in North East England', *Advancement of Science*, Vol 6, 1950, pp 325–31.

11 Mess, H. A. *Industrial Tyneside, a social survey.* E. Benn, 1928. Northumberland and Tyneside Council of Social Service. *Tyneside Local Government Areas.* 1960.

12 *Report of the Royal Commission on Local Government in the Tyneside area.* HMSO, 1937, Cmnd 5402.

13 *Newcastle upon Tyne Development Plan Review.* 1963.

14 Burnett, J. *The history of the town and port of Sunderland and the parishes of Bishopwearmouth and Monkwearmouth.* J. S. Burnett, 1830.

Potts, D. *Sunderland: a history of the town, port, trade and commerce.* R. Williams & Co, 1892.

15 Robson, B. T. 'An ecological analysis of the evolution of urban areas in Sunderland, *Urban Studies,* Vol 3 (2), 1966, pp 120–42.

16 *Sunderland East End. Sub-district and action area plan.* 1967.

17 *Southwick, Sunderland. District Plan,* 1967.

18 Aycliffe Development Corporation. *Aycliffe expansion. Master Plan Report.* May 1967.

19 Peterlee Development Corporation. *Peterlee. Master Plan Report.* Sept 1952.

20 Washington Development Corporation. *Washington New Town. Master Plan and Report.* Dec 1966.

21 Northumberland County Development Plan *North Killingworth. The written analysis.* Aug 1959.

22 Northumberland County Development Plan *Cramlington. The written analysis.* Apr 1962.

CHAPTER 10

North East 2000. Page 226

1 Board of Trade *The movement of manufacturing industry in the United Kingdom 1945–65.* HMSO, 1968.

2 *North East White Paper.* HMSO, 1963, pp 5–7.

3 *Challenge of the Changing North,* pp 1–4.

4 *The Intermediate Areas. Report of a Committee under the Chairmanship of Sir Joseph Blunt,* HMSO, 1969, Cmnd 3998.

5 *Outline strategy for the North.* Northern Economic Planning Council, Mar 1969.

6 *Report of the Royal Commission on Local Government in England,* 3 Vols, HMSO, 1969, Cmnd 4040.

Bibliography

Background and supplementary to the references in the text (qv).

Basic to the understanding of POST-WAR DEVELOPMENT AND THE EMERGENCE OF REGIONAL PLANNING

The North East. A programme for regional development and growth. HMSO, Cmnd 2206, 1963

Northern Economic Planning Council. *Challenge of the Changing North.* HMSO, 1966

Northern Economic Planning Council. *Outline Strategy for the North.* NEPC, 1969

PRINCIPAL WORKS, GEOGRAPHICAL AND LITERARY

Daysh, G. H. J. (editor). *A Survey of Whitby and the Surrounding Area.* Shakespeare Head, 1958

Daysh, G. H. J. & Caesar, A. A. L. 'The North-East Region of England', *Studies in Regional Planning*, G. Philip, 1951

Daysh, G. H. J. & Symonds, J. S. *West Durham. A problem area in North-Eastern England*, Basil Blackwell, 1951

Fawcett, C. B. 'North-East England', *Great Britain. Essays in Regional Geography*, 1930, pp 332–48

Headlam, Sir C. M. *The Three Northern Counties of England.* Northumberland Press, 1939

House, J. W. & Fullerton, B. *Teesside at midcentury.* Macmillan, 1960

Jones, L. R. *North England: an economic geography.* Routledge, 1924

'A Scientific Survey of North-Eastern England', British Association, Newcastle upon Tyne, 1949

Smailes, A. E. *North England.* Nelson, 1960

Turner, G. *The North Country*, Eyre & Spottiswoode, 1967

STANDARD HISTORIES

Hodgson, J. *A history of Northumberland*. 7 Vols, E. Walker, 1820–58

Hughes, E. *North country life in the Eighteenth Century: the North East 1700–50*. OUP, 1952

Hutchinson, W. *The History and antiquities of the County Palatine of Durham*. 3 Vols, Newcastle, 1785–94

Mackenzie, E. *A descriptive and historical view of Northumberland, New-castle, Berwick etc*. Mackenzie & Dent, 2nd edn, 2 Vols, 1825

Middlebrook, S. 'Newcastle upon Tyne, its Growth and Achievement', *Newcastle Journal*, 1950

Northumberland County History Committee. *History of Northumberland*. 15 Vols, A. Reid, 1893–1940

Page, W. *Durham*. Victoria History of the Counties of England. 3 Vols, London, 1905-28

Victoria History of the Counties of England. *North Riding of Yorkshire*. 2 Vols, Constable, 1914–25

NATURAL ENDOWMENT (Chapter 2)

Dunham, K. C. 'Geology of the North Pennine orefield, Vol 1: Tyne to Stainmore.' *Economic Memoirs, Geological Survey*, HMSO, 1948

Eastwood, T. *Northern England*. British Regional Geology, HMSO, 1953

Edwards, W. & Trotter, F. M. *The Pennines and adjacent areas*. British Regional Geology, HMSO, 1954

Geologists Association. *The Geology of Northumberland and Durham*. 1931.

Hanley, J. A., Boyd, A. L., & Williamson, W. *An Agricultural Survey of the Northern Province*. Newcastle: Department of Agriculture, Armstrong College, 1936

Pawson, H. C. *A Survey of the Agriculture of Northumberland*. Royal Agricultural Society of England, 1961

Raistrick, A. 'Lead mining and smelting in the Northern Pennines during the 18th and 19th centuries', *Proceedings* University of Durham Philosophical Society, 1936, pp 164–79

Smailes, A. E. 'The lead dales of the Northern Pennines', *Geography*, Vol 21, 1936, pp 120–9

Stamp, L. D. (editor). *The Report of the Land Utilisation Survey of Britain*. Pt 47 County Durham, 1941; Pt 51 Yorkshire, North Riding, 1945; Pt 52 Northumberland, 1945

Stead, J. E. *Cleveland ironstone and iron*. Middlesbrough, 1910

Sykes, E. C. 'The agricultural geography of Northumberland'. *Geography*, Vol 18, 1933, pp 269–80

PEOPLING AND INDUSTRIAL DEVELOPMENT (Chapter 2)

British Association for the Advancement of Science. *Industrial resources of the Tyne, Wear and Tees.* 2nd edn, 1864

Buckley, F. 'Potteries on the Tyne and other northern potteries during the eighteenth century', *Archaeologia Aeliana*, 4th series, Vol 4, 1927, pp 68–82

Clapham, J. 'The Manufacture of glass in England: the rise of the art on the Tyne', *Archaeologia Aeliana*, New Series, Vol 8, 1880, pp 108–26

Clapham, R. C. *An Account of the Commencement of Soda Manufacture on the Tyne.* 1869

Cochrane, A. J. H. *The Early History of Elswick*, 1909

Crawley, J. *Potteries of Sunderland and district: a summary of their history and products.* Sunderland Corporation, 1951

Dillon, M. *Some Account of the Works of Palmer's Shipbuilding and Iron Company*, 1899

House, J. W. 'North-Eastern England. Population movements and the landscape since the early nineteenth century', *King's College, University of Durham, Dept of Geography, Research Series*, No 1, 1954

Pilbin, P. 'The external relations of the Tyneside glass industry', *Economic Geography*, Vol 13, 1937, pp 301–14

Pilbin, P. *Geographical studies of the development of certain industries of Tyneside and North East England.* Unpublished MSc Thesis, Durham University, 1935

Pilbin, P. 'A geographical analysis of the sea salt industry of North East England', *Scottish Geographical Magazine*, Vol 51, 1935, pp 22–8

Pilbin, P. 'The influence of local geography on the glass industry of Tyneside', *Journal* Tyneside Geographical Society, New Series Vol 1, 1936, pp 31–45

Raistrick, A. *Two centuries of welfare: the London (Quaker) Lead Company*, 1692–1905. Friends' Historical Society, 1938

Shaw, H. *The River Tyne: its advantages and possibilities.* Andrew Reid, 1908

Tomlinson, W. C. O. *The North Eastern Railway: its rise and development.* Andrew Reid, 1914. Reprinted by David & Charles, 1968, with introduction by K. Hoole

Tyne Improvement Commission. *Centenary 1850–1950: a century of progress.* 1950

Warren, J. G. H. *A Century of Locomotive building by Robert Stephenson & Co.* 1923

PEOPLE AND WORK (Chapter 3)

Davison, E. *The mobility of labour in the North East Coast area.* Unpublished M Com Thesis, Durham University, 1932

Dewdney, J. C. 'The daily journey to work in County Durham', *Town Planning Review*, Vol 31, 1960–1, pp 107–34

House, J. W. *Papers on Migration and Mobility in Northern England*, Nos 1–9, University of Newcastle, Dept of Geography, 1964–9

Joint Committee as to Regional Planning. *Industry, Employment and Population in the North East.* Technical Sub-Committee of Planning Officers, Sept 1964

North East Development Association. *Migration.* NEDA, 1950

North East Development Association. *The Northern Region: review of employment conditions in Northumberland, Durham and the North Riding.* Issued biennially, 1950–8, then 1961

North Regional Planning Committee. *Mobility and the North.* 3 Vols, 1967
Wilson, G. C. *Social and Economic Statistics of North East England.* University of Durham, Department of Economics, Rowntree Research Unit, 1966

DEVELOPMENT AND GOVERNMENT POLICY (Chapter 4)

Board of Trade. *An Industrial Survey of the North East Coast area.* Armstrong College, Newcastle upon Tyne, HMSO, 1931

Caesar, A. A. L. 'A Survey of the Industrial Facilities of the North-East region' *North East Development Board*, 1942

Daysh, G. H. J. 'A Survey of the Industrial Facilities of the North East Coast', *North East Development Board*, 1936

House, J. W. *Recent economic growth in North-East England, University of Newcastle upon Tyne, Department of Geography Research Series*, No 4, 1964

Mess, H. A. *Industrial Tyneside: a society survey.* E. Benn 1928

Ministry of Labour. *Reports of investigations into industrial conditions in certain depressed areas of (1) West Cumberland and Haltwhistle, (2) Durham and Tyneside.* Cmnd 4728, HMSO, 1934

North Eastern Trading Estates Ltd. *Industrial Estates: a story of achievement.* J. Burrow. 1952

Northern Industrial Group. *North East Coast: a survey of industrial facilities.* A. Reid, 1949

Sharp, T. *A derelict area: the South-West Durham coalfield*. Hogarth Press, 1935

Teesside Industrial Estate. *Report and Development Plan*, 1964

Temple, A. *The derelict mining villages of County Durham*. Unpublished M Litt Thesis, Durham University, 1940

COAL (Chapter 6)

Dunn, M. *An historical, geological and descriptive view of the coal trade of the North of England*. Pattison & Ross, 1844

Fynes, R. *The Miners of Northumberland and Durham: a history of their social and political progress*. J. Robinson, Blyth, 1878

Galloway, R. L. *The Annals of Coal-Mining and the Coal Trade, the Invention of the Steam Engine and the Origin of the Railway*. Colliery Guardian, 2 Vols, 1898

Hall, T. Y. 'Rivers, ports and harbours of the Northern coalfield', *Transactions*, North of England Institution of Mining Engineers, Vol 10, 1861, pp 41–72

Hall, T. Y. *A treatise on the extent and probable duration of the Northern coalfield, with remarks on the coal trade in Durham and Northumberland*. A. Reid, 1854

Webb, S. *The story of the Durham miners, 1662–1921*. The Fabian Society, 1921

IRON AND STEEL (Chapter 6)

Bell, F. E. E. (Lady Bell). *At the works. A study of a manufacturing town (Middlesbrough)*. Edward Arnold, 1907. Reprint David & Charles, 1969

Edwards, K. H. R. *Chronology of the development of the iron and steel industry of Tees-side*. Wigan. K. H. R. Edwards, 1955

Gjers, J. 'Historical sketch of the rise and progress of the Cleveland iron trade', *Transactions*, Chesterfield Institute of Engineers, Vol 3, 1875, pp 63–75

Gleave, J. T. 'The Tees-side iron and steel industry', *Geographical Journal*, Vol 91, 1938, pp 454–67

Head, J. 'Recent developments in the Cleveland iron and steel industry', *Proceedings* Institute of Mechanical Engineers. Vol 45, 1893, pp 224–77

Stuart, A. D. *The Cleveland iron industry*, 1936

PLANNING (Chapter 9)

The statutory planning authorities, counties and county boroughs, have prepared and published development plan proposals under the Town and Country Planning Act 1947. More recently development plan reviews have been undertaken and there is, additionally, a wealth of more detailed reports, including town maps, proposals for rural areas, the coastline and for the redevelopment of central areas, among others. These reports would be too numerous to mention individually but complete lists are available at each planning office.

Some of the references below are drawn from the early post-war period of consultative planning.

Economist Intelligence Unit. *Survey of Transport Needs and Resources in the Tyneside Area*, 5 Parts, EIU, 1965

Elphick, P. 'Cramlington. Some problems encountered in building a New Town', *Town Planning Review*, Vol 35, 1964, pp 59–75

Glass, R. (editor). *The social background of a plan: a study of Middlesbrough*. Routledge, Kegan Paul, 1953

Lock, M. (Editor). *Middlesbrough Survey and Plan*, 1947

Lock, M. (editor). *The Hartlepools. A Survey and Plan*, 1949

Manley, G. 'The City of Durham', *Geography*, Vol 23, 1938, pp 147–55

Sharp, T. *Cathedral City. A Plan for Durham*. Architectural Press, 1945

Sharp, T. 'Forest villages of Northumberland', *Town Planning Review*, Vol 26, 1955–6, pp 165–70

Sylvester, D. 'Durham City', *Sociological Review*, Vol 36, 1944, pp 67–75

Teesside Survey and Plan: Vol 1. Policies and proposals, HMSO, 1969

Thorpe, D. & Nader, G. A. 'Consumer movement and shopping centre structure. A study of a central place system in Northern Durham', *Regional Studies*, Vol 1 (2), 1967, pp 173–91

Wilkinson, Ellen. *The town that was murdered—Jarrow*. 1939

Index

Illustration, diagrams or photographs, italicised thus *144*